ings

Structural Change of Property

Edited by Silke van Dyk, Tilman Reitz and Hartmut Rosa

Volume 7

Carsten Herrmann-Pillath is Professor and Permanent Fellow at the Max Weber Centre for Advanced Cultural and Social Studies, University of Erfurt and a principal researcher at the COEVOLVERS project.

Carsten Herrmann-Pillath

Havings

Steps Towards a New Economic Philosophy of Property and Beyond

Campus Verlag
Frankfurt/New York

STRUCTURAL CHANGE OF PROPERTY

ISBN 978-3-593-51976-0 Print
ISBN 978-3-593-45962-2 E-Book (PDF)
DOI 10.12907/978-3-593-45962-2

Werderstr. 10, 69469 Weinheim, info@campus.de.
Cover design: Verlagsgruppe Beltz
Typesetting: le-tex xerif
Typesetting font: Alegreya
Printed in the United States of America

www.campus.de
www.press.uchicago.edu

Klaus von dem Borne zum Gedenken

Contents

Preface[1]

In the four years preceding the publication of this book, I was one of the principal investigators of the DFG cooperative research center "Structural Change of Property."[2] In its first stage, this center gathered researchers from many disciplines to explore property in rich dimensions: historical, international, sectoral, social, you name it. This type of high-level research project in Germany aims to foster cross-disciplinary cooperation, and after four years, there is a rich harvest. This book is my individual cross-disciplinary contribution to the center, inspired by many other researchers' discussions and research outcomes. My subproject was about China: The role of shareholding cooperatives and hybrid land ownership in shaping social and cultural change in the megacity of Shenzhen. I am grateful to the team that realized this work, facing many difficulties as much of the fieldwork had to be done under the draconian COVID-19 regime in China.[3] However, this book contains only one chapter on this research, even though it inspired my thinking on property.

This book's primary rationale is critical, but it also goes beyond critical reflection in suggesting an entirely new conceptual framework for property research. This claim is trumpeted in the book's title, which features an English neologism: HAVINGS. I present a theory of havings in which the conventional notion of property is only one aspect.

When dealing with the realities in China, researchers cannot avoid noticing the glaring tension between the established notions of property and social practices. China imported the terms of property from the so-called Western

---

1 The author used Grammarly Premium for editing grammar and style. AI was not used in writing any content.

2 https://sfb294-eigentum.de/en/

3 https://sfb294-eigentum.de/en/subprojects/hybride-eigentumsordnung-im-staatskapitalismus/. I am indebted to the full-time team members Cheng Jing, Li Ling and Han Xu, the part-time members Song Sisi and Zhao Qian, and the associate SFB fellow Professor Guo Man. Specific contributions came from Professor Pan Liqun, Ren Yuxuan and Peng Ying.

discourses, often even the Western laws: private property, state ownership, collective and communal property, and public property. However, let us look at the phenomenon of "urban villages," originally fast-growing informal settlements built by native farmers and housing primarily migrant workers. The established property categories do not help in understanding how actual powers of using and controlling land are distributed and change through time. To a large degree, these categories are not institutions that determine the behavior of actors like "rules of the game," but tools to justify, legitimate and orchestrate social actions of various groups to get hold of the valuable resource of land. This is where difficulties of cross-disciplinary integration lurk everywhere. For many disciplines, the standard categories of property are given for various reasons. For example, lawyers may take them for granted because Chinese law defines and enforces them, although they also recognize the judiciary's essential role in interpreting these laws. As long as courts are not involved, practices may diverge widely from the law. When a conflict erupts and goes to court, judges often face complex equity issues in dealing with what the litigators may see as legitimate claims. In informal settlements, substantial swathes of urban land are involved, and hence, sensitive political topics such as distributional fairness among different groups are virulent. Researchers may conclude that "real life property" is not the same as in legal theory, which often aligns with economics demanding to overcome practices denounced as detrimental to urban development and income growth. This tension is salient in Shenzhen, but I learned from our sister project on informal settlements in India that the situation is the same: Standard conceptions of property do not help in understanding practices on the ground.[4] This had been argued forcefully in an influential paper by Benjamin Solomon and co-authors, a Mercator Fellow of the SFB,[5] and is further developed by Varun Patil, who emphasizes the importance of political processes in factually determining people's powers in controlling land and its use.[6] One of the PIs, the anthropologist and sociologist Martin Fuchs, stressed that a critical issue in cross-disciplinary research on property is that other disciplines often project the settled terminologies and institutions of advanced industrial nations of the so-called "West" on non-Western societies. This is certainly true for economics and sociology, as they mainly concentrate on those societies, Germany, Europe, or the United States.

4 https://sfb294-eigentum.de/en/subprojects/urbane-eigentumsordnungen-und-die-transformation-von-burgerschaft/

5 Solomon, Conover, and Shizgal 2017.

6 Patil 2024; Patil and Fuchs 2024.

Indeed, anthropologists attacked and rejected the standard terminology early, especially in the context of research on post-socialist transformation societies where the standard framework was actively transferred, such as in programs of "privatization."[7] Some authors opted for the "bundle of rights" view introduced by Hohfeldt.[8] However, it remains unclear how we can refer to these rights terminologically: Economists tend to interpret them as "property rights," along the lines of *usus*, *fructus* and *abusus* known from Roman law. As in the economic theory of commons, these rights may have the same status as conventional property, even "private," such as concerning alienation. This has also attracted anthropological critiques, pointing toward the fundamentally different nature of such rights in Indigenous societies, even if we refer to commons.[9] The question of our language of property is on the table.

Since I had done research in Shenzhen years before the SFB started,[10] I was sensitized to these issues and began considering alternative concepts. Max Weber obtained a crucial role. Max Weber does not concentrate on property but on "appropriation." The latter is undoubtedly a key concept in many projects of the SFB, for instance, the question of appropriation of specific resources such as the wind in renewable energies[11] or the appropriation of the female reproductive organs in various approaches to alternative technologies of human reproduction;[12] however, what Weber had already developed was a dynamic and action-based view on appropriation. He was already aware that even opening access to resources to others can be a form of appropriation, which stays in tension with the simple opposition between "private property" and open access to public property.[13] Therefore, I took the initiative to establish a working group on Max Weber, and researchers from different disciplines joined in various stages of their careers: Lydia von der Weth, Dirk Schuck, Verena Wolf and Markus Vinzent. Over two years, we read and discussed Weber's contributions, and I received inspiration for writing the first chapter of this book. Thank you, Max Weber team!

One important lesson from reading Weber is that we cannot analyze property independently from the economic system of which it is a part, particularly how property relates to money and finance. In the SFB, several projects reveal this close

7 Hann 2007, Turner 2017.

8 Benda-Beckmann, Benda-Beckmann, and Wiber 2006.

9 Wagner and Talakai 2007.

10 Herrmann-Pillath, Guo, and Feng 2021.

11 https://sfb294-eigentum.de/en/subprojects/windernte-und-warmeklau-als-indikatoren-neuer-eigentumsordnungen/

12 https://sfb294-eigentum.de/en/subprojects/eigentum-am-menschlichen-korper-im-kontext-transnationaler-reproduktionsokonomien/

13 This is salient today in the digital economy; https://sfb294-eigentum.de/de/teilprojekte/geistiges-eigentum/

relationship, such as the role of housing assetization.[14] For Weber, private property is a specific form of property that is critical for capitalist calculation. Most SFB members would tend to agree, but the implication is less obvious when it comes to debating so-called "alternatives to property:" Similar kinds of property may have very different social and political consequences in different economic systems and, specifically, how these organize finance. However, our fetters of language partly block the view of such interdependencies. Writing as an economist trained in the German traditions of institutional economics or, better, evoking the Weberian concept of order, "economics of order" (*Ordnungstheorie*), I know this fact well. The classical 20th-century German economists mostly believed that private property only has beneficial social outcomes if embedded in a specific economic order that establishes a "firewall" between property and power, both financial and political. This demonstrates the primacy of order over property.[15]

However, I learned that achieving analytical and theoretical progress is difficult as long as we stay within our established frames of talking property. So, the idea for this book was borne. In our research on Shenzhen, already referring to Weber's concept of appropriation, we introduced the term "ownership" to refer to a form of property that does not allow for alienation and is relational.[16] That was premature, even though I later learned that some anthropologists had moved in the same direction.[17] However, I also learned that disciplines differ widely in interpreting this term: Ownership is often seen as the most potent form of Blackstonian property in legal studies and institutional economics.

Hence, two kinds of work were necessary. First, clarify the fundamental meanings of property, and then construct a new language of property that would liberate the understanding of these meanings from the constraints of current terminological usages. For the first work, my cooperation with Frédéric Basso (at LSE, not an SFB member) proved invaluable: Our book on embodiment and political economy already contains a chapter in which we approach property from an embodiment perspective.[18] Fred also showed me the capstone that was not yet included there but is now included in the current book: Sartre's view on *faire, avoir* and *être* as the three fundamental modes of human existence.[19] Sartre's inspiration shows the importance of foundational work on property, primarily done in philosophy.

14 https://sfb294-eigentum.de/en/subprojects/das-habitat-als-pfand/

15 Unfortunately, this insight has been widely marginalized in modern economic and political thought, as Walter Oswalt has forcefully demonstrated in his critique of modern economic liberalism; Oswalt 2024.

16 Cheng, Herrmann-Pillath, and Li 2022.

17 For example, Brightman, Fausto, and Grotti 2016.

18 Basso and Herrmann-Pillath 2024.

19 Sartre 2017.

Two philosophical contributions by SFB members were highly significant for my work: Jakob Blumenfeld's book on German idealism[20] for the argument in Chapter 3 and Tilo Wesche's work on the Rights of Nature in Chapter 5.[21] Hegel had shaped my thinking for years, culminating in a book on a Neohegelian approach to institutions.[22] Therefore, Blumenfeld's argument was fully compatible with my thinking, and I could sketch a Hegelian view on property that goes beyond standard views that mainly focus on the "Philosophy of Right" and that overlook the deeper phenomenological roots of Hegelian property (Hegel also influenced Sartre). Hegel invented the German term for "private property," so we gain much insight when Blumenfeld shows that German idealism, in general, derives property from the need to create a peaceful and flourishing community. Contrary to the anglophone tradition, property is not an individual's natural and pre-social right. To put it paradoxically, private property is public: This tradition is mostly neglected in the Anglophone literature on property and has continued in the previously mentioned views of German economists of the last decades of the 20th century, though gradually fading out in following the Anglophone mainstream.

Against this background, Wesche's argument becomes even more significant: Rights to Nature should not be derived from ecocentric ethics and worldviews but as rights to property of nature that systematically follow from the existing legal and institutional framework: a revolution from within. In the same way, as we recognize women's property today and reject gender-based dispossession reigning in many societies, past and present, we may recognize other beings' property in the future, an argument also well-known in animal rights literature. Again, the problem with property is less seen in isolation but with its embedding of ideological, social, and political frames. This means that, eventually, a radical political transformation is necessary. At this point, my work in Chapter 5 could also build on the cooperation in the COEVOLVERS project, where I am one of the PIs, exploring the utopia of a multi-species body politic.[23]

Western colonialism has forced these property frames on the world as we know it today, and they are rooted in European antiquity. The SFB diagnosed and explored this fundamental fact in several projects.[24] These results highlight the need and difficulties of moving beyond these frames terminologically. The current attempts often lead to a terminological mess, most apparent in the in-

20 Blumenfeld 2024.

21 Wesche 2023.

22 Herrmann-Pillath and Boldyrev 2014.

23 Horizon Europe project 101084220: "Coevolutionary approach to unlock the transformative potential of nature-based solutions for more inclusive and resilient communities". I am grateful to Simo Sarkki and Juha Hiedanpää for inspiring collaboration on ecocentric democracy.

24 For a stimulating collection of papers, see Bianchi Mancini et al. 2024.

flation of the meanings of "commons," reaching from local to global, Indigenous to open source, and many other uses. I contributed to that mess, too,[25] and felt a sense of urgency in clarifying terms. This book is my effort to do so. In referring to modes of having and modes of havings, the new conceptual framework builds on linguistic universals.[26] These universals combine with a rich variety of practices in which alienability and forms of alienation via money-mediated social interactions play a critical role.

I hope the new terminology will receive critical acknowledgement, although I do not expect much to change with the established frames firmly entrenched in our societies. The language of havings is an attempt to create a scientific terminology that enables cross-disciplinary research on what we know as property while avoiding the many pitfalls of the established language, which is only apparently unified across the respective single-disciplinary discourses.

25 Herrmann-Pillath 2023.
26 Aikhenvald 2012.

Introduction: Beyond property

Je suis ce que j'ai.
Jean Paul Sartre, L'être et le néant[1]

When the anthropologist Luiz Costa presents his ethnographic account of ownership and kinship among the Kanamari in Western Amazonia,[2] he insists that for an adequate understanding and description of their practices and ways of life, it is necessary to use the native language words. Translations inevitably distort meanings. This is certainly true for any words that might appear semantically close to "property," hence describing a human relationship with an object that legitimately excludes others. His report is part of a fascinating collection of papers on Amazonian natives, and the authors agreed on using the term "ownership" in the introduction specified as "altering ownership"[3] for the phenomena they are exploring. However, the term ownership is not free from conceptual bias, too, as in influential English uses, the term refers to the strongest "Blackstonian" form of property, undoubtedly different from what the authors have in mind.[4]

The Kanamari raise pets, often the offspring of killed prey. They incapacitate the animals by pulling out teeth and claws, which frequently is enough to kill them. The surviving animals are trained to eat human food, including meat of their species, which is often pre-chewed by humans, primarily women, who then feed the animal. The feeding establishes a relationship of mastery between the human and the pet: The human is the pet's owner. Feeding is not just meeting a need but also creating one, hence a dependency relationship. The pet exclusively relates to the human owner. Costa shows how such feeding relationships permeate Kanamari life, merging the notions of ownership and kinship, as in the primordial relationship between mother and child. These relationships are seen as deeply embodied: Costa uses the term "body-owner" instead of "owner." The pet becomes part of the human body through feeding and vice versa. However, the relationship is asymmetric since the body-owner is the locus of agency relative to

1 Sartre 2017, 774.
2 Costa 2016.
3 Brightman, Fausto, and Grotti 2016.
4 Honoré 1961.

the owned, like the mother in relation to the child. This asymmetry also applies to the relationship between chief and followers, which is established in commensality. Commensality enacts kinship. Chiefs are the body-owners of the garden, which marks the village's location, and they allocate plots to households. There is a clear distinction between the communal garden and the household plots. Ownership is fundamental in the Kanamari worldview, as it grounds in spiritual conceptions of life where predation is omnipresent, with the Jaguar as the supreme body-owner of all life. Feeding is the human transformation of predation while maintaining the mastery of ownership. Commensality creates community via the symmetry of feeding.

Costa's study is one example of numerous anthropological contributions showing that possessive relationships are a universal feature of being human. However, they still have distinct qualities across human societies that do not allow for the generalization of the notions of property prevailing in so-called "Western" modernity. In the Amazonian examples, nurturing is a critical element of possession, raising questions about common distinctions between "care" and appropriative relationships: Care appears as mastery over the other and appropriates via embodying the other. Hence, we notice that Western biases in conceptualizing property also affect views that dissent from the mainstream.[5] A glaring example is the debate about the commons, where anthropologists have argued that the dominant property paradigm still shapes this notion and fails to grasp the nature of possessive relationships in non-Western societies.[6]

Property is a central economic institution and a topic of many theoretical controversies, often profoundly impacting society and politics.[7] Political revolutions frequently put property at their center, aiming at uprooting the distribution of wealth and power in society. Property is also at the core of the current climate challenge to society, as it is the institutional form that shapes how most humans access and use natural resources.[8] Therefore, a clear theoretical view of property is indispensable. However, this view is not ready because the complexity of property in economic life transcends the simplicity of theoretical concepts by far, often leading to severe misjudgments with practical impact. A famous example is

5 A case in point is the magistral book by Widerquist and MacCall 2021. They organize the entire anthropological evidence to refute the mainstream view of property and cast the falsifying data in the same language, such as common or public property. Although I am sympathetic with their critique, this approach stays in the mainstream in failing to recognize the nature of genuinely different ways of relating to things and people. The critical issue is how "private property" and "property" relate, and what are the minimal features of "property."

6 For the case of Oceania, see Wagner and Talakai 2007.

7 van Dyk, Reitz, and Rosa 2023.

8 Wesche 2023.

Hardin's "Tragedy of the Commons," which informed many efforts to install private property of natural resources but was refuted by Elinor Ostrom's research on real-world commons.[9] She showed that the actual workings of property are determined by complex social, cultural and political factors and, hence, cannot be reduced to abstract theoretical principles that only highlight aspects such as economic efficiency. Property, in the sense of Mauss, is a "total" social phenomenon, and limiting the view on a specific scientific discipline such as economics is like the proverbial blind men touching only one part of the elephant, thus ending up with partial and grossly misleading views.

Until today, the economic view of property is shaped by the idea that scarce resources are best allocated via markets, and markets require clear property rights assignments to reduce transaction costs. This idea has been extended to a teleological view of institutional change, suggesting that with scarcity becoming increasingly salient, such as resulting from population growth, property will evolve towards a regime of more differentiated and unequivocally assigned property rights.[10] For example, many economists recommend clarifying property rights and installing markets if water becomes scarce. Such recommendations are not universally accepted since critics are concerned about the distributional impacts of markets and issues of human rights regarding basic needs. However, overviewing historical developments, the economic notion of institutional progress driven by efficiency seems to accord with the evidence, but with a Polanyian twist: We do indeed diagnose a global diffusion of a particular formation of property, but this is also, if not predominantly, driven by the diffusion of specific ideas about property, and not necessarily by the convergence of economic determinants of institutions. In Marxian terms, the intellectual superstructure was at least as significant for the diffusion as the material substructure.

This diffusion was mainly driven by the forceful transplantation of European legal concepts and laws to the colonies, resulting minimally in a legal pluralism of local customs and the laws of the colonizers.[11] Moreover, adopting variants of European law was also seen as a critical element in efforts to modernize countries that escaped colonization, such as Japan, or even countries undergoing decolonization, which mainly substituted the colonizers' law with national laws informed by the same legal teachings. Property is shaped primarily by civil and common law, and these have defined the models for law-making all over the globe. These are mainly the versions of 19th-century nation-states. In the early period

9 Ostrom 2015.

10 A classical statement of this is Douglass North's (1981, 1990) work in earlier stages of his intellectual development.

11 Acemoglu, Johnson, and Robinson 2001.

of colonization, other trajectories were still possible, such as the transfer of feudal law in the French colonies.[12] But today, the European models prevail in many countries. Apart from customary law, one of the most developed alternatives is Islamic law. Even in the case of China, where property defines its nature as a socialist state, the civil law mainly follows the European models, after earlier receptions in Republican China that were informed by Japanese transplantations of German civil law.

For the argument in this book, one observation is essential: This process of outward colonization of the globe legitimized by European notions of property was accompanied by the internal colonization of local communities in Europe by the emerging modern nation states, epitomized in the struggle over the commons.[13] Even earlier, Roman conceptions of property evolved in the provinces of the Empire, driven by powerful interests in exploiting these lands to accumulate wealth in the Italian heartland appropriated by the Roman elites. Hence, we cannot understand modern forms of property without relating property to the outwardly and inwardly colonizing state and recognizing the tension between the state and local communities.

In the modern debates about property, this question is salient in what appears to be a relatively narrow topic: the fight of Indigenous people to regain and protect claims of their homelands against the hegemonic societies. In these debates, we learn that Indigenous claims cannot be adequately translated into the language of hegemonic law, even though native lawyers must do it to prevail in disputes and convince political actors.[14] However, reference to Indigeneity is misleading while truly inspiring: All kinds of local communities confronting an intruding state and its modern law may count as "indigenous," such as the communities in early modern rural France. Indigeneity refers to the difference between local people and a colonizing power, eventually transforming into an independent state like the USA or Brazil. This is important, but it is not far enough since we must recognize the phenomenon of internal colonization. This can refer to minorities in states that were never colonized in the past but also to local communities in the broader sense that may follow practices of property that do not accord with the hegemonic law, such as in a country like Indonesia, where modern state law, Islamic law and various local customary laws coexist. One legal domain where this is most salient is the family and inheritance, especially regarding gender. In countries such as In-

12 Greer 2017.

13 de Moor 2018.

14 McNeil 2017.

dia, local practices often prevail over formal civil law, visible in widespread and blatant violations of women's rights.[15]

I take such observations as inspiration to raise a theoretical question. We face a global convergence of legal and economic conceptions of property, driven by expert epistemic communities, business interests, and state elites pursuing modernization projects. On the other hand, we also know that other conceptions of property are being marginalized. What if those marginalized conceptions show us that something essential is missing in our modern ideas of property, a white spot that calls for theoretical extraction and systematization? What if these other ideas may show us new solutions to our challenges today? What if "they" are right, and "we" have been wrong for centuries, if not millennia?

In other words, I aim to de-colonize property, literally and metaphorically. Property is a concept that is almost by necessity shaped by hegemonic interests, even in the sense that critics are drawn into the orbit of their ideas. For example, potential intellectual property owners certainly will endorse ideas about this type of property. In the 19th century, the emerging capitalist elites favored the new private property concepts enshrined in the civil laws. Unfortunately, critics were drawn into a position that mainly defined itself as the negative, resulting in modern conceptions of state ownership and other forms of public ownership. These alternative ideas often undergirded internal colonization, too, harming local communities like capitalist colonization.

In economics, the semantic space of property is spanned by the notions of state ownership, collective or communal property, public property and private property. This list hides the diversity and richness of property in human history and fails to highlight essential components.[16] The distinctions are shaped by the legal setting of modern states, which could only be taken for granted in a quasi-Hegelian view that these represent a climax of institutional development. I take a radically different position: Even the notion of property as such is deeply problematic as it carries the burden of European history since Roman times. Via translations, it became part of many languages, and indeed all hegemonic ones. This is a global intellectual if not spiritual, colonization. I use the term "spiritual" here since property is indeed shaped by ideas that are by no means grounded in "science" but are primarily religious in origin.[17] If we confront property with Indigenous spirituality, the latter may seem easy to surrender, facing claims for science as in economics. However, the latter claims are spiritual, too, for example, regard-

15 Rao 2008.

16 This fact is mainly pointed out by anthropologists, for example Turner 2017.

17 Vinzent 2024. For lively illustrations, see the vignettes in Kimmerer 2020.

ing the negation of animals as property holders and reclaiming "soul" and personhood only for humans.[18]

How can we throw off the intellectual ballast of two millennia speaking "property"? We must change our language. This book introduces an English neologism: "havings." This is in formal analogy to "belongings," derived from "to belong." Indeed, "to have" and "to belong" are closely related, as what I have, belongs to me. However, the verb "to have" has a much broader meaning than only referring to linguistic terms of possession. In introducing the neologism "havings," I highlight these aspects exclusively. Many languages use verbs like "to have" that express possessive relationship, such as in Chinese "you," (which is then further specified in bisyllabic words, such as "zhanyou") or "ter" in Portuguese that shows the same broader meanings as "to have." Another frequent construct is using "to be" with a noun, such as in Russian where "I have" translates as "u menja est'", with "est'" "to be." Similarly, in Japanese, the construction is used "watashi ni XXX ga aru," with "arimasu" meaning "exist." In sum, across human languages we observe a close relationship between "having" and "being" in the sense that "having" extends further than mere "property" and also includes strong forms of identifying a feature with an individual, such as saying, "I have a long nose," and similarly, expressing a form of co-existence as a close association between an individual and an object.[19]

The approach to "havings" developed in this book takes these fundamental linguistic patterns as the point of departure as they reflect the universality of possessive relationships in human forms of life.[20] In doing so, in this introduction, I refer to one philosophical position explicitly, Sartre's account of possession, since this grounds the claim of universality in the ontology of being human (we will discuss in Chapter 5 whether this extends beyond humans).[21] Sartre distinguishes between three fundamental modes of human being: doing *faire*, having *avoir* and being *être*. He regards doing as being reducible to having, since we mostly need to have something to do something and do something to create what we have. Sartre distinguishes neatly between the ontological relationship of having and the rights to have, that is, property. The latter only serves to create legitimacy of having, resolve conflicts, and hence regulate social relationships that affect having. However, Sartre cannot avoid using terms such as possession or even property since there is no noun corresponding to *avoir*, similar to the situation in English. Let

18 Deckha 2021.

19 Aikhenvald 2012.

20 To be crystal clear: I distinguish this view radically from otherwise related views, which, however, deny property as "private property" being a universal feature, for instance, Widerquist and McCall 2021. This is definitively true, but I claim the universality of havings and regard private property as a specific institutional form that became hegemonial in capitalism.

21 Sartre 2017, 754 ff.

me continue to use the term "possession" here even though "havings" would be the proper term in my argument.

What does it mean that possession is ontological? This is not the place to delve into the intricacies of Sartre's philosophical reasoning. I restate his argument in plain words and add cursory observations on how we can make sense of it in terms of contemporary human sciences. Sartre claims that having is the necessary form of being because the human individual is always deficient in transcending her current status which is also untransparent (in the sense of non-thetic) to consciousness. Being (as for-itself) is a project (often written *pro-jet,* hence a projection) in which the individual enacts what is radical freedom of choice facing an open and indeterministic future.[22] Choice is radically free because the world as a totality of possibilities is underdetermined and must be fixed by acting. This differs in principle from the notion of freedom that informs economics. In economics, individuals know their preferences and face constraints (which may be uncertain in the probabilistic sense); they are free to choose which actions contribute to fulfilling their needs. In Sartre's view, the constraints are not objectively given but are determined by free choice in turn (his famous examples include the rock, which I might see either as an obstacle or an opportunity to climb and achieve a grander view). The constraints are part of the project of being which is freely chosen. Further, having an object is not simply controlling a resource to meet one's preferences. By having an object, subject and object form one unity of being, a Hegelian totality. For the individual, being requires creating a relationship with an object that is both different from the subject and also a part of it. Evidently, this view is deeply influenced by Hegelian expressivism, yet eschewing the reference to spirit (for Sartre, the human is God): In the relationship of having, the individual projects herself on the world and, at the same time, becomes herself.

Accordingly, Sartre's notion of appropriation is much wider than the common view of property. His example of skiing illustrates this point. A slope would be destroyed if we tread on it. When skiing, we glide over it and appropriate it as an independent object, preserving its shape. Our appropriation is enacted via our own bodily movements, and the gliding creates the unity of slope and individual. Obviously, this does not imply that the slope becomes the property of the human. Economists would point out that the slope is a club good, and if too many people would use it, destruction looms. Hence, rights of access must be established and enforced. However, this argument does not invalidate Sartre's point: Using is not simply a functional relationship but ontological. Accordingly, using has the

22 This fundamental orientation towards the future in even the simplest actions, like raising a bottle to drink, is also highlighted in modern cognitive sciences and philosophy of mind; Clark 2023.

same temporal complexity as being, creating a relationship through time. Depending on the object's physical nature, this implies the temporal continuity of having which correlates with the ontological complexity in terms of the totality of havings. Each single having evokes the world populated with all other objects with which the individual relates, epitomized in the phenomenon of the "home," universal for humanity, in the sense of dwellings in which humans arrange the objects they use and live together with them.

Sartre's ontology can be interpreted non-philosophically as distinguishing between the *Umwelt* and the physical environment, with the *Umwelt* being defined as the totality of affordances for action.[23] The concept of affordance in cognitive sciences converges with Sartre's analysis because affordances are what Barad calls "intra-action."[24] An affordance is an objective feature of the world which is defined by enabling and evoking action of a particular individual, such that at the same time its objectivity is rooted in the subjectivity of action, even in the strongly individualized meaning of Sartre's freedom: The individual can create new affordances in the world. In this cognitive science view, the world is the totality of individualized *Umwelten* and is constituted by the interactions of the individuals. There is no Hegelian external reference to fix the world independently, even if only in the sense of a convergent historical process. For the child, the tree is an affordance for climbing; for the adult, it is a place to rest under its shadow. Both actions appropriate the tree: For example, the tree might be familiar from regular strolls of a family, and they might all habitually refer to "our tree," absent a property right. They might feel irritation when meeting strangers under its shadow.

Following Sartre, we define having as a universal form of being human, which is incorporated in havings, that is, objects that are seen as parts of individual beings, though being materially separated. Sartre argues that this view includes several forms of action that may appear to be staying in tension with this unity. First, he regards buying an object as a strong form of appropriation that activates the power of money as a universal means of enacting desires, thus seeing money as tightly bound to having, even though money is also the medium of alienation. Second, he interprets giving away as a form of appropriating the receiver of the gift. Third, even the destruction of an object may be the ultimate form of appropriating it. Thus, having is a constitutive aspect of all human actions. For example, Sarte even interprets knowing as a form of appropriating the world.

---

23 The notion of *Umwelt* has been elaborated in detail by von Uexküll as distinguishing between the physical environment as seen by the scientific observer and the surroundings as seen by an animal; Uexküll and Kriszat 1934. The *Umwelt* is constituted by the feedback loops between action and outcomes. It is an essential concept in modern ecosemiotics (Maran 2020), combined with modern cognitive sciences and Gibson's notion of affordance; Chong and Proctor 2020.

24 Barad 2007.

Sartre's philosophical account is endorsed by modern behavioral sciences views about defining features of the human species as compared with its next closed species.[25] This is salient in early childhood development: Very young children cross-culturally display a sense of owning objects and, most importantly, recognizing and respecting ownership by others, with cultural differences in specific practices emerging later as a result of socialization. As we shall see, the cross-cultural convergence of basic notions of having in Sartre's sense can be traced by exploring the various linguistic expressions for having across human societies.

One critical insight gained from reading Sartre is to recognize having as a form of action. Hence, the first task in overcoming our intellectual blinds on property is to eschew its reification. We achieve this in chapter 1 where we learn from Max Weber's views on property, which are radically deflationary in focusing less on structures and objects, but on actions, and approach their outcomes in terms of patterns of powers of disposition. For Weber, the topic of property is one of appropriation. Property (*Eigentum*) as an institution is only one tool of appropriation. Weber also shows that for understanding modern property, its relationship with markets and money is essential, which also suggests the important distinction between property and wealth. Weber's account puts property in the context of his grand view on the rise of capitalism and rationalization, which matches the picture previously drawn here. Therefore, unlike Weber, we can ask what property might mean in a non-capitalist or post-capitalist society. Accordingly, for us, historical and anthropological knowledge of non-capitalist property is also highly informative for thinking about the future institutional design of the economy.

I do not delve into this historical and anthropological record but focus on one aspect in chapter 2: The languages of property. Even in the European context, we can gain much insight from reflecting on differences between languages and legal idioms and the resulting translation troubles. The commonalities reflect the convergences in the Weberian grand view; the differences are productive in suggesting new ideas beyond hegemonic thinking. This is even more true when we compare concepts of property between Islamic law and European law or the troubles with translating Indigenous ideas. The aim of the chapter is to identify universals of property that diverge from the hegemonic notions, such as treating property not as a right but as a mandate.

Chapter 3 builds on this analysis and presents a new conceptual framework of property. This requires substituting this term with the more general one: *Having*, both as referring to the action of *having* and as a noun, the *havings*, hence a neologism in English. In German, the terms *haben*, *Habe*, or *Haben* are still used, though

25 Tomasello 2019, 265 ff.

antiquated. The chapter goes beyond Weber's account of appropriation in distinguishing this mode of action from the other two, recognition and assignment, constituting an object as a having. I distinguish three structural modes of havings, in the sense of action results: possession, ownership, and property, with distinct definitions that partly differ from current uses, especially regarding ownership, which I define along the lines of relational property in the literature, especially on Indigenous claims on land. These three modes interplay in creating patterns of the distribution of powers of disposition across social group members. One important corollary of this approach is eschewing the notion of "rights" almost universally accepted in both mainstream and non-mainstream views. Property is not a right, but the key determinant of agential power as power of disposition.

I continue with two applications of my theory. Chapter 4 introduces the case of internal colonization, the building of the megacity of Shenzhen in three decades, partly expropriating native villagers' land. However, villagers could resist by claiming their ownership rooted in the spirituality of their conceptions of lineage and land. The result is a hybrid allocation of rights of disposition, which, however, did not constrain the emergence of a vibrant real estate market. Whereas Chapter 4 demonstrates the analytical value of my new theory, chapter 5 develops its normative potential in submitting the claim for other species' havings. I explore the possibility of creating ecosystem commons where all members have ownership and enjoy possession rights. I claim this construct can help fending off the looming climate crisis and biodiversity collapse.

The postscript concludes with a reflection on the political consequences of my theory, which overcomes the traditional divides between economic liberalism and socialism. Both positions are trapped in the modernist thought of the 19th century, which persists until we discard the shared pillar of both, namely property. Both positions are also statist and negate the autonomy of local communities. The idea of ecosystem commons liberates communities from the state's grip and safeguards their autonomy with strong havings that nourish their flourishing in multi-species cohabitation. The theory of havings allows a fresh perspective on classical topics such as labor and capital or the role of finance in the economy.

This work is labelled as "philosophy of economics." I avoid the common formula "economics of…" since this suggests a reference to economics as it stands. Philosophy of economics is mainly concerned with economic methodology and economic ethics in the wider sense.[26] These are also the main themes of this book. I approach methodology as a critique of language, which I regard as a major feature of modern philosophy. Language is the medium by which humans refer to reality. Hence, the critique of language is also powerful in freeing us from biases

---

26 For lucid overviews, see Ross 2014 or Hausman 2021.

and constraints of our language in approaching reality. In doing so, we can also reflect upon our human commitments to a good life, in which the distribution of resources, that is, of powers of disposition, is critical for achieving a just and flourishing society that lives in harmony with nature. Property is a core issue in the philosophy of economics, and we must transcend its current frameworks, which have blocked us from standing up to these commitments for millennia.

Chapter 1: Deconstructing property: Max Weber's approach to appropriation

Introduction[1]

The concept of property is a paradox, simultaneously simple and complex. Its apparent simplicity results from the linguistic transformation of reification or hypostasis. We are accustomed to treating *property* as an object, whether as a tangible thing like land or an intangible asset like a financial asset. Alternatively, we view it as an institution, either in a general sense of the laws of property or specifically as the rights of property. In both ways, we accept the existence of an entity called "property." This chapter will critically examine the concept of property, with Max Weber's work as a focal guide.[2] The focus is not merely on Weber's interpretation but on his ideas' profound implications for a comprehensive economic philosophy of property and beyond.

Weber was a multi-disciplinary scholar trained as a lawyer and economist and became active in establishing sociology as a discipline in Germany.[3] However, he was not satisfied with the developments in this emerging new academia, and we must recognize that his writings were strongly influenced by the economics of his times. His contemporaries also acknowledged that influence, and no lesser scholar than Hayek recommended the first parts of *Economy and Society* for a translation into English as a part of a series introducing continental *economics* to an anglophone audience. Today, Weber is no longer regarded as an "economist:" In economics, the only contribution that still attracts the attention of economists is his "Protestantism hypothesis," which is only a minor part of his vast oeuvre.[4] As

1 As I detail in the preface, the discussion of this chapter received much inspiration from the discussions in the Weber reading group at the SFB.

2 According to my knowledge, Weber does not play any role in philosophical or economic debates about property, even if these refer to historical sociology and anthropology, such as Widerquist and McCall 2021.

3 On the following, see the detailed exposition in Kenneth Tribe's introduction to Weber and Tribe 2019.

4 Kurz 2020.

we will see, this is deplorable since reading Weber can help to overcome conceptual confusion about property in modern institutional economics, where "property rights" have become an essential theoretical construct.[5] This view also had a tremendous impact on economic policies worldwide, for example, in the global movement of privatization in the 1980s under the auspices of so-called "neoliberalism."

Weber's approach to property differs from modern institutional economics in using a conceptual framework partly borrowed from Austrian economists of his times, especially Menger and Böhm-Bawerk, while also adopting a macro-sociological view on the evolution of property, which involves a different concept of rationality than economics introduced later. In institutional economics, in the first place, rationality refers to the psychological characteristics of the economic agent, with the New Institutional Economics mostly following the standard model of *Homo economicus* and the non-mainstream alternatives also including factors such as culture. Second, in the Coasean sense, rationality combines with efficiency, meaning that property rights are indispensable for internalizing externalities via markets. These ideas have motivated many institutional developments in recent times, such as the expansion of intellectual property rights and the creation of markets for pollution rights.

In contrast, Weber's notion of rationality refers to the institutional conditions of "economic calculation" that have emerged in capitalism, and therefore, he relates property closely to the institution of money. For Weber, property is an emerging institutional feature of complex social conflicts, tensions, and competing strategies for dominance by controlling access to valuable sources of socioeconomic advantage, individually in the first place, but in terms of institutional fixation, within and between groups. This view does not define the mainstream position in modern economics. However, there is an important exception: the recent turn of one of the leaders in the field, the late Douglass North, from an efficiency-based view to approaching property as a political means to regulate violent social conflicts among groups vying for dominance.[6] However, throughout his prolific career, North ignored Max Weber to the detriment of economics. Weber already presented a comprehensive view on the emergence and stabilization of property in the analytical triangle of economy, specifically markets, money, specifically finance, and rule (*Herrschaft*), going beyond the focus on the state in some strands of institutional economics.[7]

5 Alchian 2008. However, some economists believe that this focus on property rights has left the fundamental notion of "property" in limbo, for example, Wilson 2022.

6 North, Wallis, and Weingast 2009.

7 Barzel 2012 who also cites Weber only in passing.

However, as we will see in the next section, Weber did not use the term "property" (*Eigentum*) in the foundational sense of modern economics. At this place, and especially when it comes to the analysis of capitalism, he mainly refers to the notion of "power of disposition" (*Verfügungsgewalt*), which he borrowed from Carl Menger.[8] Power of disposition relates to another key concept, wealth (*Vermögen*), and both are conceptual elements in a broader framework of "appropriation" (*Appropriation*) as a fundamental type of social action. That means Weber used a more complex conceptual framework for analyzing property than modern economics, which exclusively focuses on "property rights." Weberian property as *Eigentum* has a much more limited meaning to which we turn now.

The distinction between *Eigentum* as property and *Vermögen* as wealth

Max Weber relegated the term "property" to a narrow and specific position in his general account of "appropriation" provided that we translate the English term into the German *Eigentum*, as usually done:

> *Chancen* that are appropriated to individuals through inheritance, or to heritable communities or associations, will be called a property (of the relevant individuals, communities, or associations), and where appropriated as an alienable *Chance*, free property.[9]

We will discuss the term *Chance* extensively below; suffice it to say that this refers to an uncertain opportunity to gain an advantage in a social struggle. This definition of property is surprisingly narrow, even though it might cover much of what is considered (private) property in modern societies. However, many observations invite questioning this quick conclusion, such as on inheritance. There is an inheritance tax in many societies, though mainly at a low rate. Many liberal economists, famously John Stuart Mill, have recommended that inheritance be taxed substantially.[10] That would imply that according to Weber's definition, the assets held by an individual during her lifetime would not count as their full "property." Indeed, even if the tax rate is low, from a systematic perspective, this means that, nevertheless, the right to property is conditional on the policy of the government and that, in principle, the individual right to inherit the assets is not a property of the

8 Menger 1971, 3, regards the *Verfügung* (power of disposal) over a thing as one defining feature of the fundamental concept of "economic good." Tribe translates *Verfügungsgewalt* as "power of disposition," see Weber and Tribe 2019, 481.

9 Weber and Tribe 2019, 124.

10 Ekelund and Walker 1996. Mill distinguished between the right to bequeath and the right to be bequeathed and rejected the latter.

heirs, and that any act of disposing of the assets after death cannot be regarded as a full expression of the original right to property since it is subject to a tax separate from the income tax that was already imposed on the sources of the heritable wealth.[11] There is no apparent reason why the complete transfer to any heir could not be a possible institutional set-up. Hence, we would need to distinguish such kind of "property" from the Weberian one we mostly take for granted, but which, strictly spoken, is even non-existent in many modern societies. We notice that Weber did not yet know the legal developments springing from the Weimar Constitution, which resulted in an essential divergence between German civil law and constitutional law, with the latter adopting a view on inheritance that recognizes the difference between property that is possessed (the legator) and a mere claim of the heirs who, in Weber's wording, enjoy the mere *Chance* on wealth accrual, creating a delicate balance between the absolute notion of property in the civil law and property as a socially embedded and circumscribed fundamental human right.

Similarly, philosophers often have asserted that the fundamental form of property is owning one's body.[12] John Locke famously grounded his influential theory of property on this assumption, arguing that one's bodily effort of labor literally "infects" an object with our primordial ownership of the body. However, in modern societies, there are very tight constraints to alienating our bodies or parts of it. We cannot trade our organs; we cannot sell ourselves into slavery; there are many international differences in the legal setting for surrogate motherhood, or similarly, for prostitution; in other words, if we follow Weber's definition, in modern societies, citizens are denied the full rights to property of their own body.

Weber's definition is thought-provoking, but he did not further pursue the implications that could follow for a general theory of property. We are left alone with the question of the proper English translation of his *Eigentum*, given that property in our modern societies is different; so to be scientifically precise, we would need to coin another term for this, perhaps using a set of distinct specifications, thus considering a spectrum of various types of property. "Private property" is an option that jumps to the eye. However, Weber does not use this term systematically: In the previous example of modern German law, civil law appears to define "private property," whereas constitutional law, also employing the term *Eigentum*, seems to refer to a different kind.[13] In the parts of *Economy and Society* authorized

11 On this point and the following see the detailed legal analysis in Harke 2020.

12 Waldron 2023.

13 This is salient when considering American views on the German duality of concepts of property, for example, Alexander 2003. German constitutional law embeds property into the *Sozialstaat* and is hence directly compatible with "liberal" American approaches, such as recently Dagan 2021.

for publication by Weber, we find various uses of "private" that appear to allude to the notion of *Privateigentum* (such as *Privatwirtschaft*), but the term as such appears only once.[14]

The difficulties in extracting Weber's approach to property from his works partly result from the fact that the monumental *Economy and Society* is an amalgam of different manuscripts, and the publication of most of them was not authorized by Max Weber himself. Look at the version edited by Marianne Weber and Johannes Winkelmann and search for *Eigentum*.[15] The result is strange, as this term is only indexed 11 times, including combinations such as *Eigentumsklage*. For *Privateigentum*, there is no entry at all. Hence, we might conclude that Weber does not have to say much about property.

Not at all: Property plays a critical role in two other key published works, Weber's dissertation and his habilitation.[16] However, we must be careful about the German equivalents. The dissertation deals with the emergence of a specific form of legal construct in medieval times, the root of German civil law's modern legal entity promulgated during Weber's lifetime, the "public mercantile association" (*Offene Handelsgesellschaft*). However, the critical concept is *Vermögen*, not *Eigentum*. This term often translates as "property,"[17] but this is seriously misleading and reflects the ambivalence of "property" in English. As we will discuss below in more detail, *Vermögen* refers to appropriated assets that are evaluated and aggregated in monetary terms. This definition includes two different perspectives: One is the capacity of *Vermögen* to generate financial income, and the other is that it might serve to satisfy claims of creditors for whatever reason. The latter closely relates to the notion of liability (*Haftung*), a critical theme in the dissertation. The proper translation of *Vermögen* is a matter of dispute; in his new translation, Tribe uses "wealth."[18] He follows Menger here, also observed by Weber, who defines *Vermögen* as the totality of economic goods at disposal.[19] These considerations show that Weber does not equate *Vermögen* with property as *Eigentum*. This fact is especially significant when we consider those parts of *Economy and Society* that were authorized by Weber and recently published in Kenneth Tribe's new translation. *Eigentum* is introduced in chapter 1, which deals with fundamental forms of *social* action, and *Vermögen* in chapter 2, which deals with *economic* action.

This distinction is of fundamental importance for the general argument in this book, even though, as we shall develop step by step, the translation as "wealth" is

---

14 Weber 2014b, 69.
15 Weber and Winckelmann 2009.
16 Weber 2012 and Weber 2014a.
17 Ford 2010.
18 Weber and Tribe 2019, 484.
19 Menger 1871, 89,

not followed in my approach developed in chapters 2 and 3. We use this term here provisionally. The critical point is that Weber relates *Vermögen* to money and markets exclusively, whereas *Eigentum* generally is independent of the market context. The modern uses of "property" conflate these distinct views and institutional contexts.[20] Weber defines *Vermögen* as follows.

1. "Wealt"" is not, of course, only made up of material goods. Rather, the wealth of its holder includes all *Chancen* of powers of disposal reliably secured, whether by custom, interest, convention, or law (and even a business's "clientele"—whether the business is that of a surgeon, a firm of solicitors, or the retail trade—is a part of the "wealth" belonging to the owner if, for whatever reason, they can be relied on, and where these are legally appropriated, they can of course be "property" as defined in Chapter 1, § 10).[21]

This definition does not conceive wealth as being owned as property but controlled by "powers of disposal reliably secured." Property is only a specific form of appropriation; it circumscribes only a subset of wealth. This definition is highly significant as there is a clear difference between property in Weber's sense and wealth, revealing a distance from modern legal conceptions of property. In these conceptions, the notion of wealth plays an important role and defines even differences in the same legal sphere, such as in continental Europe. For example, German civil law refers property to *Sachenrecht* (property law), hence to material objects exclusively, so that, for example, financial claims are not property (belonging to *Schuldrecht* (law of obligations). However, the European Court of Justice adopts the broader perspective close to Menger's definition of *Vermögen*. It regards all possible sources of economic gain as property.[22] However, it does not go as far as Weber, who even mentions the regular customers of a business as *Vermögen*. These differences reflect the emergence of new forms of wealth before the Industrial Revolution, mainly land, then real capital such as machinery, followed by financial capital in various types of assets, and today, knowledge and other immaterial goods.

This observation shows we can take two different analytical stances when analyzing appropriation.

- One is to start from the endogenous dynamics of the economy, where continuously new chances for economic advantage emerge, which then can become objects of appropriation in various forms, of which property is only one. In this

20 These conceptual distinctions have been lost in contemporary economics but were well noticed by earlier generations of economists trained in the intellectual history of economics, such as Krüsselberg 1984. In these traditions, property is seen as a legal concept, wealth and capital as economic concepts.

21 Weber and Tribe 2019, 177.

22 Praduroux 2017.

view, however, all these appropriated chances become rights and form wealth, with some of those rights even taking the legal form of property.
- The other is to start from a given pattern of practices and unearth the underlying order that stabilizes these practices, which may also constrain and channel forces of endogenous economic change. Both analytical stances are productive for understanding historical developments, such as the expansion of intellectual property in recent decades.

In conclusion, conflating wealth and property in one single concept, as in English, is wrong in Weber's framework, and we cannot even say that property is the right to wealth as an object. Wealth is an independent form of appropriation in the form of powers of disposition and, as we shall see below in more detail, relates to the economy and the market specifically. In contrast, property is a form of appropriation that includes but also transcends the economy.

The concept of "order" *Ordnung*

As we see, the proper translation of "property" is not evident in the context of Weber's work. We will deal with the language of property in the next chapter, but we will use Max Weber as a case in point in this chapter. If we accepted Weber's definition, most of what we regularly include under the term "property" would need to be referred to with another term. In English, "property" shows the ambivalence of object and institution, as property can even refer to landed assets, that is, real estate. At the same time, the term is also used in philosophical literature to refer to the most fundamental institutions of social life. These varieties call for conceptual clarification, perhaps even new terms for the different uses. Max Weber is an essential inspiration because Weber adopts a specific methodology and epistemological position that prevents him from using overly general, aggregate, and abstract concepts in a reified manner. His approach is the antidote to reification because Weber's sociology is action-centered. Hence, property is secondary to the action of appropriation, or it is one of its specific institutional forms. Let us look at what appropriation means in more detail.

For Weber, social life is a struggle between individuals and groups over what he calls *Chancen*. In the definition above, "property" appears as a particular type of *Chance*. We need to add another essential definition provided in the same paragraph: "Appropriated *Chancen* can be called 'rights'."[23] This is another example of

23 Weber and Tribe 2019, 123.

the intricacies of translation, as the English "can" translates the German *sollen*, which means it is being defined as rights. The Weberian notion of "right" is not exclusively related to the concept of "law." Weber writes:

> 2. For the concept of "law" as employed here, the existence of a staff dedicated to its enforcement is its most decisive feature, although for other purposes it might be defined quite differently. This agency, of course, does not have to resemble, in any respect, those with which we are familiar today. In particular, there is no necessary requirement that a "judicial" body exists.[24]

That means enforcement is essential, but it is not necessarily bound to the existence of the modern state.[25] We will discuss this question later in more detail; suffice it to note here that in modern civil laws and the variants of common law, property is indeed enforced by the government, so that rights are also legal rights. However, Weber's rights also exist in other forms. The conceptual frame of right is broader than law and relates to Weber's concept of "order" *Ordnung*.

> § 5. Action, especially social action, and even more specifically, a social relationship, can be oriented by an actor's conception of the existence of a legitimate order. The *Chance* that this actually occurs will be called the "validity" of the relevant order.[26]

And:

> 2. We will call the substantive meaning of a social relation a) an "order" only when action is (on average and approximately) oriented to definable "principles." We shall b) only speak of this order being "validated" if this actual orientation to those principles is also in practice followed because these principles are in some way or another recognised as binding or exemplary for the action. In fact, the orientation of action to an order occurs for a wide variety of motives. But besides other motives, the circumstances that for at least a proportion of actors the order seems exemplary, or obligatory, and hence is something that should have validity, naturally increases the *Chance* that action will be oriented to this order, often to a very significant extent.[27]

Weber's concept of order neither refers to something exclusively external to the social actors nor is accessible to an external observer without considering the internal states of actors, such as their beliefs or emotions. An order is a particular type of meaning, manifesting in certain principles accepted as legitimate by the actors and validated in their practices. Whether the actions manifest the order is itself contingent. Hence, expectations are critical for stabilizing an order. They are grounded in past experiences but mostly in conceptions of legitimacy and the following acceptance of an order, which can result from many factors that We-

24 Weber and Tribe 2019, 113.
25 As we will see, this is a bone of contention in modern institutional economics; Hodgson 2015.
26 Weber and Tribe, 2019, 108.
27 Weber and Tribe 2019, 109.

ber explored in much detail in his sociology of rule, such as tradition, belief, and rational consent.

Further, Weber explicitly rejects the idea that order is a monolithic and society-wide phenomenon. Indeed, even single individuals may follow various orders by acting in different social domains and following conflicting orders (such as moral versus economic). Further, there is also the possibility that individuals intentionally act against an order, yet this action also confirms its validity. Therefore, we notice that Weber's concept of social action is individualistic in the sense that individuals always can take distance from order and pursue their own goals, although in interdependence with others, and they recognize this interdependence in preparing and conducting their actions (which for Weber is the defining feature of "social action").

An order constitutes rights. This term is foundational and overcomes dualities often taken for granted in discussing property, namely the duality of law and custom, sometimes referred to as "customary law" or, in economics, a related distinction between "formal" and "informal institutions." In Weber's action-centered view, the theoretical notion of order is the counterpart to what Weber has not yet used as a theoretical concept, namely "practice." If we approach property as denoting a pattern of practices of appropriation, we will not look primarily at the law as shaping these practices but at the order. As said, that would not imply a society-wide property order but a variety of orders specific to certain domains. For example, appropriation orders differ across science, family matters, or finance.[28]

What does an order put into order? In the context of appropriation, these are the social actions and their consequences. People strive to appropriate *Chancen*. This term has proven challenging to translate, and it is highly significant that in the most recent state-of-the-art translation of the first chapters of *Economy and Society*, Kenneth Tribe opts for the solution to keep the German term in italics, even though "chance" is also an English word. However, the English "chance" has no plural, so the German plural *Chancen* is usually translated as "odds" or "prospects," which would not make sense for Weber's usage. As a result, the English language literature has often mistakenly emphasized the probabilistic aspect of the term, distorting the German meaning, where, however, the probabilistic aspect is also salient in the definition of order, as seen. Uncertainty, resulting from struggle and social complexity, is essential for Weber. But the uncertainty of what? This question relates to the other meaning of "chance," which is covered by "opportunity," hence the prospect of gaining an advantage of any kind. Accordingly, when looking at what sort of *Chancen* Weber mentions when employing the term appropriation, these are not only resources as material objects but also, for example,

28 This matches with Bourdieu's approach to fields and habitus that we will introduce in Chapter 3.

privileges such as diplomas, rights of access to professional circles, or formalized status. Considering these references, the concept of exclusion seems most relevant. Appropriation is a means of exclusion, but at the same time, there are also *Chancen* that result from other mechanisms of exclusion and, therefore, become targets of appropriation.

Appropriation is a specific type of action that is critical in social struggle. This term poses another difficulty in translation as it evokes social-Darwinist thinking, especially as it is also explicitly linked to selection. However, Weber uses the term "selection" in a broader sense and includes forms of selection that do not result from struggle but from the general conditions of life. He also considers the selection of norms and other forms of social relationships. In this sense, Weber adopts a general evolutionary framework for understanding social and economic change. However, struggle is omnipresent and, by definition, requires the intention to compete with others. Hence, competition is the general form of struggle, which can also take more specific forms, such as contests or conflicts, the former being more regulated than the latter, including all kinds of violence.

To sum up, Weber starts by viewing social life as a struggle where appropriation is a crucial means of gaining an advantage over others. However, this is not a Hobbesian state of nature but a state of order which governs social action. Order is not necessarily imposed by an external force such as the government but emerges endogenously as a complex conjunction of institutions, norms, or rules on the one hand and internal individual states such as beliefs, affects, or rational choices. Law is a specific force of order that defines a particular form of appropriation as property.

Appropriation and closure of social relationships

The counter pole to struggle is community. Unlike Tönnies, Weber adopts the action-centered perspective again and speaks of two primary forms of social relationships, namely "communalization" versus "sociation," These are technical English terms that translate the German *Vergemeinschaftung* and *Vergesellschaftung*. The terms are essential for discussing property, so we look at the definition.

§ 9. A social relationship will be called a "communalisation" (*Vergemeinschaftung*) if and to the extent that the disposition of social action rests—in the individual instance, or on average, or as a pure type—on a subjectively felt (affectual or traditional) mutual sense of belonging among those involved. A social relation will, on the other hand, be called "sociation" (*Vergesellschaftung*) if and to the extent that the disposition of social action is directed to a balance of rationally motivated interests (whether value rational or purposively rational), or to the connection of inter-

> ests motivated in the same way. *Vergesellschaftung* can typically be based on rational agreement arrived at through mutual consent, but not exclusively so. In such a case, sociated action is rationally oriented (a) by value, to a belief in one's own obligations; or (b) purposively rationally, to the expectation of loyalty from one's partner.[29]

Like Tönnies, Weber relates communalisation to the stance of belonging grounded in affects and tradition, whereas sociation rests on rational actions. Weber's notion of "rational" is broader than the economic one as it also includes forms such as value rationality that may engender stances such as feelings of obligation and expectations about commitments of one's own and others. Further, following the action-centered approach, both concepts can apply to social entities of different scopes and sizes. For example, sociation does not refer to "society" as in Tönnies's uses, but, for example, to establish a company. Communalisation may also include governments mobilizing a country for war and sacrifice. In focusing on action, Weber avoids reifying terms such as *Gesellschaft*, which he rarely uses and shuns as technical terms. For example, in the unfinished manuscript draft on markets (published in the Winckelmann version of *Economy and Society*), he speaks of *Marktvergesellschaftung*, not *Marktgesellschaft*.[30]

The distinction is of great significance in the context of Weber's dissertation, although he does not yet use these terms. Weber considers the transition from the "solidarity" of primary groups to the legal forms of "liability" related to formal associations, such as companies resulting from sociation. This distinction relates to the debates among lawyers of his times about the origins of the categories of civil law, where forms such as the "open mercantile association" appear to be independent of the traditions of Roman law but rooted in purported Germanic traditions of community. Weber discusses how the needs of more complex business operations required the formal separation of different types of *Vermögen* among the company and the members and their families, such that the reach of liability became transparent and predictable. This differentiation resulted in the emergence of the "firm" as a separate entity. Therefore, the need to clarify financial rights and obligations in business drove the specification of property assignments in terms of *Vermögen*. In Southern Europe, the transition to sociated business forms took a different track but implied such a separation. This separation also reveals the interest in protecting the family wealth from claims of business creditors (for example, immobile property as excluded from business concerns and the resulting liability).

Hence, we confirm what has been stated in general terms already, the emerging social differentiation of the economy as a separate domain, specifically in the

29 Weber and Tribe 2019, 120.

30 Weber and Winckelmann 2009, 382 ff.

form of markets, created the interests of certain groups to legally define their relationships as distinct arrangement of rights of disposing over wealth as *Vermögen* of business entities.

This distinction between communalization and sociation differs from another duality, namely between openness and closure.

> § 10. A social relationship, whether communalisation or sociation, will be called open to outsiders to the degree that participation in the mutual social action oriented to the substantive meaning that constitutes such action is not proscribed by prevailing valid rules to anyone so inclined and able to participate. By contrast, a social relationship is closed to outsiders to the extent that its substantive meaning or its prevailing rules exclude such participation, or restrict or permit it only according to specific conditions. Openness and closedness can be defined traditionally or affectively, by value or by purposive rationality.[31]

In the ideal-typical case of communalization, the internal social relationships would be open, reflecting solidarity among members. Although Weber does not use this term, we might refer to this as "sharing," meaning that all potential kinds of action that engage with specific sources of advantage, hence *Chancen*, are open to everyone. However, this is rarely the case in communities if sources are rivalrous (if only a seat and position at the dinner table). In external relations, communalization is often accompanied by closure since criteria such as kinship constrain membership. In contrast, sociation can be more flexibly arranged with varying degrees of external closure and openness, as these are determined by institutional fiat, such as agreements, and can be adapted to members' needs. Again, what matters is the degree of rivalry of the sources of advantage.

Now, we can further specify the meaning of appropriation since appropriation is a significant means of closure by exclusion. Weber also uses the term "monopolization" in this context. This term applies to both internal and external relationships. Once an individual or subgroup appropriates a certain *Chance*, this becomes a right. That means communalization and sociation are manifest forms of internal appropriation by rights, confirming the previous observation that law is only a specific form of enabling and stabilizing appropriation. In general, the order that is valid in the domain where the actions of communalization and sociation unfold sustains a specific pattern of appropriation. Weber identifies various forms of appropriation that we do not need to discuss now. As introduced previously, *Eigentum* is one of these forms.

However, one important aspect deserves mentioning, which is that social relationships do not only involve appropriation, but also "imputation" (*Zurechnung*):

31 Weber and Tribe 2019, 123.

§ 11. A social relationship can, for those involved according to tradition or statute, have as a consequence a) that particular kinds of action are imputed by each participant to all (in "solidarity"), or b) the action of particular participants ("representatives") can be imputed to the other members ("the represented"), such that they both enjoy the *Chancen* or bear the consequences.[32]

As we have seen, in the development of Weber's thinking about property, the concept of "liability" looms large. Imputation is a general analytical term, and we may reserve "liability" to the term "property." In his dissertation, Weber shows that the emergence of the legal person as the holder of rights to assets and the concomitant differentiation from the assets of the members of that entity resulted in the formation of modern forms of property related to wealth. In other words, certain forms of property emerge from the functional needs of ordering increasingly complex market transactions and, therefore, differ from forms of property that transcend markets and may even be primordial, such as property held by families.

We can illustrate the significance of this distinction with the social and political struggle over aristocratic landed wealth in the 19th century, which bears many resemblances to Weber's analysis of the Roman agrarian economy that we visit in the next section. The new civil laws and emerging national states legally annulled or tightly constrained constructs such as the *fidei commissum* or perpetual trusts, which aristocratic families employed to shield their wealth as property protected from creditors' claims. These traditional legal forms achieved even more vital significance than under the old regime because the current holders of the estates were also firmly engaging in the credit market, so their indebtedness could entail the loss of the family estate for future generations. Hence, the modern legal concepts abolished these prerogatives. The main goal was to bring the landed property into the reach of the market, which was accompanied by technical measures similar to the Roman case, that is, the creation of land registers. So, we observe an interesting twist that we can only grasp if we distinguish between property and wealth: In a sense, the old institutional forms represented property, whereas the new ones were wealth, a view that also transpires in Piketty's analysis of the transition to the rentier economy where the new bourgeoisie followed the aristocratic precedent treating landed estate primarily as a source of regular flows of rents.[33] The land was conceived as "capital," generating monetary profits (see below).

This historical transition has a highly significant modern sequel, which is that in common law, the old forms persisted with some modification and are widely used in modern finance to create myriad varieties of entities in which the current holders are not property holders, enjoy the flow of income generated from the

32 Weber and Tribe 2019, 127.
33 Piketty 2013, 206 ff.

assets and are shielded from full liability, thus minimizing their risks and maximizing their profits.[34] Hence, the "capitalists" even avoid property but aim to appropriate rights of disposition related to wealth. This confirms Weber's approach to focus on *Vermögen* when analyzing appropriation in the economy, particularly regarding capitalism.

Economic action and appropriation

The last observation highlights the need to distinguish clearly, like Weber, between the economy and other societal domains and to differentiate concepts of property accordingly. Indeed, when discussing property, we need to focus on the economic aspect, which is not explicitly mentioned by Weber in his definition, though implicitly alluded to in the context of "alienation," because one of the most critical forms of alienation is via the market. As we will discuss below in detail, the question is how this criterion relates to the other, namely inheritance. Inheritance, as such, is a means to transfer a certain status as defined by appropriated *Chancen* across generations, so it is a significant means of closure. However, it is essential to distinguish between inheritance in general, which includes all variants of descendants' claims on the property, and "testaments", in which an individual is free to dispose of assets to anyone, in the most liberal case.

This distinction reveals a tension between the two elements of Weber's definition, which we can only resolve if both types of action, inheriting and alienating, are entirely under the control of the individual holder of the property. As we have seen above, in the case of inheritance, this may be limited concerning claims of the state, but most importantly, historically, to claims of the family. The family or kinship group, as one of the essential primordial forms of communalization, may govern inheritance and constrain the leeway of the individual holder of assets, even to the degree that the latter only has the status of a steward, as in the case of *fidei commissum*. Modern inheritance laws mainly recognize specific minimum claims of close relatives, but, as in Germany, observing different degrees of relatedness such that second-degree relatives would face a higher tax rate, thus actually expropriating them partly, or better, revealing that these claims do not have the status of Weberian property. In other words, modern inheritance law regulates the inheritance of wealth and contains Weberian property in the transition

34 Pistor 2019.

between generations.[35] This is salient when the testator wants to bequeath property but has negative wealth: In this case, heirs can only appropriate the property when redeeming the debt.

In his habilitation on Roman governance of agricultural land, Weber explores how conceptions of private property emerged from the interests of individual wealth owners to disenfranchise even many of their sons. A leitmotif of the dissertation is relevant, too, as this was also a requirement to create security for creditors since wealthy Romans were engaging in increasingly sophisticated financial transactions.[36] At the same time, Weber also shows that this went along with further accentuating the distinction between private property and public property since the Roman Empire opened its vast acquired territories ("public," *ager publicus*) for agrarian settlement, including for the disenfranchised, in the legal form of tenancy. Most interestingly, both tied up in a topical focus of Weber's habilitation, which is the role of land registers and field surveyors. These served different purposes, such as assigning plots to tenants and, most importantly, assessing tax duties. They eventually enabled the emergence of a market for land rights with distant holders of the rights, thus fostering the emergence of large private landholdings. This land market was deeply integrated with the financial market, so Weber speaks of "agrarian capitalism." This characterization follows from the diagnosis that for the status of the wealthy landowners, the financial gains from agriculture mattered essentially to maintain their urban lifestyles (and even political position, as in the case of senators).

In both the dissertation and the habilitation, Weber's notion of property is operative in analyzing *economic* change. What is Weber's idea of "the economic"? Again, this is action-based:

> § 1. Action will be called "economically-oriented" inasmuch as its intended meaning is oriented to meeting (*Fürsorge*) a desire for utilities. "Economic activity" (*Wirtschaften*) will refer to a peaceful exercise of a power of disposition primarily oriented to "rational economic action," which action is primarily rational by virtue of being directed to a purpose (*zweckrational*), and hence is planfully oriented to economic ends. "Economy" is autocephalous economic action; "the pursuit of economic activity" (*Wirtschaftsbetrieb*) is continuously ordered (*betriebsmäßig geordnetes*) economic activity.[37])

35 Recent research on testaments in Roman law (Harke 2023) has confirmed this distinction. The original freedom of bequeathing by testament was constrained by enforcing mandatory shares for family heirs; however, the former related to property, hence indeed a pristine form of private property, whereas the latter referred to wealth.

36 Goetzmann 2017, 103 ff.

37 Weber and Tribe 2019, 143.

We notice the distinction between "economically-oriented" and "economic." The former includes all kinds of goals where the economic goal is only secondary, such as a religious war that requires the mobilization of economic resources. Further, even when economic goals dominate, violence disqualifies an action as "economic." As we shall see later, it is crucial to exclude violent means of appropriation from the economy, which, however, is a complicated matter insofar as we need to distinguish between violence and power.

In this definition, there is another intricacy of translation, as the term *Fürsorge* oscillates with the German *Vorsorge* (which Weber also uses) since Sorge, in general, implies being future-oriented, thus reflecting uncertainty, which is not just "meeting" a need in the present. So, perhaps a better choice is "provisioning" (also used in the quote below). The other tricky question is the meaning of "utilities," which translates *Nutzleistungen*. As Kenneth Tribe explains in detail, this term was taken from Böhm-Bawerk but never sedimented in German language economics since there were also receptions of the merging neoclassical economics, hence using the term *Nutzen*. Weber accepted the idea that this means *nützlich* in the eyes of the beholder, hence containing a strong dose of subjectivity. Still, we should keep his use separate from the meaning of modern economics. Hence, we get the following English translation:

> § 2. By "Utilities" (*Nutzleistungen*) will always be meant those concrete (real or putative) *Chancen* of present or future possible uses that one or more economic agents deem solely appropriate to become objects of provision, to whose presumed significance as means capable of serving the economic agent's or agents' ends his (or their) economic activity is consequently oriented. Utilities can be services (*Leistungen*) realised either by a human or a nonhuman (material) intermediary (*Träger*). These latter material intermediaries for utilities, of whatever kind, are called "goods," whereas human utilities, insofar as they arise from actual action, are called "services." Social relationships are also the object of economic consideration insofar as they are thought to represent a possible source of present or future powers of disposal over utilities. "Economic *Chancen*" are opportunities that arise through custom, interests, or a (conventionally or legally) guaranteed order with respect to an economy.[38]

As we see, the term *Nutzleistungen* does not refer to a universal psychological construct, even if based on subjective assessment, but relates to the domain of economic action, which is, by definition, social, hence intersubjective. Further, economic action is about safeguarding future utilities, which points to the essential role of rights that guarantee access and continued use, which unpredictable actions of others could otherwise jeopardize. That means the context of the struggle over economic advantage determines what a "utility" is, and this context is patterned by a broader range of institutions, also beyond the economy, especially

38 Weber and Tribe 2019, 150.

rule and domination. Most basically, we can distinguish between needs and market-related utilities, which boil down to the *Chancen* to generate income from appropriated sources of utilities. This contextualization of *Chancen* in the realm of money and markets establishes the connection between the concepts of *Nutzleistungen* and *Vermögen*.

Weber is very clear about exclusively confining the notion of *Vermögen* to the monetary economy, which is one reason why the translation as "wealth" may be problematic (in English, mostly "property" would be used[39]). Nevertheless, the point in favor is twofold. One is that Weber strictly confines *Vermögen* either to capacities of generating future income or to assets tradable via markets and, therefore, having a price. Second, only if there is a price can wealth be considered as an aggregate. Weber's definitions are pure economics:

> The income of a household is the sum of goods calculated in money that, employing the accounting principle stated in 4. above, can be rationally calculated to have been available to it in a previous period, or for which there is the *Chance* of such availability in a current or future period according to rational assessment. The total calculated sum of goods at the disposal of a household for its permanent and direct use, or for the acquisition of income (estimated in market *Chancen* as in 3.), is called its wealth. The premise of purely monetary budgetary accounting is that income and wealth consist either of money, or of goods that can in principle be exchanged at any time for money, and hence are to the highest degree absolutely marketable.[40]

These observations raise important questions about property, which we will answer step by step in the following chapters. Weber states that there is only possession (*Besitz*) in an economy without a monetary standard of value. This distinction reveals a critical point: Weber approaches property as an epiphenomenon of the more fundamental processes that led to the emergence of rational economic action and capitalism as a comprehensive system. Therefore, he spends much space in Chapter 2 of *Economy and Society* elaborating on money in technical detail, which today may appear surprising in what counts as a "sociological" work. The emergence and the use of money create the conditions for calculation, hence rational planning, and allow the social construction of the entity named *Vermögen*. Therefore, as argued previously, the analytical step from economic change to property is most significant in this perspective because the institutions emerge as fulfilling specific functional needs implied by the former.

This causal primacy of economic change becomes apparent when considering the "capital" concept derived from *Vermögen*. Weber gives a highly significant example, comparing the rentier and the capitalist (which relates to the Piketty argument that we alluded to previously). For the rentier, land is wealth because it gen-

---

39 As in Ford 2010.

40 Weber and Tribe 2019, 175.

erates a flow of monetary income, such as from tenancy. Nevertheless, the rentier does not optimize his wealth in terms of rationally considering alternative uses of the monetary capital embodied in the land. *Vermögen* becomes capital only if the use of assets is subject to a comprehensive accounting system for costs and potential profits from alternative uses. At this point, *Eigentum* in Weber's meaning becomes important because only specific institutional forms of property enable this full-scale economic calculation, most importantly, free labor and private ownership of means of production. Notice the difference to Marx: Whereas Marx emphasizes exploitation and analyzes this based on the labor theory of value, Weber follows the economics of his times and sidelines this theory. Instead, he emphasizes the functional needs of rational calculation: "Capitalist calculation, then, in its most formally rational guise, presupposes the struggle of man against man."[41] This translation is unfortunate, as *Kapitalrechnung* is not referring to "capitalism" as an economic system, but to "capital accounting," hence not "capitalist accounting:"

> Proper to rational economic acquisition is a particular form of monetary calculation: capitalist calculation. Capitalist calculation is the estimation and review of *Chancen* for acquisition and successful outcomes of the same by comparing the estimated monetary amounts of all acquisitional goods (in money or in-kind) present at the outset of an acquisitive undertaking with the stock of (remaining and newly manufactured) acquisitional goods present at the completion of a particular undertaking, or where continuous acquisitive activity (*Erwerbsbetrieb*) is involved, comparing the opening and closing balance in an accounting period. Capital is a monetary estimate of the sum total of means of acquisition at the disposition of the enterprise for its own purposes shown in its balance sheet; profit or loss is the surplus or shortfall of estimated values disclosed by a closing balance compared with an opening balance; capital risk is the estimated *Chance* of loss to the balance sheet; and an economic undertaking is action that can be autonomously oriented to capitalist calculation. This orientation derives from calculation: prior calculation of the anticipated risk and profit arising from a measure under consideration, and subsequent recalculation reviewing the actual resultant profit or loss.[42]

Weber defines capital in financial terms, unlike earlier economists, whom he followed otherwise, such as Menger, who treats capital as real capital. Therefore, his concept seems closer to Marx. However, in this translation, we should substitute "capital" for "capitalist" since Weber carefully distinguishes between the technical aspects of calculation as necessary conditions of rationality and the social conditions for realizing this calculation. In Chapter 2 of *Economy and Society*, Weber develops a complex taxonomy of objects of appropriation, especially concerning labor and means of production. This distinction is economically important as the

41 Weber and Tribe 2019, 182.
42 Weber and Tribe 2019, 179.

appropriation of labor can combine in various ways with the appropriation of the complementary means of production. Further, appropriation of labor can take different forms concerning the proper activity, the *Leistung*, and its product. Weber assumes that only specific combinations of forms of appropriation can also sustain a regime of rational calculation:

2. The greatest degree of rationality as a calculative means of orientation for economic activity is achieved by monetary calculation in the form of capitalist calculation; materially presupposing the most extensive market freedom, meaning the absence of either compulsory and economically irrational, or voluntary and economically rational monopolies (i.e., monopolies oriented to market *Chancen*). The competitive struggle over the sale of products that is linked to this situation generates a range of expenditures, especially with respect to sales organisation and advertising in its widest sense, which, in the absence of such competition, would simply cease to exist (hence, in the case of planned economies or rational comprehensive monopolies). Furthermore, rigorous capitalist calculation is linked socially to "factory discipline" and the appropriation of material means of production, and thus to the existence of a relation of rule.[43]

Here, a crucial point comes to the fore, which is that the conditions of economic rationality include a "relation of rule", that is *Herrschaft*. The locus of this rule is the factory. This is highly significant as modern economics does not resolve a paradox that results from the coexistence of a supposedly free labor market and hierarchical subordination in companies, neutralizing the latter via the assumption that the labor contract implies agreement with subordination, and allows for leaving the company at will. However, this distorts social realities and thus should be taken at face value as a profound contradiction at the heart of economic liberalism.[44] For Weber, this is not a contradiction at all since this is a requirement of enabling full-scale economic calculation. Ruling in the factory also requires that workers do not own the means of production that are complementary to their work. In conjunction with that, the freedom of the labor contract means that the employers do not appropriate labor; hence are also free from any other obligations to workers than those stipulated in the contract, which is a condition for reducing uncertainty about labour costs.

The difference to Marx is significant: Marx treats property as a given and does not explain in detail how this emerges in the process of economic change. In this sense, Weber provides a microeconomic and sociological explanation for phenomena that Marx analyzes mainly as macro-processes, following the tradition of classical economics. Weber received inspiration from the transition to modern, later "neoclassical" economic theory, combined with his action-based analytical stance, which matches the methodological individualism that came along with

43 Weber and Tribe 2019, 202.
44 Armbrüster 2005, Anderson 2019.

it. Weber's view allows a more nuanced view of "capitalism" as a system, with important implications for the theory of appropriation.

Appropriation of *Chancen*, power of disposition, and property in capitalism

Weber describes the emergence of capitalism as follows:

> Development into capitalism: α. Actual monopolisation of money capital (*Geldbetriebsmittel*) by entrepreneurs so that they might make advance payments to workers. Associated with this is the management of goods production through producers' credit and disposal over the product, despite the formal continuation of the appropriation of the means of gainful activity (*Erwerbsmittel*) to the worker (in industry and mining). β. Appropriation of the right of sale of products on the basis of previous actual monopolisation of market knowledge, and hence of market *Chancen* and money capital through forcibly imposed and monopolistic guild regulation, or privilege of political force (as a source of rental income, or against a loan). γ. Inner disciplining of the labourer dependent on domestic industry: delivery of raw materials and equipment by the entrepreneur. A special case here is the rational and monopolistic organisation of domestic industries on the basis of privileges granted for financial purposes and for the gainful employment of the population. The granting of a concession with respect to gainful activity was linked to the compulsory regulation of working conditions. δ. Within the enterprise, creation of workshops without rational specialisation of work where all material means of production are appropriated to the entrepreneur. In mining, this implies the appropriation of deposits, shafts, galleries, and equipment by the owner. In transport, shipping came into the hands of large owners. Everywhere, the outcome was that the workers were expropriated from the means of production. ε. The final step in the capitalist transformation of productive enterprises is the mechanisation of production and transport, together with capitalist calculation. All material means of production become "fixed" or enterprise capital. The entire labour force becomes "hands." The transformation of undertakings into associations owned by those holding securities results also in the expropriation of the manager and his transformation into an "official," the owner becoming a trustee for those who supply credit (banks).[45]

This description reveals that in analyzing the emergence of capitalism, we need to distinguish between various and specific mechanisms of economic action and the ultimate stage where they play together in forming a comprehensive system. As such, the mechanisms can already be capitalist if they result in specific forms of social action. Therefore, Weber acknowledged that capitalist forms of economic action can emerge within settings that have not yet been completely transformed into a capitalist regime. In his habilitation, he speaks of "agrarian capitalism"

45 Weber and Tribe 2019, 260.

without claiming that the entire Roman economy has developed into capitalism, with significant constraints such as the continuation of slavery, which is unfree labor. This analysis puts his argument in a two-pronged relationship with Marx: On the one hand, as for Marx, the material conditions of slavery were essential in blocking the transition to capitalism, but at the same time, slavery could become an object in capitalist practices, which is a contradiction in adjective for Marx.[46]

Similarly, in his scientific and political analyses of East Prussian agriculture, he draws comparisons with Southern Germany, showing that capitalist practices had become dominant only in the case of the former. Property arrangements play an important role here: Landlords did not interfere with tenancy relationships and commons in Southern Germany because they were more profitable than directly controlling land in full-scale private ownership. Peasants lived close to marketplaces and engaged in economically productive activities, generating sufficient income to safeguard the rents paid to landlords. In comparison, the Eastern landlords were interested in creating large estates where hired hands did the agricultural work, driving emigration to America and immigration from Poland. Hence, Weber diagnosed dire political consequences for the national cohesion of the young German nation.[47]

Capitalism appears as a set of mechanisms and practices that can coexist with other forms of economic organization, such as in different regions of Germany. Property is one of the critical institutional elements, but this does not mean that in non-capitalist arrangements, certain groups do not profit substantially from them in terms of accumulating *Vermögen*. Hence, the interests of various groups and their resulting actions explain why specific arrangements prevail and persist: In Eastern and Southern Germany, landlords pursued their economic interests and gained from the existing arrangements, but only in the Eastern regions, creating the institutional conditions for capitalist agriculture.

Weber does not ignore the distributional consequences: Weber distinguishes between formal and substantive (*materiale*) rationality and recognizes that real-world capitalist systems can manifest many violations of material rationality, which includes distributional pathologies or interference by irrational elements such as political interests or speculation.

§ 9. The formal rationality of economic activity can be characterised here as the degree of calculation that is technologically possible for that activity, and the extent to which it is actually applied. By contrast, the substantive rationality of economic activity concerns the degree to which

46 Wiener (1982) points out that *Economy and Society* differs sharply from Weber's earlier analysis. But this is perhaps a distortion resulting from the problematic status of that book. The parts authorized by Weber match with his earlier work. I am grateful to Dirk Schuck for pointing out this source.

47 Stienen 2022, 127.

the given supply of goods for particular human groups (however delimited), organised through economically oriented social action, was, is, or could be subjected to particular evaluative postulates (however constituted). These postulates are extremely ambiguous.[48]

To this paragraph we add the important remark:

Beyond these general circumstances, the undertaking oriented to market *Chancen* furthers this form of expropriation a) by rewarding the rational and technological qualities of capitalist calculation where there is complete appropriation to the owner, as compared with any other economic process of lower calculable rationality, b) by rewarding the purely mercantile qualities of management as contrasted with their technological qualities, and the maintenance of technological and commercial secrets, c) by favouring speculative management, which presupposes such expropriation. This is ultimately made possible without regard to the degree of technological rationality involved: d) through the superiority possessed α. in the labour market, by virtue of possession of any property, with respect to partners in exchange (workers), β. in the goods market with respect to any commercial competitor inferior in methods of calculation, less well situated with regard to credit-worthiness, and less well provided with capitalist calculation, installed capital goods, and access to commercial credit. A further specifically material irrationality of the economic order is that the greatest extent of formal rationality in capitalist calculation is possible only where the worker is completely subject to the rule of entrepreneurs. Finally, e) discipline is optimal where there is free labour and the complete appropriation of the means of production.[49]

Property is less significant than the power of disposition to understand the material consequences of specific institutional arrangements. This insight is evident from Weber's comparison between Eastern and Southern German agriculture: As said, in the latter, landlords had no economic interest in changing property arrangements because the existing allocation of powers of disposition was more beneficial in securing flows of economic benefits to them. At the same time, this left more room for improving living standards for the farmers, who also retained traditional powers of disposition. In contrast, the Eastern regions faced more severe economic disruptions, with political consequences, such as heightening societal tensions over Polish immigration.[50]

Hence, property is a less general economic concept for understanding appropriation than the power of disposition. As I mentioned, Weber relied on Carl Menger's work from whom he borrowed *Verfügungsgewalt*. This notion is essential for Menger in defining an economic "good." To qualify an object as a good, it must relate to a (human) need and have a feature that enables fulfilling that need. At the same time, this causal connection must be recognized by a person, and this person must have, in principle, the power of disposition over the object. The

48 Weber and Tribe 2019, 172.
49 Weber and Tribe 2019, 245.
50 Stienen 2022.

latter observation is essential, as this means that there is no abstract notion of a good disconnected from a relationship between the object and a person who can act upon the object.

This notion of good gives us an essential hint at how to translate the term *Chance* into English. A Mengerian good is an intermediate between subject and object, different from the view in modern economics, which neatly separates the realm of subjective utility assignments from the domain of objects to which these refer, the goods. In modern scientific terminology, a term that comes close to this constellation is "affordance." Affordances in cognitive sciences or design refer to objects that elicit specific actions, such as a seat affording the action of sitting.[51] Hence, on the one hand, affordances are features of the material world, such as a tree being an affordance to climb. However, at the same time, they are subjectively material in that they relate to actions of specific beings with certain embodied capacities to act: The tree is affordance to climb for a cat, but not for a duck. Weber's *Chance* similarly refers to properties of the material world that enable economic actions. Therefore, we might translate the term as "affordance." Individuals can realize affordances without appropriating them, excluding others, yet they must have the capacity for this action. If individuals appropriate the *Chancen*, these turn into rights, which can also be legally enforced. Economic affordances relate to the economy and, in Western modernity, markets. They are defined as *Chancen* to reap monetary gains in economic transactions.

In differentiating the economic domain from other societal value spheres, we must distinguish property and wealth as *Vermögen* and, eventually, capital. Market development has driven the transition to full-scale capital accounting, constitutive of economic rationality. A fundamental internal contradiction of capitalism is that, on the one hand, for gaining an advantage in economic struggle, appropriating powers of disposition is the key; on the other hand, the social conditions of deploying capital require establishing factory rule, which grounds in a conception of property as *dominium*, hence transcending the economic domain.

Conclusion

Weber's approach to appropriation is essential for the economics of property in many respects. The first and most fundamental insight is that *Eigentum*, in the Weberian sense, emerges endogenously in markets as a form that enables rational

51 Chong and Proctor 2020.

calculation of economic benefits for certain groups of actors. This view transcends the Coasean notion of economic efficiency because one of the critical conditions is the peculiar combination of free labor markets and hierarchical discipline or rule in the factory. This results in material irrationality of the distribution of the gains from economic action among groups. Therefore, the institutional arrangement requires stabilization via legal fixation of the corresponding forms of appropriation and the resulting allocation of powers of disposition among various groups. This constellation motivates the widespread political and social critique of property, often directed at "private property," which is effectively referring to *Eigentum*.

Hence, capitalism as a comprehensive system is only sustainable with a strong state that enforces property. This statement radically differs from the common liberal, even libertarian view that the state is necessary to protect the rights of property holders: here, the state enforces a regime of inequality between property holders and free labor. Weber has the notion of "political capitalism" that refers to more specific forms of direct participation of government in the economy, which also results in specific forms of material irrationality. However, capitalism in general, can be seen as a close conjunction of state and market, such that state-enforced property becomes the means to impose a particular economic order on people:

> 4. Commercial economic sociation (*Vergesellschaftung*) of economic activity presupposes the appropriation of the actual holders of utilities on the one hand, and market freedom on the other. Market freedom increases in significance (1) the more complete is the appropriation of the actual holders of utilities, especially of means of production and of transport; for their maximum degree of marketability implies a maximum orientation of their economic activity to market situations. It also increases (2) the more that appropriation is limited to actual holders of utilities. Every appropriation of human beings (slavery, bondage) or of economic *Chancen* (client monopolies) places a limitation on human action oriented to market situations. Fichte was right in his Closed Commercial State to regard this restriction of the concept of "property" to material goods (while at the same time extending the content embodied in property to autonomy of powers of disposal) as the characteristic feature of the organisation of property in a modern commercial economy. All those with an interest in the market had a stake in the way such a reorganisation of property eased their orientation to those *Chancen* of gain that the market situation provided, and the development of this particular form of property order was consequently largely due to their influence.[52]

Weber's views can help clarify the distinction between "legal" and "economic" property rights in modern economics.[53] Clearly, economic property rights correspond to Weber's *Verfügungsgewalt*. This reveals the problematic status of the

52 Weber and Tribe 2019, 208.
53 Hodgson 2015 versus Allen 2015.

concept of "property" in the concept of "property right." In the Weberian sense, this cannot be put together since it would imply that the "property right" must be defined by being inheritable and free. Using the term "property" indiscriminately results in conceptual and analytical confusion. Only legal rights of a particular type can be property, whereas "property rights" are powers of disposition. We will further pursue this argument in Chapter 3.

However, there is a deeper issue at stake. The modern legal concepts of property are a hybrid of new institutional forms that ease market transactions to the highest degree possible or even create markets, but at the same time, they are rooted in pre-modern notions that emphasize property as a form of rule, that is, *dominium*. This may explain why economics shows an ambivalent stance towards property: In a "radical" view, property should wither away in a market regime which would not allow for any fixation of ownership, rendering it negotiable at any point of time.[54] This reveals that in real-world market economies aka capitalism, power is at stake, not efficiency. As Weber writes in the chapter on the sociology of law in *Economy and Society*:

> The result of contractual freedom, then, is in the first place the opening of the opportunity to use, by the clever utilization of property ownership in the market, these resources without legal restraints as a means for the achievement of power over others. The parties interested in power in the market thus are also interested in such a legal order.[55]

Hence, the profound paradox of capitalism is that capitalists do not need property to control the power of disposition that enables them to appropriate economic affordances, aka *Chancen*. They even shun property to avoid the consequences of liability. At the same time, they need property to cement capitalist rule, which also requires transgenerational protection of status.

In Figure 1.1, I summarize Max Weber's conceptual framework. The objects of appropriation are not "things" but *Chancen*. What counts first is powers of disposition over *Chancen*, which can result from many different social forces which are arranged in a social order. If *Chancen* are appropriated, they become rights. Property is one institutional form of right, but not the only one, though dominant in capitalism as private property. In capitalism, *Chancen* are subject to markets as the central institution in the economy which require and enable calculation. Calculation transforms *Chancen* into wealth, which is not co-extensive with property. For wealth, powers of disposition are critical, but not all powers of disposition are subject or amenable to calculation. Hence, property transcends the domain of the economy.

54 Posner and Weyl 2018. We discuss this contribution in Chapter 3.
55 Weber, Roth, and Wittich 1978, 1169.

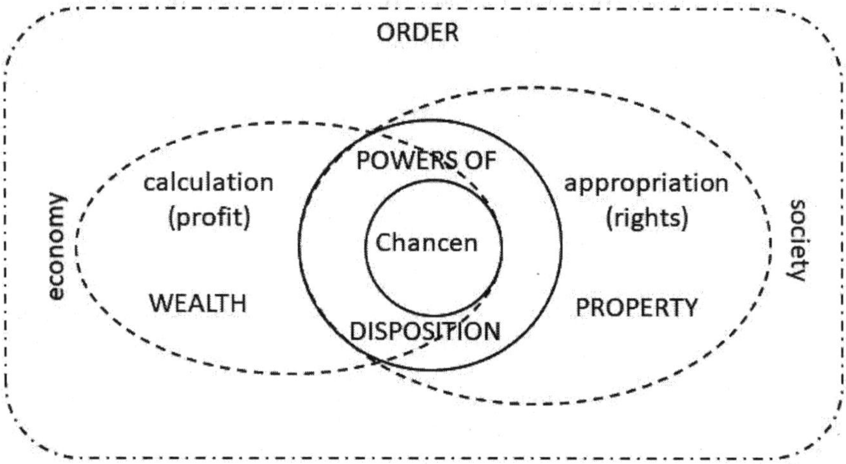

Figure 1.1: Max Weber's approach to appropriation
Source: author's diagram

Despite these essential Weberian insights, Weber's focus on appropriation does not elucidate all the phenomena of order that constitute property, such as the role of legitimacy. Weber's work concentrates on the relationship between property, wealth and capital in the emergence of capitalist forms of economic order, such as Roman agrarian capitalism. This focus blanks out the variety of property across other types of order, and even within capitalism, across diverse social domains, or value spheres, in Weberian parlance. Therefore, a comprehensive theory of property must transcend capitalism and treat its form of property, private property, only as one form among many. The next chapter explores this diversity while looking for conceptual unity.

Chapter 2: Exploring the languages of *property*

The semantic domain of *property*

Ludwig Wittgenstein once quipped that philosophy is like bumping the head against the walls of language.[1] This certainly applies to property. Our discussion of Weber's views on property showed that one of his main concerns was to clarify the meanings of terms such as *Eigentum* and *Vermögen*. This chapter will examine such terminological issues, focusing on etymologies and translations of property-related terms. This approach is not intended to be a Heidegger-like creative use of words. Still, my main concern is to draw philosophical insights from language analysis that eventually help us to develop analytical and conceptual frames for understanding property in the real world. By reflecting on languages and their differences in meanings, we aim to reach through the institutional realizations of property, for example, property in contemporary capitalist societies, and get hold of the lifeworld of having as an existential dimension of being human. The structures of having, as reflected in languages of property, will provide the ground for formulating a new theory of having beyond property in the subsequent chapter.

My starting point is the diagnosis that our (meaning: English) language of property is impoverished in many contexts, and unfortunately, especially in the social sciences and related fields.[2] Scholars often speak of property as a generic term and even neglect distinctions clearly defined in legal language, such as possession versus property. Ignoring the linguistic diversity of property across cultures and societies is an even more severe flaw. A general theory of property must start by recognizing this diversity. Just assuming that there is a catch-all concept

1 Wittgenstein 2009, § 119. "The results of philosophy are the discovery of some piece of plain nonsense and the bumps that the understanding has got by running up against the limits of language. They – these bumps a-make us see the value of that discovery."

2 For a lucid critique of studying property in Imperial China, see Ocko 2004. Translation issues loom large in anthropological research on property in contemporary non-Western societies, such as Oceania, Wagner and Talakai 2007.

that is valid everywhere and at any time is not a priori justifiable. General theories of property, such as in economics, aspire to apply universally, such as explaining the emergency of property rights among North American native people and claiming that this grounds a universal theory of property in advanced capitalism, and vice versa.[3] However, this has led to severe blunders with many scientific and political implications.[4] One of the roots of the problems was the failure to correctly translate indigenous terms into European languages, claiming the absence of property, which was seen as an indicator of "savage" status akin to animals.[5] Against this background, we become aware of the fact that language is power: In translating indigenous terms in specific ways, colonizers negated existing practices, justified their appropriation of native territories, and provided legitimacy to the institutions of colonial rule.[6] This continues until today when former dispossession is renegotiated at the courts, and the question is still problematic of how to depict the nature of Indigenous claims in the language of hegemonic law of the respective nation-states.[7]

Furthermore, a kind of self-colonization in Western modernity reflects the history of the European nation-states, which intruded and often forcefully incorporated local communities in the context of property, the crusade against the commons, and the enclosures.[8] Consequently, the new language of the European civil laws also shaped the colloquial notions of property. In our modern world, there is a struggle over new words, often in the legal sphere, to overcome this poverty of language. For example, in German, recently the notion of "Verantwor-

3 Classically, Demsetz 1967. It is illuminating to compare the entries on property in the 1987 editions of the "New Palgrave. A dictionary of economics" with the 2008 edition. In the first, Ryan 1987 offers a broad perspective on the economic and philosophical aspects, whereas in the latter, we have specialized entries on "property rights" with emphasis on private property, Alchian 2008, and a technical analysis of the Law & economics of property law, Lueck 2008. This shows how economics has become increasingly context-insensitive and a-historical.

4 Greer (2017, 60 ff) gives a detailed account of the misperceptions underlying Demsetz' analysis.

5 Möllers 2024.

6 For example, in Africa, the British introduced a terminological juxtaposition between traditional "communal" land and modern private ownership systems, which did not adequately reflect the diversity of property relations in villages, which also included market-oriented land transactions, though not cast into the colonizers' legal language, Chimhowu and Woodhouse 2006. Since we cannot reconstruct the historical situation, we only have the colonisers' accounts using their terminology. Even today, this gap is discernible since there are few field studies of native villagers' views, such as Sawadogo and Stamm 2000. These conceptual troubles are endemic: compare the case of Oceania, Boydell 2010.

7 These issues are salient in Australian court proceedings over Indigenous land issues. Keenan (2015, 112 ff) shows that even in one judgement, the three judges disagreed about the meaning and nature of Indigenous claims on land.

8 Padoa-Schioppa (2017, 451 ff, 473 ff) overviews the landmark event of the Napoleonic codification of property law and territorial administration.

tungseigentum" ("responsible property") has been coined to denote a new form of socially responsible enterprise that generalizes over certain forms of family business.[9]

A general theory of property could build on a survey of property practices across many societies. I choose another approach: exploring the languages that reflect those practices, extracting theoretical insights from differences in meaning, and distinguishing these cases from observations on commonalities. However, we must define a starting point in identifying the broader range of references of these linguistic phenomena. In doing so, we must immunize our thinking against all biases resulting from our own language. The term "property" is the most problematic, as it carries all the baggage of the history and current understandings of property in hegemonic modern societies. Therefore, from now on, I will use ***property*** in bold italics when I speak about the generic phenomenon that we are exploring, a semantic domain referring to a range of actions, and will use "property" with inverted commas to refer to the established uses in contemporary law and related disciplines. I use simple italics when I cite words in the original language. In the next chapter, we will resolve this terminological tension by introducing an entirely new terminology of ***property*** that refers to "having" as the foundational type of action and "havings" as its outcomes.

Weber's concept of appropriation defines one reference point of ***property***: We refer to a particular type of action and not to an institution. These actions exclude others from using a particular object, announcing that an object belongs to someone, or quarrelling over such assignments. Early Roman law expresses this fundamental appropriative action in the formula "meum esse."[10] It is important to avoid projections of established notions of "property" right from the beginning. For example, assigning an object to someone, such as a prey to a hunter, does not necessarily imply that the corpse belongs to the hunter exclusively, as in European traditions. In many Indigenous societies, the assignment implies the obligation of sharing the prey.[11] However, this does not invalidate the assignment; on the contrary, the assignment is also an assignment of a specific obligation and the corresponding agency. In fact, this is also true for established modern concepts of "property" since the owner of an object is also assigned responsibility for it. For

---

9 Reiff 2024, Schlömer-Laufen, Reiff, and Kay 2024.

10 Kaser (1985) discusses the complexity of this expression insofar as it refers to specific legal norms in disputes where, in the first step, it expresses an absolute claim, ritually enacted in touching and grasping an object. This ritual is the *mancipatio;* von der Weth 2024. In many languages, the basic form of possessive verbs is derived from actions of grasping and holding, such as Spanish *tenere*, Aikhenvald 2012, 28.

11 Trosper 2022, 54. Most significantly, this obligation often is not based on claims of others vis à vis the hunter but on claims of the prey and the spirit that owns it.

instance, the owner of a car is seen as being responsible if she neglects necessary repairs and causes an accident. That means the assignment of obligations and the recognition of appropriation are three aspects of one form of ***property***.

As these examples show, the Weberian emphasis on appropriation is an expression of a distinct cultural form, possessive individualism, which puts the individual at the center of the action, abstracting from the embedding social relationships.[12] However, there is also the possibility that a community assigns an object to an individual without that individual taking the respective appropriative action. On the surface, both appropriation and assignment may result in the same form of "private property," but the actual social meaning is very different. For example, the Cree Hunting Law of 2009 (§ 9.8)[13] clearly establishes ownership of individual kills as a rule of assignment, which the community can adapt depending on environmental conditions, and there are sharing obligations. The appropriative action, the hunt, is thoroughly monitored by the *Kaanoowapmaakin*, the hunting leader and steward of the hunting ground. The Cree (Eeyou) Hunting Law has the following comment on the terminology of the document:

> The drafting of this document has required many choices to be made. While this document was drafted originally in English, the choice was made to use Eeyou terminology for each of the important concepts it sets out, for this is a document that is conceived and articulated by Eeyou for Eeyou. It is intended, therefore, that it reflects Eeyou concepts, Eeyou values and the Eeyou way of seeing things. The Eeyou terms chosen were themselves the object of much discussion and reflect the consensus reached. At the same time, an attempt has been made to make it clearly understood by non-Eeyou and by the non-Eeyou legal system, so the decision was made to try to use a tone and style easily understood by most non-Eeyou, but that still reflects the role of law in Eeyou culture. The great challenge of this process has been to find a way to describe accurately in writing, and in a language that is not the original language of the Eeyou, what is an oral tradition expressed in the Eeyou language. It reflects a balancing of the need to remain faithful to the oral law while producing a written law that would be clearly understood by Eeyou and non-Eeyou alike.

As we learn from that quote, we must expand the established notions of ***property*** in various directions to catch the entire semantic domain. In the European tradition of possessive individualism, ***property*** is reduced to the action of appropriation, which is also manifest in treating "property" as a right mainly, both in the civil law and the human rights context. However, this creates a bias that blinds the view on the other components of ***property***. In Weber's approach to order, the second element is recognition or legitimacy. Recognition can imply that there is

12 Macpherson 2011.

13 https://www.cerp.gouv.qc.ca/fileadmin/Fichiers_clients/Documents_deposes_a_la_Commission/P-640.pdf, last access March 23, 2024.

no need for appropriative action since the status quo is taken for granted. Most of our daily life proceeds on that basis: I enter a fast-food restaurant, buy a burger, and take it away. Most other people will acknowledge that this is "mine," and I do not need to take particular appropriative action in defending my claim. My appropriative action was buying the burger and handing over the money. I may even leave the receipt on the table, as I expect no one will challenge my appropriation.

As already noticed, the third element of ***property*** is the assignment of agency and responsibility. Consider, for example, the difference between selling the watch inherited from my grandfather and bestowing it to my child. From the modern legal point of view, these are different ways to transfer "property" from me to another person. Yet, there is a fundamental difference, depending on recognized social norms. If I sell the watch, no one, including myself, will see any restraint on the buyer what she will do with the watch, even throwing it into a lake. But if I bestow it to my child, I expect that my child will keep and care for it, and the child may feel the same. Yet, we will also think it is legitimate to sell the watch if the child runs into dire financial straits in the future. Hence, the two actions of transferring "property" are, in fact, two different actions in terms of assigning agency to the receiver, i.e., ***property***.

Property has a systematic relationship with agency, in two senses. One is that ***property*** is part of the actor's identity, the other is that it is a constituent of agential power. This connection is universal across the languages of ***property*** and is salient in Indigenous views that relate ***property*** to mastery, even in the ontological sense: There are conceptions of all entities being owned by spirit-masters, of which human claims are only derivations.[14] This notion of mastery is still visible in Slavic languages where terms related to ***property*** mostly have roots in notions of force and power, such as the Russian *obladat'* for *owning* relating to *vlast'* (power), or *sobstvennost'* (property) to *sila* (force, power).[15] This is also a defining feature of the difference between the Roman *dominium* and *proprietas*, with the former emphasizing the aspect exerting power, especially over other beings.[16] These obser-

14 For example, Cesarino (2016) describes the rich multiple ontology of the Amazonian Marubo, where everything is assigned to an owner, yet this differs radically from private property since ownership is always referred to as a double of spirit and human, and thereby constitutes universal relationality. However, this is not flattened collectivity but refers to mastery in the specific sense that in the human domain, the chief is the supreme owner as master. Wood (2012) explores similar ideas among the Kamula of Papua New Guinea, including new things such as logging and mining technology in this doubled spiritual sphere and mediating conflicting appropriative claims.

15 Ivanchikova 2018.

16 In canonical law, the reception of the Roman terms paved the way for later linguistic developments in Western Europe where *proprietas* became the root of terms such as *property* or *propriété*. *Dominium*, extending the notion of the unlimited power of *pater familias*, referred to the authority of the church over people, whereas *proprietas* referred to people's relationship with things. The latter became controversial

vations suggest that conceptualizing ***property*** as a right may be wrong in mixing up with "property:" ***Property*** is a form of power, hence closer to Weberian power of disposition.

Identity is salient in one of the classic examples of ***property***, the home of a person, family, or group.[17] A home is also recognized as belonging to someone in the sense of privacy (not necessarily individual). At the same time, a home is also an indicator of status, especially if combined with land in an estate. In many societies, ***property*** is, therefore, an essential indicator of status and hence, social identity. ***Property*** is also the means available for an individual to act, hence, agential power. Identity and agential power are closely related since status is also a determinant of agential power (often theorized as social capital). The relationship is salient in various languages' distinct semantic fields of ***property***. For example, the German *Eigentum* is located in the field with the root *eigen*, which includes meanings such as what is a characteristic feature of a person and what a person claims to be *eigen*.[18] In English, the term *property* originally referred to the features of a certain individual as a member of a group, and only after the 17th century acquired the distinct meaning of "property."[19]

One important aspect warrants consideration that is salient in the often-made distinction between perishable items for consumption and durable items, which partly overlaps with another distinction, whether the items can be moved or not. Land is the paradigmatic case of an immobile and durable item, food of a perishable and mobile item. Generally, we observe that the languages of ***property*** are shaped by the need to deal with durable items. The reason is that only durable items can become a constituent of identity and a sustainable basis of agential power. Perishable items become significant for identity and agential power precisely by conspicuously wasting them, with famous examples like the potlatch.

when considering, for example, *proprietas* of clerics who were subject to *dominium* of the church (Demoulin-Auzary 2005). This distinction reappeared in imperial colonization, where *dominium* referred to the imperial appropriation of land, different from the individual property of imperial subjects (Greer 2017, 355). In the Eastern European regions, rooted in the different social and economic structures of the Byzantium Empire, as seen for the Russian case, ***property*** remained associated with *dominium*. These differences even show up in contemporary legal practice in cases where a unified formal law exists; Mendelski and Libman (2014) discuss the case of Romania, where the Byzantium legacy worked through the stage of Ottoman rule.

17 Aristotle refers to possessions in general as belonging to the household, so the ***property*** of things is derived from the ***property*** of the home; Miller Jr, 1986.

18 https://www.dwds.de/wb/Eigentum

19 https://www.etymonline.com/word/property. A universal pattern across languages of ***property*** is that the grammatical possessive is used for both properties of entities and their relationship to other entities assigned to them, Aikhenvald 2012.

Durability must be distinguished from productivity, with another paradigmatic case being cattle, which are movables. The individual cattle have a limited lifetime, but the herd is durable in the sense of reproducibility, hence its productivity. Durability has one important implication: The items can be stored and accumulated. Therefore, in most societies, ***property*** is seen as a potential cause of inequality, leading to specific forms of assigning ***property***, for example, when recognizing a fact of appropriation, assigning the obligation to share, from potlatch to progressive taxation.[20] In many Indigenous societies, the obligation to share is a critical means to contain inequalities in the group.[21] Most religious conceptions of ***property*** impose a similar obligation to share, with Islamic law being a foremost example, with the *zakat* being a mandatory sharing of wealth with poor Muslims.[22] There is an interesting twist, though, as Islamic law even recognizes the importance of personal wealth since it creates the agential power to do such actions beneficial to others, fulfilling Allah's commandments. In Germany, the constitutional law recognizes the social responsibility of ***property*** and stipulates that ***property*** must serve both individual and communal interests, which goes beyond just stating that the exertion of private "property" should observe current laws and regulations.[23]

Another important observation is about the combination of perishability and immobility, where labor is paradigmatic, which is spent in the moment of enacting it, and cannot be transferred to another place without moving the agent doing the labor. Many societies have distinct forms of ***property*** relating to such items, such as slavery. A labor service cannot be owned but only be claimed via a contractual obligation of the provider, still leaving much uncertainty regarding effort and quality. So, ***property*** can only take the form of appropriating the provider him- or herself. A slave may provide sexual services as the prostitute does, but the latter retains ***property*** of the body while entering a contractual relationship with the

20 In European notions of ***property***, this was seminally formulated in Aristotle's view on ***property***, Mayhew 1993. He distinguished ***property*** and its use and for each, private and common. In doing so, he did not regard the combination of private ***property*** and private use as feasible and recommended combining private ***property*** and common use. This combination implies the obligation to share by morally inspired voluntary actions reflecting virtue, not by legal obligation. This view was commonplace in medieval notions of ***property***, and sharing was even enforced by the church, Kauffmann 2005.

21 Trosper (2022, 112 ff) shows that the potlatch is an institution that stabilizes common pool fisheries in neutralizing the "tragedy of the commons." Widerquist and McCall (2021) survey the anthropological records on sharing extensively.

22 Tripp 2006, 56 ff.

23 Kingreen 2016. The German constitutional view is closer to so-called "liberal" conceptions of property in the Anglo-saxon sphere (e.g., Dagan 2021) than to the common law notion as interpreted in the Law & economics view (e.g., Serkin 2016).

client. However, many societies curtail the rights of using this ***property***, such as outlawing prostitution.

Finally, once objects become constitutive of agency, there is a universal distinction between alienable properties and non-alienable properties.[24] This follows from the embodied nature of agency. Inalienability applies to all bodily features, such as my nose. Still, it can also be a feature of physically separate objects, such as a sacred item that signals the status of a person. Vice versa, alienability may refer to physical separability but also to all kinds of alienation by intermediation. For example, even my nose can be alienated via a transaction with another person who gains the rights to an exclusive view of that unique part of my body, so that I am always obliged to carry a veil unless the new proprietor lifts it for her exclusive enjoyment. Hence, the duality of alienability and inalienability defines a rich spectrum of specific forms of agency that refer to handling the underlying ***property***. As we will see, a critical aspect of orders of property across societies is which forms of social relationships embed, enable and constrain alienability, and foremostly, what is the role of markets and money.[25]

As a result of the discussion, we get a simple map of the semantic domain of ***property***. In the following, we will explore how the various languages of ***property*** fill this semantic space.

The universality of *property*

In comparing the diversity of ***property*** across languages, we also aim to identify the universals of ***property***. This does not mean that always and everywhere, all the exact constituents of ***property*** are manifest; to the contrary, depending on many contextual factors, certain constituents are dominant, and others may be lacking. Yet, we can say that ***property*** is a universal phenomenon. This is sometimes disputed, especially in the Western intellectual discourse accompanying the rise of capitalism. ***Property*** was seen as a civilizational achievement, hence as non-existent among so-called "savage" people.[26] The Marxist literature followed this view

24 Aikhenvald 2012.

25 This has been classically formulated by Aristotle, for whom alienability was the essential feature of individually owned ***property***. However, he combined this criterion with strong ethical constraints on profit- and market-oriented action which he saw as eroding the social relationships essential for a good life; Mayhew 1993. This primacy of social relationships in determining legitimate forms of alienation is universal across all human societies, completely independent from Western intellectual traditions, such as Oceania; Lieber and Rynkiewich 2007.

26 Möllers 2024.

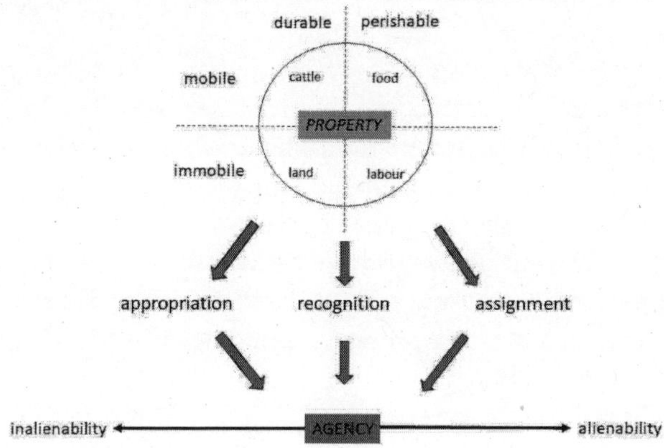

Figure 2.1: The semantic domain of ***property***
Source: author's diagram

by assuming a sequence of civilizational stages starting from primordial communism. However, these views emphasize a specific form of ***property***, "property," that dominates capitalist societies and downplays the variety of ***property***.[27] Unfortunately, this has also shaped the development of the economic theory of ***property***, even reproducing the 19th-century misperceptions about the progress of expanding "property rights," which are theoretically conceived as the historically specific form of ***property*** in capitalism. The rise of the New Institutional Economics since the 1970s had severe political implications, as the false Whiggish idea of progressing private "property" in human civilization was also invoked in the radicalization of privatization programs worldwide.[28] Only Elinor Ostrom's theoretical and empirical rehabilitation of the commons could unveil these misconceptions in economics while remaining in its orbit.[29] However, this also shows that ideas about alleged Indigenous alternatives to ***property*** inadvertently stand in the tradition of

27 For example, Brightman, Fausto, and Grotti (2016) show that exclusive forms of appropriation can be found across a wide range of native Amazonian people, which play a central role in ordering social relationships. Yet they also argue that this is fundamentally different from the capitalist form of private "property" because the appropriative claim is always seen as mediated by relationality, for which they coin the term "altering ownership."

28 Kennedy 2011.

29 Ostrom 2015. For an anthropological critique, see Wagner and Talakai 2007.

colonial denials of it. There are alternatives to "property," but ***property*** is universal.[30]

We must also notice that the argument presented here also works in the other direction: Recent research has revolutionized our conceptions of earlier periods in human civilizations, showing that capitalist structures and hence, forms of "property," had always existed in societies with a certain level of economic complexity.[31] Further, in contemporary societies of the Global South the juxtaposition between modern "property" and traditional ***property***, especially communal one, is often the construct of Western colonizers and fails to see that these traditional forms allowed for many ways of alienating ***property***, including via markets, yet without the Western legal framing.[32]

One straightforward way to state the universality of ***property*** is to define it negatively. In all human societies, theft is morally disproved and mostly punished.[33] This means recognizing a special relationship between people and objects: ***property***. We are not allowed to take away what others have for whatever specific reason beyond situations of dire straits and appalling injustice. Considering the semantic domain, recognition and assignment are more important for defining this opposition of theft and ***property***, than appropriation: ***Property*** is not a Hobbesian confrontation between two thieves who both wish to appropriate an object. A person morally protected from theft does not need specific actions to appropriate the object: passive ***property***, so to speak. This constellation can be analyzed in terms of Weber's concept of order: The primordial form of ***property*** can be defined as the *recognized assignment of the dispositional power over an object to particular people*. In this definition, the often-made juxtaposition of ***property*** as the relationship between people and things versus a relationship between people implodes because recognition entails the latter. By implication, social norms that regulate how this dispo-

30 This needs emphasis against the views expressed by Widerquist and McCall (2021). Refuting the widely held view in liberal economics and political philosophy that private property is a kind of "natural" state does not imply that ***property*** is not universal. In their refutation, the authors project the capitalist "property" taxonomy on non-capitalist societies, such as "common" or "public property" as alternatives to private "property." This fails to recognize that non-capitalist ***property*** is neither of them. This is the gist of the anthropological critique of Ostrom (see previous footnote).

31 For the case of ancient Greece, see Bresson 2014.

32 For Africa, Chimhowu and Woodhouse (2006) speak of "vernacular markets." The blanking out of markets is a corollary to constructing "traditional" property and was a general phenomenon in colonial African studies, finally demolished by Sundström 1974.

33 For the case of Imperial China, Zelin (2004) takes the draconic laws punishing any kind of theft as an indicator of the strength of ***property***. There is the case of the so-called "tolerated theft" among hunter-gatherer societies, which Widerquist and McCall (2021: 117) interpret as a "last resort" if, for some reason, sharing breaks down. The concept has been widely debated in anthropology and biology and can be interpreted as reflecting mechanisms of group selection in small groups with close social relationships, hence as a form of cooperation benefitting individuals and groups alike; Wilson 1998.

sitional power is used, such as demanding sharing, do not invalidate the original assignment of these powers.

This definition implies that formal law is not a necessary ***property*** component, especially in the sense of enforcement by the government.[34] The role of government in ***property*** is indeed close to a Hobbesian scenario in the sense that the proprietor might rely on the government for forceful appropriation.[35] But this view would also be one-sided because forceful appropriation is only an ultimate means. Mostly, the "government" takes the shape of the judge, which is salient in the development of Roman law that profoundly shaped modern civil law. In practices of ***property***, judges often take many aspects into consideration of recognition and assignment, such as in situations of legal pluralism when customary law and formal law differ.[36] In invoking notions such as equity, judges often invoke Weberian order, and less the formal law.[37] This is possible because formal law often leaves leeway for interpretation when it comes to civil law, which is even wider in common law that follows precedents,

The Hobbesian scenario also suggests another observation: Theft is often accepted or even applauded when this appropriation aims at outgroup people. Raiding is an accepted form of warfare in many societies. It has only been outlawed in modern conventions of war, which, alas, are not always followed (for a recent example of "civilized" war, consider the raids of Russian soldiers in Ukraine). Hence, the negative definition of ***property*** as outlawing theft is directly linked to the ingroup/outgroup distinction unless we refer to modern law, which in principle applies universally, hence, for example, protecting people of another nationality from theft when staying in a country the laws of which punish theft. Yet, we can keep the vital insight that the elementary form of ***property*** by recognition and assignment is bound to a community with shared moral norms sanctioning theft, a Weberian order. This is also salient in the opposite case when theft is seen as legit-

34 Institutional economists often maintain this view; Hodgson (2015), for example, even argues that customary law cannot fully constitute ***property*** of course, he means "property."

35 Cai, Murtazashvili, and Murtazashvili 2020.

36 Legal pluralism may be seen as the more common situation in most societies, past and present, and prevailed in Europe until the transformative transformations of nation states; Padoa-Schioppa 2017, 167 ff. Today, countries such as India and Indonesia systematically recognize legal pluralism, and even the United States must be included by recognising tribal law. In all such cases, we cannot equate government and the law, and judges are pivotal in the Weberian order of ***property***.

37 Weber is implicitly contradictory, even though we must notice the editorial issues mentioned in Chapter 1. The critical issue is the juxtaposition of *qadi* justice and rational law, which has been thoroughly criticized in Chinese studies considering the "substantive rationality" of court proceedings in Imperial China; Huang 2006. In modern common law, equity stands apart from law in certain contexts, such as jurisdiction on covenants; Serkin 2016, 181 ff.

imate if the moral economy of a community is violated by existing distributions of ***property*** across members.[38]

The corollary is that quasi-modern forms of ***property*** can be found universally in contexts where one group subjects another group seen as "non-human:" For example, Amazonian Indigenous warfare went along with widespread slavery with no substantial difference to Roman conceptions of *dominium* over people.[39] Slaves were also traded, hence even establishing a connection between ***property*** and markets. In the Roman empire, market-based forms of "property" of land emerged in the subjugated provinces where the notion of sacredness of the Italian lands did not hold.[40] We can observe this transition also in Greek Antiquity.[41] In the Homeric period, there were clear ***property*** assignments for war booty and land. However, regarding land, there was a distinction between types of exchange: alienability of land was restricted to gift exchange, whereas transactions with strangers were seen as illegitimate.[42] The latter distinction between types of exchange was also an important feature of trade since inter-city traders were confined to specific places beyond the core area of the *polis*, thus marking the distinct nature of "property" transactions with strangers. Hence, the emergence of such transactions without strong forms of community embedding transcends the two forms of violent appropriation and moral circumscription. With the increasing monetization and commercialization of trade, neutral forms of transactions gradually encroached on morally confined domains, such as in the context of mortgage. However, there was also a close connection between ***property*** and war because of the military innovation of the Hoplite phalanx in which the soldiers, as owners of ***property*** in the polis, defended their own status as citizens.[43] In this sense, notions of ***property*** and "property" coexisted in Antiquity, and the ingroup/outgroup distinction was of paramount importance.

This view of ***property*** is close to Hannah Arendt's distinction between property and wealth.[44] For her, a fundamental phenomenon of modernity is precisely the

---

38 A case in point is medieval Europe, where the idea of the poor's natural right to claim the surplus of the rich emerged that could even be enacted by theft. Alternatively, the church could threaten to excommunicate a rich person who did not give to the poor; Kauffmann 2005.

39 Santos-Granero 2016.

40 Interestingly, as Kantor (2017) analyzes, these forms were not cast into fully-fledged *dominium*, thus revealing its role in indicating social status of the citizens of Rome. As Max Weber had already argued, agrarian capitalism emerged from tenure arrangements of Imperial land in the provinces.

41 Economou and Kyriazis 2017.

42 Gottesman 2010.

43 Mann 2012, 199 ff.

44 Arendt 2018, 58 ff, 109 ff. Arendt receives the Aristotelian views on ***property***, which are easily misunderstood if we use the term *property* in its modern meaning, even if major elements of ***property*** are recognized, such as the individual right to alienation; Miller Jr, 1986.

opposite of the Whiggish views on "property:" a gradual loss of the original sacred role of ***property*** and the growth of a propertyless class of people. She writes:

> Originally, property meant no more or less than to have one's location in a particular part of the world and therefore to belong to the body politic, that is, to be the head of one of the families that constituted the public realm. (...) The wealth of a foreigner or a slave was under no circumstances a substitute for this property, and poverty did not deprive the head of a family of this location in the world and the citizenship resulting from it.[45]

Within the community, ostracizing a member also means confiscating his ***property***, even destroying it. This tight relationship between community and ***property*** can be traced back to pre-historical times. The archeological evidence is clear.[46] First, from earliest times onwards, humans have developed a sense of identifying things with people, for example, burying individuals with precious objects they own. This also hints at the sacred nature of this relationship, which is directly visible in the demarcation of land belonging to a community by religious artifacts, including graves.[47] Another observation points to the universality of warfare and raiding that motivated the fortification of settlements. Both religion and warfare involve the community in ***property***, resulting in a notion of layers of ***property***, such as giving a leader special right to claim objects and resources to recognize and enable the functions of organizing collective action. As Arendt writes, early ***property*** associated objects and places, a relationship that continues until today when people embellish their homes with personal items. The fundamental unit emerging in pre-historical times, fully visible in Arendt's references to Antiquity, is the family, which itself can take many forms depending on the specific rules of kinship. Finally, an important aspect of primordial ***property*** is that some objects were seen as inalienable, unless being transferred in certain ritualistic frameworks such as gift-giving.[48]

We cannot know the linguistic reflection that accompanied the behavior leaving material traces. However, we know about the conditions among various Indigenous people for which anthropological records exist since the 19th century. At this point, only one essential observation needs mentioning: This is the spirituality of primordial ***property***.[49] In all records, there are indications that ***property*** was

45 Arendt 2018, 61.

46 Earle 2017.

47 Research on contemporary Indigenous people has also shown that the strongest forms of ***property*** refer to ritual objects that are inalienably assigned to their holder; Gordon 2016.

48 An important case in point is Roman law, which exerted deep impact on Western ideas of ***property***. In earlier stages of legal practices, property transactions of certain items, the *res mancipi*, most importantly land, could only take the form of specific rituals; Harke 2016, 242 ff.

49 Sahlins 2023, 145. The volume edited by Brightman, Fausto, and Grotti (2016) presents many examples in detail; see also Wagner and Talakai 2007 and the related special issue.

tightly connected to the idea of spiritual mastery. For example, a human would not be seen as the ultimate proprietor of an animal, but the spirit who is embodied in it or guards it. Even humans are not seen as "owning" themselves but as being subject to spiritual masters. A critical corollary of this is that the realm of spirits is conceived as a governance structure, with one supreme entity from which all spiritual powers of disposition originate. In such a worldview, all ***property*** is sacred, and human ***property*** is stewardship, even in relation to one's own body.

Sacred ***property*** played an important role in Antiquity, although a remarkable observation is that legal theory mostly advanced in the secular domain, driven by the interests of wealth holders to make the best use of their ***property***. Roman law took the distinction between sacred and public forms of property versus personal secular property as fundamental but did not develop the former in detail since law was seen as regulating human matters, but not the gods.[50] Already in Greece, this led to considerable ambiguities between the sacred and the public, since, for example, a temple may be seen as assigned to a god, but nevertheless is managed by the public authorities, and hence is appropriated, for example, regarding the flow of revenues generated by temple land leased out to tenants.[51] Roman law assigned a special status to the original Italian lands, implying that transactions must be ritually governed, hence assuming a quasi-sacral status. This view corresponds to Indigenous conceptions that ownership of territory ultimately rests on the sacred authority of the chief:[52] This idea has been dominant in many societies, such as assigning the territory to the ultimate authority of the king in feudal regimes, but also the case of China, where the entire territory of *tianxia*. that is the civilized world, was seen as being subject to the Emperor. The question is open how far modern constitutional assignments of certain resources to the "nation" have a similar status of imbuing public ***property*** with an aura of sanctity.

Spiritual views have been influential on more formal and legal conceptions of ***property***. A significant example is the Islamic idea of ***property***. ***Property*** is ultimately grounded in the supreme being, Allah, implying that all individual ***property*** is stewardship.[53] Stewardship has twofold meanings: First, humans receive ***property*** for productive and responsible action, and second, this requires concern for the community. Hence, ***property*** obliges moral action, defined by the *Quran*

50 Bloch 2006. Interestingly, one of the most famous Roman texts on ***property***, Cicero's *De Domo Sua*, focused on clarifying religious law, as he had to defend expropriation by means of sacralization of his property; Rüpke 2019.

51 Rousset 2013.

52 Costa 2016. This is also recognized by Widerquist and McCall (2021, 213 ff) who argue that chiefs act both as owners and "monarchs," that is combining economic and political powers (which would contradict purist conceptions of private "property").

53 Sayın et al. 2017.

and *Shariah* law, with no distinction between the aspects of durability and mobility, as is salient in religious norms of consumption. In this sense, ***property*** is mainly grounded in assignment, both assigning rights and duties to human proprietors. For example, Islamic inheritance is not a right of the testator but accrues to the next generation by assignment as defined in the sacred texts of Islam, such as the *Surah An-Nisah*.[54] Islamic law also includes the ingroup / outgroup distinction, as in the context of the Holy War. However, the notion of "community" is itself universalistic in referring to the *Umma*. This is radically different from the European civil laws tied to the nation-state, though it also maintains principles such as equality of membership status. This difference is also essential when considering Islamic law in countries such as Indonesia, where it co-exists with customary law in the various communities included in the nation-state and covered by its civil law, hence a situation of legal pluralism.[55]

We can conclude that it is highly misleading to inform the study of ***property***, as normally done in economics, by the conditions of Western modernity. ***Property*** is a human universal and, as such, manifests a much richer semantic domain than "property." However, as we will see in the following sections, this semantic space is also present in Western modernity, though partly silenced because of the impoverished language of ***property*** and due to capitalist colonization of societies, including the Western heartlands.

The economic language of *property*

A brief reflection of economic language is necessary before we explore the semantic domain of ***property*** in more detail. Economics only uses the terms "property" and "ownership," and this is almost indiscriminately, with the exception that

54 Taqiyuddin, Millah, and Luthfi 2023. Assigning inheritance as a right of the heirs is a widespread phenomenon. In Roman antiquity, a special arrangement, the *testamentum per aes et libram*, strengthened the rights of testators vis-à-vis the family, meeting the demands of the growing market economy; von der Weth 2024. In the late Empire, this was bolstered by a new form of the spirituality of land, since Christians saw themselves as heirs to God and his Son, thus individualizing claims to ***property***, radically deviating from Jewish practices of family-bound inheritance; Vinzent 2024. Interestingly, as Goody (1983) has argued convincingly, the church later endorsed freedom of testament against family claims, especially extended kinship, to bolster the bequeathment of land to the church, a paradoxical move of endorsing individualization of ***property*** to strengthen corporate ***property***.

55 Universitas Islam Negeri Sunan Gunung Djati Bandung, Indonesia and Gojali 2023.

sometimes "property rights" are distinguished from full ownership in the sense that one proprietor holds all the rights.[56]

The most important differentiation of ***property*** in economics is by type of subjects: private or individual, collective or common, public, and state. This distinction was enshrined in the first codifications of civil law, which also created the fundamental ambiguities of the terms "public" and "state." The article 542 of the *Code Civil* states

> Les biens communaux sont ceux à la propriété ou au produit desquels les habitants d'une ou plusieurs communes ont un droit acquis.[57]

This formulation originally served to recognize the traditional rights of rural communities separate from feudal ***property***, but in the wake of Napoleonic administrative reforms, the term community was interpreted in terms of the lowest level of territorial administration of the national state; thus, in fact, disenfranchising the native communities.[58] Since the term "public" is understood as referring to a generic notion, the *Code Civil*, in its factual application, does no longer recognize the specific status of communities in the sense of Tönnies' *Gemeinschaft*. This is also true for economics, which only reinstated the specific status of communities as subjects of ***property*** following Elinor Ostrom's seminal work.

The distinction between different types of ***property*** raises the question of whether the underlying relationship remains the same, only with different subjects. This can undoubtedly be the case since economics mostly follows the concept of a legal person as proprietor, that is, does not distinguish systematically between natural persons and, for example, firms as subjects of ***property***. In this case, identifying private "property" with individual ***property*** would be misleading as all types of subjects can be proprietors in the sense of private "property." For example, a cooperative may relate to non-members as a private proprietor, or a state-owned company can have the legal form of a public corporation with the government as a sole or majority shareholder. In these cases, the distinction between assignment and appropriation applies since we can conceive state ownership as a legal means of appropriation that still requires assigning the ***property*** to a particular representative. One typical example is that the constitutions of many countries assign natural resources to the ***property*** of "the people," which is then appropriated by the government as "property," which eventually renders these resources tradable on international markets.[59]

---

56 Many institutional economists follow the classic text here: Honoré 1961.

57 https://www.legifrance.gouv.fr/codes/article_lc/LEGIARTI000006428841

58 Vanuxem 2022.

59 Wenar 2017. Wenar classifies this as "theft" since the profits from trade are appropriated by certain elites usurping the government.

However, such a continuity of a specific form of "property" across all types of subjects is not even maintained in economics. An important example is the role of public ***property***. Public ***property*** refers to "the public" as an open category without clearly demarcating this group of people regarding access. For example, a public square may be assigned to the government as proprietor, but appropriation is left unspecified as anybody can enter the square including non-nationals. In other words, the notion of "public" partly suggests open access. This applies with a vengeance when considering the common economic distinction of goods according to the dimensions of the rivalry of use or consumption and excludability. This distinction does not relate to ***property*** per se. Still, economics suggests that certain types of goods are associated with certain types of ***property*** subjects, such as a public good with the government as caretaker and regulator, for example, on air pollution. This view always considers whether, alternatively, individual appropriation in the form of private "property" would be feasible, which is seen as the most efficient institutional arrangement. For example, in the case of air pollution, private rights to pollute may be created, which does not create private "property" of the air but enables individualization of rights to use that air as a repository for wastes.

The same applies to the notion of common ***property***. Common *property* refers to a group that shares the ***property***. In practice, this leaves the definition of the community open, as there can be different rules for defining membership. This can mean relating to a group delimited by kinship, which draws a line between ingroup and outgroup, or to a local municipality that has no restriction on who takes residence. As in the previous case, private "property" can apply here once we distinguish between the material objects and the form of access. For example, if a forest commons assigns full private "property" to plots, this would effectively annul the commons. However, the logging rights may be fully privatized since this does not imply alienability of the plots. The effect of privatization of use rights is visible in the composition of the members of the commons while keeping the common forest intact.

One peculiar, though universal reference of "community" is the family, which is not recognized at all in the economics taxonomy, even though in many societies, past and present, households, not individuals, have been seen as holders of ***property***.[60] The notion of "household" is not necessarily coextensive with "family" if the latter includes extended kin. The neglect of the family also implies that economics systematically ignores the gendered nature of ***property***.[61] This is particularly rel-

60 An important case in point is Imperial China Zelin 2004, Gates 1996.

61 Federici and Linebaugh 2019. A case in point is the gendered nature of slavery in the American South, where women were excluded from appropriating land and other forms of wealth, except for slaves. As a

evant if we consider the deep impact of Roman law on capitalist conceptions of ***property*** as private "property:" The Roman *dominium* assigns ***property*** to the male head of the household, thus preparing the ground for the gendered individualization of property, neutralized as private "property." In contrast, the household head in Chinese customary law is only a member of the agnatic family, so in critical areas such as inheritance, there are fundamental differences in assigning ***property*** to the household: Inheritance in China is household division according to custom and contractual arrangements but is not a will of the male household head.[62]

The examples show that it is misleading to conflate all these different relationships in one concept of ***property*** unless the domain of ***property*** is approached in a wide range, as done in the previous section. Economics, as said, tends to reduce ***property*** to the type of "property" because New Institutional Economics, in the tradition of Coase, refers ***property*** to markets and to the dimension of appropriation via markets.

This raises the question of whether using the same term for all these types should be discarded. Is a commons ***property***? Is state ownership ***property***? Consider the commons: In principle, all specific rights, such as fishing rights, can be seen as "property" rights in the economic sense.[63] However, what is the status of the commons proper? If we approach the commons as the topmost and universal ***property*** of the commons, such as a forest commons, this can be approached as ownership in the sense of the most complete and powerful form of private "property," implying, for example, that the community can alienate the forest. In this case, there would be no difference between common ***property*** and other forms of "property."

We can also consider these questions in another context: the relationship between subjects and objects in a company. Economics suggests, for example, that the CEO is not the proprietor of the company's assets if this is listed and therefore owned by the shareholders. However, the shareholders have no power of disposition over these assets, only indirectly via voting rights in the general assembly. In economics, the CEO is not regarded as having "property." In the semantic domain outlined in Figure 2.1, the CEO does have "property" via assignment.

One way to resolve these terminological muddles is to conceptualize "property" rights as powers of disposition, tantamount to reducing "property rights" to possession.[64] Hence, there is a discussion about whether genuine ***property*** can

---

result, they became active participants in the slave market, specializing on female slaves; Jonse-Rogers 2019.

62 These conceptions continue to hold sway in modernizing rural China; Cohen 1992.

63 Schlager and Ostrom 1992.

64 In principle, this is the notion of "economic property rights," which many economists see as the fundamental form of ***property***, independent from the legal form, for example Allen 2015.

only take the legal form, as in the case of negating the status of the proprietor to a CEO. This would imply that customary forms of ***property*** would not count as such. The wider view on the semantic domain rejects this narrow understanding and avoids reducing ***property*** to possession. The dimensions of recognition and assignment imply that beyond possession, there are other means than legal enforcement to create stable forms of ***property*** independent from manifest possession.

In sum, the standard economics distinction of types of ***property*** hides its complexity which encumbers our understanding the specific actions and structures of ***property***. In terms of disciplinary contexts, anthropology is a more powerful framework.[65] This insight emerged from research on the postsocialist transition economies, where economic approaches failed to see the social realities of ***property*** beyond the simple taxonomy of ownership types.[66] We will discuss a Chinese case in Chapter 4. These issues are not only of academic interest: As we have seen, one area of neglect has been the notion of communal property, which stays at the center of socioeconomic transformation in Africa, conventionally referred to as "customary tenure" of land, which still makes up the majority of ***property*** arrangements.[67] The conditions vary widely across African countries, but a common theme is the awkward positioning of customary tenure between state and private ownership of land. Paradoxically, state ownership can often imply that after decolonization the new states continue with colonial legal ordering of ***property***, thus failing to empower local communities.[68] On the other hand, introducing modern institutions of "property" often creates hybrid regimes with many social and political consequences, such as changing the composition of local elites while still failing to improve the living conditions for most of the community members.[69]

The many terms of *property*

Language issues lurk everywhere when we discuss *property*:

65 This assessment follows the more extensive discussion in Benda-Beckmann, Benda-Beckmann, and Wiber 2006.

66 Hann 2007.

67 Wily 2017.

68 Another important case in point is Indonesia, a global hotspot of the deforestation crisis. Indonesia has firmly entrenched state ownership of forests, in continuity with Dutch colonial law. There are deep conflicts over the recognition of communal rights, and the solution is blocked by the framing in terms of the duality of state and private ownership; Larson et al. 2017.

69 See Chimhowu 2019 for the African cases.

- There is often a divergence between legal language and colloquial uses of terms relating to ***property*** (for example, in German colloquial speech, *Eigentum* and *Besitz* are almost synonyms, whereas civil law neatly distinguishes the two).
- This difference also affects translations since many countries have adopted legal terms that originated in a European language and were not originally used in the native language (for example, the modern Chinese term for ***property***, *suoyou* was borrowed from Japanese *shoyū* in place of the old term *ye* which is no longer used today in that meaning).
- In general, translations often reveal distinct connotations of terms that appear as synonymous in the first place (for example, the French *proprieté* as a translation of the English *property* refers to "property" in the sense of absolute ownership).
- Even within one language, the words relating to ***property*** often dictate a particular structuring of the pragmatics of *property* (for example, the English common law terms of property law employing *fee* insinuate a "bundle of rights" view rooted in feudal land law which used *seisin* as holding the rights to the benefits of land, though as a freeholder).
- Finally, the meaning of ***property*** as such is often ambiguous, which relates to the distinction between the substantive and the verbs describing the relationship (for example, in German, *Eigentum* and *Besitz* combine with the same verb *besitzen*).

These various terms denote ***property*** in the sense of demarcating certain sectors in the semantic domains of ***property***. For example, ***property*** as wealth tends to highlight the aspect of durability: We would not think of a banana as constituting our wealth, although we bought it and own it. However, the term "property" confuses the relationship with the object. What kind of relationship is defined by ***property***? Legally, one criterion to specify the ***property*** relationship is that a *property* claim is valid *erga omnes*, that is, against everyone, whereas contractual claims only count against the contractual party. This distinction is extremely important regarding exchange: If I buy a second-hand car from a private person, I want to be safe that this contract is a genuine transfer of power of disposition. It would not be enough just to be safe that the seller would relinquish her claims. What if her brother would come up later, claiming that he was also a user of the car and co-owned it and that his sister had no right to sell it? If the transfer creates a claim *erga omnes*, this is not possible. This example points to a critical issue in developing modern "property" law: Such issues were highly significant in the case of landed ***property*** involving families, often extended. Only relying on a contract between two parties would not suffice to create future certainty of dispositional powers.

Therefore, the institution of "property" evolved as a claim against any potential future claimant.

In this sense, ***property*** is a public phenomenon. Most modern legal systems distinguish between property law and contract law. However, this depends on how the notion of the public is interpreted. The claim *erga omnes* reflects the expansion of the reach of transactions and, hence, diminishing transparency of the contractual history related to a specific ***property*** object. This may change by employing blockchain technology more widely. In old China, deeds securing land rights were contracts only, but with enough witnesses co-signing the contract.[70] Here, the *omnes* is defined by the community in which the transaction was conducted and of which the witnesses are members. Combining this with the tax payment led to the contract's recognition with a red official stamp, which extends the protection of ***property*** vis à vis anyone.

Such issues are critical until today. Understanding ***property*** as wealth defines a difference between the German legal approach to *Eigentum* and the European one. German civil law refers "property" only to *Sachen*, hence material objects, but not to other claims constituting wealth as *Vermögen*. In the European context, this creates a terminological fuzziness with deeper significance for our concerns. In the "Protocol to the Convention for the Protection of Human Rights and Fundamental Freedoms, as amended by Protocol No. 11 of the European Treaties (1952)", ***property*** is explicitly protected as a basic right.[71] What kind of ***property*** is it? Let us look at the key paragraph in various versions.

Article 1 – Protection de la propriété

Toute personne physique ou morale a droit au respect de ses biens. Nul ne peut être privé de sa propriété que pour cause d'utilité publique et dans les conditions prévues par la loi et les principes généraux du droit international.

Article 1 – Protection of property

Every natural or legal person is entitled to the peaceful enjoyment of his possessions. No one shall be deprived of his possessions except in the public interest and subject to the conditions provided for by law and by the general principles of international law.

Artikel 1 – Schutz des Eigentums

Jede natürliche oder juristische Person hat das Recht auf Achtung ihres Eigentums. Niemandem darf sein Eigentum entzogen werden, es sei denn, daß das öffentliche Interesse es verlangt, und nur unter den durch Gesetz und durch die allgemeinen Grundsätze des Völkerrechts vorgesehenen Bedingungen.

---

70 Hase 2013. Witnesses were also essential in Romal legal practice; von der Weth 2024.

71 https://rm.coe.int/168006377c

Статья 1 – Защита собственности

Каждое физическое или юридическое лицо имеет право на уважение своей собственности. Никто не может быть лишен своего имущества иначе как в интересах общества и на условиях, предусмотренных законом и общими принципами международного права.

As we see in the title, all versions refer to what is regarded as an adequate translation of ***property***. But in the first sentence, conceptual confusion emerges. The English version no longer refers to ***property*** but to *possessions*. Since this is a legal text, this seems problematic because, in common law, there is a clear distinction between *property* and *possession*. In German, *possession* would be rendered as *Besitz*, which German civil law treats as systematically different from *Eigentum* as "property." So, strictly speaking, the protocol does not seem to protect "property" in English.[72] The German text is consistent, whereas the French text is not. The first sentence uses *biens*. This term has a broad meaning, generally as "good" (*Gut* in German). In the plural and in the legal context, *biens* is wealth (*Vermögen* in German). Interestingly, the Russian version inverts the French use: The first sentence refers to "property" as *sobstvennost*, whereas the second speaks of wealth as *imuščestvo* while the French switches to *proprieté*. This is remarkable because the French expressions for wealth also include *patrimoine*, which also means "legacy." This points to Weber's definition of *Eigentum*.

These distinctions matter.[73] Strictly speaking, the German *Eigentum* in the protocol cannot be the meaning of "property" since the German civil law only refers this to *Sachen*, whereas the French *biens* is expansive in including all kinds of resources that generate economic benefits. Hence, the German translation is informed by the meaning of German constitutional law, which seems appropriate in the context of the protocol. However, if we look at how the European Courts deal with ***property***, they follow an interpretation of *biens* which clearly emphasizes the economic benefits, hence the aspect of wealth. The consequence is that the Court tends to include claims such as financial ones or intellectual property, perhaps even business opportunities, thus coming close to Weber's use of *Chance*.

Apparently, the emerging understanding of ***property*** is shaped by two aspects: the first is the broader notion of the power of disposition, the other is the emphasis on economic benefits, even in the sense of legitimate expectations, and implicitly the reference to monetary valuation. As we already mentioned in the previous chapter, this can be traced back to the transition to a monetary conception of *pat-*

72 In the English translation of the German Civil Code, *Eigentum* is rendered as *ownership*. https://www.gesetze-im-internet.de/englisch_bgb/englisch_bgb.html#p4585

73 Praduroux 2017.

rimoine as the aggregate means to earn a reliable flow of monetary income, that is, rents.

If we turn to the relationship proper, this complexity is reduced in the dimension of the verbs. Let us begin with the German. Remarkably, no verb corresponds to *Eigentum* specifically. The verb that is used relates to *Besitz* at the same time: *besitzen*. There is a systematic difference between *Besitz* and *Eigentum*: This is salient when considering BGB § 958 (1) "Wer eine herrenlose bewegliche Sache in Eigenbesitz nimmt, erwirbt das Eigentum an der Sache."[74] This is automatic, whereas in § 959 "Eine bewegliche Sache wird herrenlos, wenn der Eigentümer in der Absicht, auf das Eigentum zu verzichten, den Besitz der Sache aufgibt."[75] Here, the intention is necessary. The interesting point is that there is no reference to any legal title or contract. This underlines another Weberian point: Action is essential in the first place when analyzing practices. Then we notice that there is a verb which is not used in legal sense, *aneignen*, which, however, is not used to refer to the status of *Eigentum* (there is the antiquated *zu eigen sein*).

Our final observation is: § 985 "Der Eigentümer kann von dem Besitzer die Herausgabe der Sache verlangen."[76] This means that once the claim to "property" is proven, "property" is stronger than possession and is not tied to any state of action; it can only be based on making the claim. "Property" is a legal claim, possession is a state of action. Yet, for both, the same verb is used: *besitzen*. This is different in English, where we have the verb *possess* and the verb *own*. However, we have three terms: *ownership*, *property* and *possession*. The relationship between *ownership* and the other two is complex. In English law, *ownership* is often seen as the most potent form of "property."[77] Indeed, the correct translation of *proprieté* would be *ownership*, not *property*. At the same time, *property* and *ownership* are verbally conflated, both referring to *own*. There is an ambiguity, then, because there is another way to distinguish *ownership* from "property:" *Ownership* refers to the relationship, "property" to the object, so that it is possible to say, "own property."

In American legal language *ownership* is mainly seen as a colloquial term that does not add something legally relevant to "property."[78] In English common law, "ownership" has been theorized as absolute "property," often labelled "Blackstonian property" which would indeed correspond to the French and German civil

74 "(1) A person who takes proprietary possession of an ownerless movable thing acquires ownership of the thing." https://www.gesetze-im-internet.de/englisch_bgb/englisch_bgb.html#p4585

75 "A movable thing becomes ownerless if the owner, in the intention of waiving ownership, abandons the possession of the thing." https://www.gesetze-im-internet.de/englisch_bgb/englisch_bgb.html#p4585

76 "The owner may require the possessor to surrender the thing." https://www.gesetze-im-internet.de/englisch_bgb/englisch_bgb.html#p4585

77 Honoré 1961.

78 Gretton 2007, 829.

law notion. But this specific meaning of *ownership* is not universal in the anglophone world. English common law knows various forms of ***property*** when it comes to land. The word *ownership* is not used but the term *fee simple* (absolute). This reflects the feudal legacy of common law: ***Property*** of land could take many forms depending on the obligations between the ultimate owner of land and the actual possessor. This defines the fundamental difference between common law and civil law: The former conceives ***property*** as a legal order of relationships between people, the latter as a relationship between people and things.[79] This difference has far-reaching consequences.

The common law tradition of focusing on relationships is an intellectual root of the modern "bundle of rights" view which has been received in various disciplines that deal with ***property*** theoretically.[80] In this view, owning a thing can involve many different rights open to design, which is factually close to feudal practices, without invoking a supreme owner. This is the theoretical perspective on *property* as a continuum of "property rights." These rights are mostly classified into the categories of *usus*, *fructus*, and *abusus*, which only fall in line with absolute ownership if all are assigned to the same entity. Otherwise, owning an object can involve many variations of specific rights. In general, ***property*** is rarely absolute in the strict meaning of the term, as there are two kinds of constraints: one type relates to claims of people that directly interact with the owner, such as neighbors, and the other is claims of the community or political entity of which the owner is a member.[81] Basically, these can refer to allowing for concurrent uses of the object (easements) or dealing with externalities (nuisances) that an owner generates in using the object.[82] A typical example of the former is the right to trespass on an estate if the neighbor cannot access her ***property*** in any other way. An example of the latter is polluting a river and harming downstream residents. This results in many varieties of ***property*** which can be covered in the bundle of rights view.

An important question is whether all terms of ***property*** discussed so far fail to grasp certain notions of ***property*** that exist in practice. The most significant case is the question of how to translate Indigenous claims to their homeland. Indigenous lawyers regularly emphasize that no existing term in the colonizers' languages grasps their specific relationship, which has serious legal consequences: Since the legal matter is often to give them a title in the first place, these cannot yet count as "property," but if their relationship is only possession, many Indige-

79 Graziadei 2017.

80 Hohfeld 2022, Benda-Beckmann, Benda-Beckmann, and Wiber 2006.

81 Even the Art. 544 of the Code Civil has constraints on "property" : « La propriété est le droit de jouir et disposer des choses de la manière la plus absolue, pourvu qu'on n'en fasse pas un usage prohibé par les lois ou par les règlements. »

82 Serkin 2016, 14 ff.

nous people did not live in their homeland for a long time, as a result of forced resettlement.[83] The key point is not just that the homeland is seen as sacred but that it is a fundamental relational good.[84] This means there is no ontological distinction between the subject and the object of the property relationship. However, we notice that such terms are also known in Western languages: For example, the German term *Heimat* does not have a meaning independent from a particular person who regards the *Heimat* as belonging to her, but also as she belonging to it. This can be covered by the notion of assignment, though, since, given the unity of subject and object, any reference to the latter implies a reference to the former: *Heimat* always entails the question, whose? Similarly, we can also formulate that the homeland is part of the identity of the Indigenous person and, therefore, cannot be appropriated at all.[85] As we will see in the next chapter, we can distinguish this as a form of *property* that is neither "property" nor possession.[86] This form of ***property*** is mostly hidden in white spots of Western languages and is only present in notions of *res sacrae*. The reason is that the relationship between subject and object cannot be inverted ontologically, as in Indigenous notions that people are also owned by the land. One remnant of the inversion is the notion of *belongings* or German *Zugehörigkeit*, which can be interpreted as counting in both directions, as in the example of *Heimat*. We may grasp this as a specific form of assignment: If the watch inherited from my grandmother belongs to me, this expression can also imply that I belong to the watch or that the assignment is bi-directional. My belonging to the watch means that the watch is part of my identity.

Widening the scope of this discussion and generalizing further, there are linguistic universals in expressing possessive relationships.[87] The linguistic perspective is much broader than what we discussed so far as it includes all kinds of possessive, such as in the formulation "Mary's intellect" or "The color of the car is blue." All languages distinguish between three broad categories of possessives, namely ownership, whole-part relationships, and kinship, and

83 McNeil 2017. This circumstance applies especially for Australia and North America. However, the legal issues also emerge in contexts that do not involve resettlement, such as Oceania; Boydell 2010.

84 Trosper 2022.

85 Dixon (2012) explains the deep relationship between language and land, often implying that the language belongs to the land, and both constitute what makes a person. Therefore, neither land nor language can be referred to in many languages with standard grammatical constructions of possession.

86 This is also salient because local people often do not see the point of introducing modern "property" institutions. For example, in the case of Burkina Faso, the native people have a strong sense of owning their ancestors' land; Sawadogo and Stamm 2000. At the same time, there are flexible arrangements for "borrowing" land, even for immigrants, without monetary compensation, so there is a workable mechanism to allocate land to productive users. Indeed, making and keeping the land fertile is a key criterion for lending out land. Further, borrowers are judged on whether they will cohabit well in the community.

87 Aikhenvald 2012.

they highlight alienability in the most general sense of separability. Further, all languages assign a more powerful ontological position to the possessor compared to the possessee. We do not go into details here; what is significant is that the issue of alienability is strongly contextualized by culture and social setting, which becomes visible when social and economic changes affect perceptions of alienability. This creates a wide area of variation between ownership in the more specific sense of ***property*** and the more general of ascribing a feature to the subject of a sentence. This is visible in English, where the adjective *own* can be used most flexibly, whereas the verb is much more restricted. For example, I can say "my own wedding" but cannot say *"I own a wedding" even though it is "my wedding." The restricted areas of possession mostly refer to inalienable parts, such as when some languages distinguish between body parts and excrements in possessive constructions. In our context, what is most significant is that many languages allow for the incorporation of external objects, such as the knife of a hunter being treated grammatically like the hand. The case of land is a strong example of this incorporation.

For our discussion in the next chapter, it is important to notice that most languages have an equivalent to the two notions of *have* and *belong*. These verbal constructs can help to distinguish between the general grammatical possessive and the narrower meaning of possession as owning an object. For example, many languages have noun phrases with copulas, such as the English *of* or the Mandarin *de* or various kinds of genitives. A simple way to filter out the narrower ***property*** is transforming such expressions into a verbal clause, such as switching from "Peter's promotion" to "Peter has a promotion", which sounds awkward, and finally, *"Peter owns a promotion", which is clearly wrong. Non-Western languages often have very nuanced ways to distinguish these differences (for example distinguishing temporary borrowing from permanent having grammatically). In contrast, Western languages are more streamlined, reflecting that in the transition to modernity, the limits to alienability were pushed back evermore. However, the distinctions also exist. For example, I can say, "I have a PhD degree", but I cannot say, *"The PhD degree is my property", even though I can say, "I own a PhD degree." Using *property* would imply alienability, which is legally prohibited, and the title is seen as a part of the personal identity.

As said, narrower possessive relationships imply a status difference between possessor and possessee and a capacity of control by the former: A linguistic universal is that the relationship cannot be grammatically inverted without shifting to belonging, such as "I have a car" and "The car belongs to me." Most languages, therefore, distinguish between phenomena that can be controlled and those beyond any control. So, I can say "my illness" but cannot say *"I own an illness." This is one reason why the Western assumption of controlling nature has changed linguistic framing, whereas in many Indigenous languages natural phenomena cannot be expressed linguistically in possessive terms since in their ontologies nature is beyond human powers of disposition.

The productivity of *property*

Let us explore these complex matters in some more detail, beginning with the observation that ***property*** is productive. This idea takes many shapes, such as the Indigenous notion of "authorship," which means that appropriating an object requires nurturing its creative powers that are harnessed by its holder and which are conditioned by a relational web reaching into the spiritual world.[88] Often, this is not stated explicitly, as in German civil law. But it is mostly implied, such as in the French *biens*. Islamic law is explicit about this point as it stipulates that only objects used for benefit can become ***property***.[89] This is defined as a benefit to humans, so it excludes benefits to non-humans. As we shall see in chapter 5, this is important when considering ***property*** in the context of ecosystems where "ecosystem services" rendered to humans ground in complex indirect productive webs of ecological interactions. In pre-modern conceptions of ***property***, this is reflected in two stances. One is to exclude nature from appropriation, only allowing for appropriation of specific benefits to humans (such as logging), while recognizing spiritual mastery, hence maintaining a strong notion of non-human ***property***.[90]

The emphasis on benefits for humans can be explained easily from the perspective of theft. Only what benefits humans is also a motivation for theft. What is useless, will not be stolen. Meanwhile, the same point on non-humans applies; taking benefits away from non-humans is not seen as theft, and so there is no need to protect them with ***property***. On the other hand, animals can be seen as invading ***property***, if they are owned by a human, such as herders letting cattle roam freely on fields for cropping. In sum, centering ***property*** on the human domain is a distinct phenomenon not limited to Western modernity, since there is also the widespread idea that ***property*** belongs to spiritual entities who are not embodied in natural entities. The classical case is the distinction between *res sanctae*

88 As an example, see Cesarino 2016.

89 The notion of *mal* excludes all objects from property that cannot be controlled by humans for their benefit, especially future benefit, which implies storability and durability; Islam 1999.

90 As seen, the paradigmatic case is Indigenous conceptions of land which is claimed as homeland. However, this land and its spirits are ultimately the owners of the people, as they nurture their bodies and relational selves; for example Henry 2012.

and *res humanae* in Roman law which, however, resulted in the Roman law mostly exploring the human dimension, and only canon law further deepening the legal handling of the former.[91] But there is an important shift in factually approaching a corporate body, the church, as holder of the ***property***, whereas, in earlier conceptions, the gods were seen as its holders, in the sense of assigning an object, such as a temple and its sacred land, to the god.[92]

In English, "property" refers to an object and the relation between subject and object at the same time. The term is even used in the narrower meaning of real estate. This reflects the history of ***property***, which converges globally regarding agricultural societies: the primordial ***property*** is land, and hence, many words in this semantic field originate with reference to land. However, this also reveals that *property* is often seen as wealth, and until today the English use of ***property*** in the narrow sense relates to wealth. Before the advent of the Industrial Revolution, wealth was seen as grounding in landed estates. This idea was rooted in the belief that only land can be productive, which was theoretically articulated in physiocrat thinking that may have been inspired by similar ideas in China. The notion of the primordial productivity of land motivated the widespread practice of approaching land as pivotal for taxing the population.[93] These views have profoundly shaped European law. For example, the section on *Eigentum* in the German BGB (§§ 903 ff) spends much detail on land. The German *Eigentum* originally directly referred to the landed estate, as in English.

The other primordial form of productive ***property*** as wealth is cattle, from which the term *capital* originated etymologically. In both land and cattle, one key defining element of wealth is salient that was also emphasized by Weber: Wealth is productive in the sense of generating future streams of economic benefits. In European languages, there is an etymological relationship between land and cattle: In common law, the "property" in land is called a *fee*, which goes back to the feudal fief. The Indo-European root is "peku-" which refers to movable wealth and cattle and is also the root of "pecunia", Latin for money.[94]

91 Bloch 2006.

92 Thomas (2011, 207 ff) discusses the medieval case of a monastery where the last monk passed away which raised the question of who the ultimate owner was. In these debates, we observe an emerging social ontology which has much in common with Indigenous spirituality as abstract bodies become "doubled" ("doublé," ibidem 232) with concrete bodies in constructs as the legal person or as embodied in the building of the monastery. This allows for two legal options: Treating the church's legal person as receiver or seeing the monastic community as a legal person embodied in the building, even without a living member.

93 Chinese ideas have influenced European enlightenment thinking via scholars such as Quesnay in France and Wolff in German-speaking regions; Mungello 1999, 88 ff.

94 https://www.etymonline.com/word/fee

The productive role of ***property*** is highlighted in the Chinese terminology for ***property*** before the advent of modern civil law, which was transferred from Germany via Japan. The old Chinese term for ***property*** was *ye* which is still widely used in many composites, such as in denoting trades and economic sectors or various terms relating to professions and skills (for example, *nongye* for agriculture, or *biye* for graduating).[95] There is one composite that still directly relates to ***property***, meaning wealth, *chanye*, but narrowly as estate, and again also referring to a branch of industry. However, this has not been received in modern legal language. The old term *ye* cannot be rendered as "property," indeed, and accordingly, modern law stands in principled tension with the older uses of *ye*. A possible translation is "productive capacity of which someone has a recognized power of disposition." This is salient when it comes to land. In Imperial China, land was seen as the ultimate productive resource, and there were many ways of appropriating it. This resulted in distinct forms of ***property***, which included permanent tenancy over generations. These constructs were still fundamentally different from "property," so the British in Hong Kong took immediate steps towards modernizing land registers with the aim of identifying the ultimate owners.[96] In Imperial China, such a notion existed, in principle, but this was tied to the obligation to pay taxes. That means, in case of conflicts, ***property*** was assigned to the taxpayer.[97]

The discussion so far allows us to separate the relationship from the object: ***Property*** appears to be the means to secure control of wealth since there is always the risk that future control of the benefits may be jeopardized for some reason. Accordingly, it is essential for durable items, even more so when they are productive.

Philosophically, the connection between ***property*** and productive wealth was seminally established by John Locke, who argued that ***property*** accrues to someone who spends labor on the object of ***property***, with the archetypical example of land that is made productive by the tiller.[98] Locke's theory is highly ambivalent, as it has been invoked by himself to justify the colonization of North American land, expropriating the natives who were depicted as savages who did not labor on the land.[99] Hence, this turns out to be "terra nullius." But his theory has also been invoked by squatters who legitimize their actions in claiming fallow land owned by holders of large estates.[100] A key question is how productivity is defined. As salient in the etymology of ***property***, this can be interpreted as productivity in terms of

95 Wang and Li 2019.
96 Hase 2013.
97 Osborne 2004.
98 Waldron (2023) overviews classical theories of property.
99 For a critique from an Indigenous point of view, see Trosper 2022, 40, 88 ff.
100 Keenan 2015, 68.

monetary income generated from ***property***.[101] If so, ***property*** is deeply connected to markets, and assimilates to wealth as a monetary category, as in Weber's definition of *Vermögen*. This is important because Locke's definition raises the question of how far the reach of one's labor may limit the extent of ***property***: Accumulation of ***property*** becomes feasible if its productivity is manifest in generating monetary income.[102]

The distinction between material productivity and monetary productivity is highly significant for understanding the Indigenous notions of ***property***: In the Cree Hunting Law previously mentioned, the hunting grounds are clearly seen as an essential productive resource, and there are meticulous procedures in mapping their boundaries and the assignments to different kinship groups. But alienation via markets is strictly forbidden, including more specific forms such as the hypothetical case that a *Kaanoowapmaakin*, a hunting leader, would sell hunting rights, even within the Cree community. However, such restrictions can also be found in mainstream Western contexts. For example, it might be allowed to forage in a forest but not for commercial purposes.[103] There may be restrictions on how to handle donated goods, which may not be resold for profit by the intermediating organization, if not legally, but as a moral norm.

Imperial China is an interesting example of this relation between productivity and money. Land appropriation was hierarchically ordered according to a system of payments.[104] Traditionally, the ultimate owner of the land was the Emperor, which legitimizes the obligation to pay tax to him. In the long run, the taxpayer is the next-layer holder of the ***property***, which refers to the so-called subsoil rights. The surface rights are more flexible and regulate the rent paid to the holder of the subsoil right. The holder of the surface right further leases the land to the farmer who tills the land. The farmers pay rent and retain the residual income. So, productivity relates to monetary categories but is based on the physical productivity of land and labor. The difference between Chinese ideas and modern Western ***property*** is that there are multiple landowners who all partake in the productivity of land, while only one group works on the land.

This discussion reveals a distinction that is fundamental across most societies. This is between a source of benefits and the benefits themselves, such as the tree

---

101 This is by no means only true for Western modernity, as we find this already in Antiquity, Economou and Kyriazis 2017, and even in earlier societies of the Middle East; Jursa 2014.

102 Trosper (2022, 201) emphasizes this point since the original Locke argument could also be employed on Indigenous people without market context. Historically, a critical observation on land usurpation in North America is its early financialization; Goetzmann 2017, 388 ff.

103 Valguarnera 2017.

104 Kroker 1958. For more detail, see Chapter 4.

and the fruits.[105] Someone can have ***property*** of the tree or not, but she might still claim the fruits as her own. Often, this is debated in legal scholarship, such as in Islam.[106] There are several reasons why this relationship is not easy to define. One is that the source may be less clearly circumscribed than the benefit. ***Property*** of the tree may or may not include the land: The tree would not be productive without pollinators, so how about their share, especially when beekeeping is involved?

The distinction between source and benefit often relates to moral considerations of using ***property***, especially the question of whether ***property*** necessarily relates to an acquisitive motivation, also in the sense that ***property*** nurtures it when it does not yet exist. This applies especially to the use of benefits for market transactions, hence earning monetary income, and as seen, often results in prescriptions that allow for enjoying benefits but prohibit the sale for profit.

Rights and obligations of *property*

The observations on the "bundle of rights" view show that a common bias in approaching ***property*** is putting too much emphasis on the rights compared to obligations. One of the fundamental obligations is the proper use of a productive resource. Nobody is obliged to sit on a stool he bought for his private home. But leaving his allotment garden untended is not only frowned upon but maybe even legally sanctioned. The concept of productive use is a key connection between possession and "property," in the legal construct of adverse possession known since Roman times, as *usucapio*, a term that continues to be used in Romance languages. That means if someone holds a building and does not use it, squatters might use it, and if the owner does not complain, after some period, the "property" accrues to the user. In this sense, a user is obliged to use it in a double meaning: First, effectively using it, and second, taking action to claim it. One version of this reasoning is the economic stance towards monopoly, which is said to have the greatest benefit in allowing for an idle life. Strictly speaking, ***property*** gives a monopoly position to the proprietor, such that a truly competitive market must minimize

105 This is a most common misunderstanding about so-called "communal" property among Indigenous peoples. For example, Amazonian people mostly have a strong sense of individual and family ownership of tools, utensils and harvested items, while regarding the productive resources as shared by the community, however, owned by a spiritual master represented by the chief; for example Matos Viegas 2016.

106 Islam 1999.

"property" holdings, which are protected against any attempt at appropriation by a more productive user.[107]

Beyond this obligation to be productive, externalities of ***property*** are pervasive and ubiquitous. Accordingly, absolute "property" is only possible if the owner also has the power to fend off all other claims resulting from externalities he imposes on others. This is the systematic reason why ***property*** and power are deeply related. This connection is salient in the Roman notion of ***property*** as *dominium*. However, as soon as the notion of absolute "property" was created, it was increasingly circumscribed to deal with the pervasive externalities.[108]

The issue of externality is significant in many respects. The definition of ***property*** in terms of exclusion is purely negative and does not give any information about the status of the excluded. If we reverse the perspective, we can also define ***property*** as resulting from the excluded individual's recognition of the freedom of choice of the proprietor. In this case, we can conceptualize ***property*** as legitimate externalities *erga omnes*, i.e., which everyone recognizes as allowable. One example of this view is the Jewish conception of ***property*** as a gift of God, especially land.[109] As such, it is defined by responsibilities and obligations to the community which recognizes this ***property***. One of the critical consequences is that within the community, one cannot use ***property*** to gain an advantage over another member, such as taking interest from a loan or accumulating land as a gift of god. In the Jubilee year, all original owners are reinstated by returning the ***property*** and loans. Hence, ***property*** of land as the key resource went hand in hand with the agricultural commandments *mitzvot*.

There has been a rich debate in Islamic law for more than a century, following the Ottoman efforts to modernize the country, which shows that ***property*** can be contextualized very differently from the case of the countries where the civil laws were inaugurated originally.[110] The reason is that if the introduction of modern "property" is part of modernizing the state, it is per se seen as a public right in the sense of contributing to the public good. This view was compatible with Islamic law that obliges the proprietor to use it in a productive way, even for accumulating wealth, because this, in turn, enables him to do the deeds that are beneficial to the community. In this sense, modernizers could argue that Western private "property" also serves a public purpose. However, there is also the possible implication that the state appropriates resources for development, which would, in fact, contradict Islamic law. In Chinese constitutional law today, "property" as private is

107 Posner and Weyl 2018. We come back on this in the next chapter.
108 Serkin 2016, 14 ff.
109 Aluffi and Francavilla 2017.
110 Tripp 2006, 21 ff, 56 ff.

explicitly protected, but contextualized in a similar way as a means to foster national prosperity and economic growth.[111] In Russia, the reforms of Cathrine the Great introduced "property" as a privilege extended by the Imperial power. This has created a deep tradition of seeing "property" as derivative of state power, and not as a natural right in the Lockean sense.[112]

In general, legal spheres differ in the extent to which ***property*** weighs rights and obligations. Western civil laws emphasize the rights dimension, and assign the obligations to government regulation, whereas other regions, though copying these laws partially, emphasize obligations of the proprietor, if only in the sense that the holder of ***property*** takes responsibility for moving the country forward economically. Yet, this focus matters regarding actions such as expropriation for public projects, where most laws include this sovereign right of eminent domain. Suppose private "property" is seen as having the function of fostering economic development. In that case, there is no principled protection if the government plans to implement a project that also contributes to that goal, such as building a highway and expropriating farmers, as in the case of China. This also affects the judgments about the amount of compensation. So, even if the legal norms may be similar, the different contextualization of ***property*** results in large differences in practice.

The issue of rights versus obligations relates to the important difference between two kinds of holding rights to an object, often seen as transcending ***property***. This is the distinction between stewardship and ownership. In some constellations, the steward is a person who can enjoy full rights of possession and enjoy the benefits of the object but is still not regarded as the proprietor.[113] This construct was dominant in defining the ***property*** of family lines in Europe, such as in legal constructs of trusts and *fidei commissum*. The difference is crucial when it comes to potential liabilities of the steward in her or his economic concerns: Since a steward is not the proprietor, she can only be liable with her personal wealth, that is, her own ***property***, but not with the ***property*** of the family line which she does not own, although being responsible for managing it. This construct is by no means only relevant historically. Many modern financial instruments in the fund industry use the trust model to reduce the liability of proprietors.[114] Medieval constructs of trust law create the durability of the financial entity of capital here.

111 Long 2009.

112 Herrmann-Pillath 2019. As Widerquist and McCall (2021) show, this is true for many emerging capitalist nations in history. The only difference is whether the monarch grants the rights or whether the elites themselves grant them, such as the members of the British parliament during the enclosure movement.

113 Emerich 2017.

114 Pistor 2019.

Historically, modern civil laws aimed to block any attempts at separating stewardship from ***property*** to create the conditions for foreclosure in case of bankruptcy of the steward. This reveals the deep connection between "property" and credit since "property" provides the means for being able to redeem a loan and, hence, being creditworthy in the first place. However, this presupposes adequate information about the value of the "property," which requires that there is a sufficient volume of trading such items on the market. A major concern of modern civil laws was reducing all impediments to the alienability of land and, hence, establishing a market and market price for land. This also allows for the use of land as collateral for loans, thus enabling other forms of investment.[115] If a steward is doing business without the backing of alienable land, this type of guarantee for lenders is lacking.

In our context, there are two important consequences. The first one is that the difference between wealth and ***property*** assumes even greater significance: Someone can own "property" but may even have negative wealth if she is indebted. This comes to the fore if, eventually, foreclosure is necessary to redeem a loan. This does not only refer to land, as in the early stages of capitalism, and in much of informal finance in developing countries today, pawnshops play a critical role in providing loans. In this case, even minor goods could become pawns if they are only durable.[116] This leads to the conclusion that in a monetary economy with widespread debt relations, most "property" is never absolute but relative to the wealth status of a borrower-proprietor.[117] In times of financial crisis, therefore, many proprietors suddenly lose their "property." Here, the state's role becomes crucial since, with the civil laws, the state also became the ultimate enforcer of debts. One consequence is that we must distinguish between ***property*** that is absolutely protected from any debt enforcement, which is the legally protected existential minimum. Only this ***property*** is truly absolute. In most cases, this refers to ***property*** necessary to lead a decent life, and which is necessary to earn a living. For example, a luxury car may be pledged to buy a cheaper one for someone who needs the car for business. Importantly, pension claims are mostly protected, which strengthens the case for treating such entitlements as ***property***.

The second consequence is the dissociation between the material ***property*** and its value, which relates to the special treatment of pecuniary externalities in modern capitalism. If my estate is damaged by some nuisance, such as blocking sun-

115 This aspect has also been emphasized in the context of Global South informal settlements, where lack of legal "property" blocks access to finance, as emphasized by the influential work of de Soto 2001. However, as Benjamin and Raman (2011) argue, this view does not recognize the complexity of embedded social relations governing assignments of powers of disposition among groups and individuals.

116 Woloson 2012.

117 The central role of debt in understanding societies is the theme of Graeber's (2014) influential work.

light and access to the shore, I may take legal action. But I cannot take legal action if market conditions change and its value plummets, with the possible consequence of driving me into bankruptcy if I am heavily indebted and confident about its value. Even if this loss of value is caused by reckless speculation on real estate, I cannot claim compensation from the speculators. This is remarkable, as financial claims are often legally protected, but not the expectations about "property" values: A proprietor holds an object, not its value. From that point of view, stewardship implies that the steward may lose value in terms of discounted future streams of income generated from an estate, but this does not translate into a change in its subjective value, including the certainty that it can never be foreclosed at conditions that might reflect the declining discounted value.

This shows that the distinction between wealth and "property" acquires a distinct meaning in the context of a fully developed market economy. In a specific sense, "property" does not fully protect wealth since the latter depends on market conditions. This is salient in the context of capital markets and explains why we still observe that family businesses tend to shun the capital markets, given the risk of being forced to relinquish their "property" by hostile takeovers reflecting divergent market valuations. On the other hand, shareholders of listed companies are not protected at all against the loss of value of these shares. The share may be a title of "property," but the wealth defined by that title, which is manifest in its value, is highly uncertain.

This discussion shows that stewardship of inalienable property is only one form of disconnecting ***property*** from markets. In our semantic domain of ***property***, we may say that we have cases of ***property*** that is fully assigned but not appropriated. This constellation has distinct forms in modern societies, such as endowments as legal persons. Here, the distinction between subject and object of ***property*** is neutralized because the object owns itself. In Western conceptions of ***property***, this notion emerged in the context of canon law and its creation of the legal person, such as in the famous dispute over the question of who owns a monastery when the last monk passes away: Is it the church or does the monastery own itself, due to its continuing material presence that embodied its legal personhood?[118] Similar constructs can be found in many societies, such as the heritable foundations of the *waqf* in Islam or the lineage trusts in Imperial China.

118 Thomas 2011.

The objects of *property*

The previous discussion points to the question of what are possible objects of ***property*** and in which specific sense? The difference between common law and civil law raises several important issues. As common law focuses on relationships between people, in principle, it is flexible regarding objects. German civil law and similar laws are more constrained in only referring to corporeal objects.[119] This raises the question of whether objects are just anything, whether particular objects are excluded, and whether different kinds of objects also define different types of relationships. In theory, the abstract notion of ***property*** means that anything can become object, and that the relationship is the same over all kinds of objects. This not true in practice, and at a closer look only refers to "property." Indeed, the dynamic of capitalism builds on what we will conceive of the performative power of "property," in the sense of transforming any object into something that can be appropriated and traded via markets, and even stronger, in the sense of creating objects as new elements of social ontology.[120] These performative powers of language ultimately undermine the distinction between corporeal and incorporeal entities, since this distinction itself is performative.[121]

Regarding the first point, the range of objects is structured and constrained. The most important relates to humans as objects of ***property***. Slavery is outlawed in most societies today. This constraint is only limited to humans; there is "property" of animals. At the same time, as in German civil law, there is a legal twist: Despite being objects of "property," animals are explicitly excluded from the domain of corporeal things, which reflects their special moral status. However, this is a recent development, and in many legal domains, this is still the case, implying that owners of animals should be allowed to handle them as they like. There is another important variation of this theme, which is ***property*** held in one's own body. On the one hand, this is clearly implied by ideas about ownership, essential also to Locke's theory of ***property***, but at the same time "property" is tightly limited, as we are not legally permitted to sell ourselves into slavery or trade our body parts.

The latter observation shows that the nature of the object matters for conceptualizing the relationship with it: The human body is a special object, and hence ***property*** takes a specific shape, affecting many issues in social life, such as the debate about legalizing prostitution. However, often, it is the legal relationship

119 For a discussion of the differences and their historical roots, see Gretton 2007.

120 Searle 1995.

121 For example, single fish in fisheries may not be objects of "property" since there are technical limits to appropriation, but via fishing quotas, they become "doubled" as virtual entities that can be appropriated; Holm and Nielsen 2007.

that defines the object and even creates it performatively. Most importantly, this relates to land. Consider a parcel of land: this consists of myriads of different objects, such as different kinds of sand, worms, and plants, as well as animals that live there continuously. "Property" of land does not refer to all these objects directly, as this would imply that the "property" would be subdivided into the same number of rights.[122] Instead, "property" refers to the abstract notion of a parcel, in principle, a segment on a map. All objects within such a segment are assigned to the "property" holder. We can also interpret this as creating an object by means of legal procedures of mapping land.[123] It is important to distinguish this from possession: In reality, an owner of a parcel of land has only limited possession of all objects there, in the sense of controlling them.

In fact, this performative dimension of law is pervasive. The example of land shows that there is the fundamental problem that once a right exists, all corporeal things are, in fact, incorporeal, namely rights, like the parcel of land identified in a cadaster. This can be reversed in the sense of reifying incorporeal rights, such as rights on an idea, that is, an intellectual property right.

One important following phenomenon is the reflexivity of "property." This means, there is "property" of an object, and there is "property" of the right of property. The latter may be itself corporeal, such as holding a title on an object without which the claim would become void if contested successfully. This is the key condition for separating "property" and possession phenomenologically: "Property" is independent of factually relating to an object physically. Yet it does not mean that it has powers independent from action, which is a dispute that ultimately leads to an assignment by a third party.

The reflexivity of "property" has one crucial consequence: If we consider "property" of rights, all ontological distinctions between objects become neutralized. This has been especially true for the recent decades, which saw an expansion of "property" to many new domains, such as genetics. However, in most societies, there are restrictions on what becomes an object of "property," as said, even in capitalist modernity. This is most salient when considering societies in which the modern notion of "property" had been introduced. An illuminating example is 19th-century Russia.[124] Following the reform initiatives of Catherine the Great, a concept of absolute "property" was imported into Russia, which turned out to create obstacles to economic development, for example, regarding the exploita-

---

122 This has been labelled the "tragedy of the anti-commons": Heller 1998.

123 Vanuxem 2022. As Max Weber had already shown, the surveying of land in the provinces was a transformative power in creating "property" in the Roman empire, even though this was not "absolute;" Kantor 2017. The transformative role of land registries is also emphasized in the context of colonial dispossession, see Bhandar 2018.

124 Pravilova 2014.

tion of mineral resources or the extension of waterways. Hence, there was a society-wide debate about whether private "property" should be transformed according to public interest. Interestingly, this also raised the question of the subject of ***property***. In the earlier reforms, the notion was that this was either private or the state. In Russian debates, the public was invoked as a third domain. For example, there was a discussion about intellectual "property" and ownership of artworks in which not only a public interest in access to cultural goods was emphasized, but also the important point of who was the actual producer of a cultural good. One opinion was that this is not the individual artist alone but also the community to which he belongs, historically and contemporarily. This leads to a different assignment of "property" compared to individualistic intellectual "property."

In many societies there are ideas that certain goods are basic needs and therefore cannot be appropriated, such as in Islam water. This example belongs to the wider domain of ***property*** of nature. There are large differences between countries with regard to the question of whether privately owned land, such as forests, must allow access for non-owners, not only for trespassing or hiking, but also, more specifically, for foraging.[125] One example of this is the Swedish *allemansrät*, which goes back to vague customary rules but even obtained a constitutional level in the late 20th century. In practice, that means there is a distinction between the *tomt*, an area surrounding a dwelling, and the larger parcel of land that is legally private "property." Non-proprietors can use the land beyond the *tomt* freely, up to a certain limit. However, this may even include commercial uses, such as guiding a hiking group and camping for two days. This differs radically from the situation in England where any economic use is strictly prohibited. In France, foraging is prohibited, even for personal consumption.

Hence, in general, we can say that the nature of the relationship between the subject and the object of ***property*** is also determined by the specific status of the object. Yet, reflexivity implies that this is not simply an ontological given. This is salient in the economic uses of the "bundle of rights" notion. Here, this notion can relate to absolute "property" when it comes to "property" of those rights. For example, someone may only have a claim on the fruits of a tree, but not the tree itself. Yet, this right of the fruits can itself be absolute, for example, including the possibility of alienation, and may not allow anybody else to interfere with my uses of the fruits, such as my relatives. Economics does not make this explicit, but this point seems to distinguish two very different conceptions of the "bundle of rights" notion: One is in anthropology, where the notion is invoked to describe the complexity and embeddedness of ***property***,[126] the other is economics, where the em-

125 Valguarnera 2017.
126 Turner 2017.

phasis is on the exactness and clarity of rights in bundles.[127] Hence, in economics, the private "property" notion as ownership prevails even in the view of the "bundle of rights." This is important, for example, when it comes to analyzing institutional arrangements such as a commons: A group of people may jointly own a commons, but their use rights may have very different statuses, especially when it comes to alienation via markets.[128]

Objects also have a different status for purely practical reasons. ***Property*** of perishable and movable items is mostly by recognition of possession. There are objects in which possession is difficult to achieve and secure, an issue that economics mostly deals with, distinguishing canonically between private goods, common goods, club goods, and public goods. However, this distinction is only treated in the context of "property," which led to very misleading ideas such as the so-called "tragedy of the commons." Economics only focuses on creating means of appropriation via "property" but does not consider the full semantic domain of ***property***, which is only adumbrated in Ostrom's approach to the commons. However, even in the case of purely public goods, recognition and assignment can establish forms of ***property*** without appropriation.

Finally, the language of ***property*** is itself the object of the various actions creating ***property***, which thereby assumes a performative function in a literal sense, as a strategy of political pursuit of interests, in the Weberian sense. This is especially true for contexts of legal pluralism and contested states of legal transformation, as in decolonizing countries, where this process is often far from being completed because the new governments often stand in the legal traditions of the colonizers.[129]

Conclusion

The essential insight of this chapter is that ***property*** is a universal feature of human existence, but this does not mean that appropriation is universal. Appropriation is only one mode of ***property***. If we own our body, contra Locke, this does not mean that we appropriate our body; we recognize it as our own, and others might agree, unless they appropriate us, for example, enslaving us. Recognition

127 Stiglitz 2013, Ho 2013.

128 As mentioned, the divergence between economics and anthropology is salient in the anthropological critique of Ostrom's theory of the commons, arguing that it marginalizes the centrality of social relationships in handling ***property***; Wagner and Talakai 2007.

129 Lund and Boone 2013.

is a mode of ***property*** that is universal across all human societies and takes different institutional forms. The most elaborate institutional form of recognition is the law. However, this does not mean that the law determines practice. The law mostly becomes relevant only in case of conflict, especially when disagreement in recognition results in appropriative conflicts. Hence, in such cases, the law becomes an institutional means of appropriation. Yet, the judge does not enact appropriation: The judicial action is in the mode of assignment. In fact, as we have seen, ***property*** is assigned and not appropriated in many societies, such as in traditional inheritance, which is the dominant mode in land-based pre-industrial societies.

These distinctions are essential for acknowledging the centrality of alienation, which is universal in defining ***property*** in specific social contexts. Whether a certain object or feature in the real world is alienable from the person who is recognized as having it defines entire social ontologies. Alienability is independent of physical separability, and it can materialize in different institutional forms. If we approach this in most abstract terms, inalienability means that the feature is a constitutive part of the identity of the person who has it. For example, this book may be seen as inalienable from me as its author. However, this does not imply that others cannot appropriate the printed text and copy it so that what seems inalienable is only its ideational content. Even in this case, others may claim that I have stolen their ideas, perhaps inadvertently. Or they may believe that a spirit possessed me and planted them in my brain. As we have seen, diverse beliefs about alienability are a defining feature of orders of ***property***. To a large degree, alienability is a performative feature of ***property*** orders.

This insight is critical for distinguishing capitalist modernity from other types of society since much of the current theorizing about ***property*** unduly generalizes over these specific conditions. Weber's views are seminal, as they highlight the centrality of specific forms of alienating appropriation that are mediated via markets and money, resulting in crucial conceptual distinctions such as between *Eigentum* and *Vermögen*. In many societies, appropriation often takes the form of legitimate theft targeting out groups and is shunned within communities. This constellation has been consistently misinterpreted as showing that these societies do not have ***property***. They do not have "property," but ***property*** mainly by recognition and assignment. The centuries of debates about the origin of "private property" have been wasted intellectually, as they generalize over the specific capitalist form of ***property***. This debate is mostly a delusion of our modern language of ***property***, which is endogenous to the economic system which now dominates most of the world economically, but not necessarily the diverse life-worlds of people living under its reign, if only at its margins. Accordingly, the critical task for developing a new approach to ***property*** is creating a new conceptual and terminological framework, which we will discuss in the next chapter.

Chapter 3: The theory of havings

Economics and *property*: An uneasy relationship

Building on the insights gained from our explorations of the languages of ***property***, this chapter develops a new theoretical frame for the economic philosophy of ***property***, with the radical move of discarding the concept and suggesting the alternative of "having."[1] In English, this involves the creation of a new word, "havings", akin to "belongings," from the root verb "to have." In German, this only means to revive words that are still in use but are antiquated: The verb *haben* relates to *Habe* or *Haben*, similar to the English *belongings*. We also have the meaning of assets in referring to bookkeeping as *Soll und Haben*. I will argue that the term "havings" is appropriate to denote the full breadth of ***property*** as salient in the previous chapter.[2] More fundamentally, we will approach having as a constitutive form of human existence related to living beings' universal notion of autonomy. As we will see, this goes back to the idea of ***property*** in German idealism, though eschewing the idealistic component, as in Sartre's view of having *avoir* as one fundamental aspect of an existential triad with being *être* and doing *faire*.[3]

Although my concern is the economic philosophy of ***property***, this is far from doing economics of ***property***. I do not use the expression "economics of property" because this would imply approaching ***property*** from the viewpoint of markets and viewing the functions of "property" in their context. As we have seen, this is precisely the critical issue in differentiating between different *property* dimensions. ***Property*** is a condition for markets to operate. Still, it cannot be treated

1 Of course, many authors tend to use the verb "have" to discuss generic aspects of ***property***, for example, Lomasky 1989. In his classical article, Honoré (1961) discusses the relationship between "own" and "have" and refers to the latter only as "having rights" to be distinguished from owning a thing by having this right. My approach differs from such uses as it introduces havings as a foundational term.

2 In the previous chapter I have already pointed out, following Aikhenvald 2012, that in many languages the basic form of a possessive verb is an equivalent to "have."

3 Sartre 2017, 754–785. We briefly explored Sartre's views in the introduction to this book.

as endogenous to markets in both the empirical and the normative sense, being transformed and degenerated into "property."[4] Empirically, ***property*** as a constituent of agency goes far beyond market agency and reaches into all social domains, such as family and politics. ***Property*** is a necessary condition for human action. Normatively, reducing ***property*** to market functionality leads to pathologies of "property" in these other domains. We meet a Polanyian paradox: ***Property*** is necessary for markets, but market forces erode ***property***.

This paradox must be stated clearly. ***Property*** and markets stay in principled tension because ***property*** is a barrier to competition while being undermined by competition at the same time. The German ordoliberal economists had argued that private ***property*** is only beneficial to society if reigned by competition because otherwise, it becomes a source of economic power and inequality.[5] Their idea of the competition was neoclassical, hence oriented towards the conditions of perfect competition. This requires a particular economic structure in which all economic actors, entrepreneurs, firms, and customers are units that are small relative to the size of the market so that they cannot influence the parameters of the market, most importantly, the price. Obviously, this idea has not been realized in modern markets. Hence, there are always two dysfunctional tendencies; the first is the creation of market power, aka monopolistic structures. Second, externalities result from actors with market power shifting liability away. For the Ordoliberals, therefore, one key aspect of the institutional design of ***property*** was full personal liability and the rejection of all legal forms of limiting liability.[6]

This tension between markets and ***property*** has been most succinctly stated in the "radical markets" approach championed by Posner and Weyl.[7] They go far beyond the Ordoliberal critique of "property" and design a system where *property* would effectively wither away from the established meaning of absolute private "property." This works via a universal system of subjecting all assets to an auction system where bidders can constantly challenge the current holder of the asset and take it over. We do not go into the details here. Suffice it to say that the condition for this is a procedure well designed in auction theory, where holders of assets truthfully announce their estimate of its value if this estimate also serves to assess their tax rate on this asset. The original model for this is land ownership and

---

4 For a related view, see Blumenfeld 2024. He criticizes the current mainstream view of approaching ***property*** either in the legal or the economic sense, sometimes combined, thereby obfuscating what I have referred to as its ontological dimension, following Sartre.

5 The classical exposition is Eucken 2004.

6 This position was already regarded as anachronistic at Eucken's time and was rarely maintained later. Bannas and Herrmann-Pillath (2020) put it at the center of their alternative view of economic system. The reactions are similar as in Eucken's times, Frühbrodt 2021.

7 Posner and Weyl 2018.

land tax. Still, Posner and Weyl expand this to all durable assets, thus envisaging a computerized registry of all valuables (cars, washing machines, or expensive watches). All holders of assets enter their assets into this registry and are obliged to join the auction so that any other bidder who thinks the asset is more valuable can take it over. This incentivizes the holder to state the actual value, which also resolves the assessment problem for the government, which taxes the asset. Similarly, the bidder must be truthful about her estimation as her tax duty would increase at the inflated values.

Here, the realism of this proposal does not matter. The proposal implies that ultimate ownership is by the government representing the market community, as in the original models for land ownership championed by Henry George or Silvio Gesell.[8] In this sense, private "property" is discarded. The market is based on public ***property*** held by the government as a steward. The economic actors only have powers of disposition continuously reshuffled by the competitive auctions. This universal auction becomes the pillar of the market system. Hence, markets without private "property" are not only feasible but also amount to the perfection of the market system.

Another way to demonstrate the contradiction between market and ***property*** is by showing the irrelevance of ***property***, which follows from the Coase theorem.[9] The Coase theorem also underlies the auction model. It states that if transaction costs are close to nil (which would be technically achieved by the computerized auction system) the initial assignment of property rights does not matter for market outcomes because these rights will be reshuffled by the market such that the most efficient holder of the rights will obtain them. However, this also means that in a world with significant positive transaction costs, ***property*** matters.[10]

This brief discussion reveals a severe misunderstanding of much of the literature on ***property***, especially the critical approaches: Capitalism does not need ***property*** in the Blackstonian form. Or, another possible interpretation, capitalism endorses ***property*** to enforce economic power, but not market efficiency.[11] In the latter case, we must sharply distinguish between capitalism and what economics theorizes as market system. The misunderstanding perhaps originated

8 Gesell 2022; George 1879.

9 Coase 1960.

10 In Russia, the Coase reasoning produced the catastrophic result of nurturing the oligarchy since Russian economists argued that following the Coase theorem, the market would reshuffle the property rights independent from initial assignments to end up with the most efficient holder; Sutela 2012, 11, 27, Frye 2006.

11 As we saw in Chapter 1, this was Weber's view: ***Property*** is necessary for imposing the factory discipline on propertyless workers. Accordingly, early social movements against budding capitalism such as the *Levellers* emphasized universal rights to smallholdings to ensure independent livelihood; Oswalt 2024.

with Marx, who confronted the enclosure movement as a young journalist. However, as the Ordoliberals pinpointed, if ***property*** is endogenous to markets, there are strong incentives to design it so that liability would be reduced, hence weakening one side of ***property*** as much as possible. At the same time, control is desirable. Therefore, in practice, capitalists prefer forms of ***property*** that are remnants of the feudal system, with the ***property*** being fragmented so that they can claim the profits from exerting their powers of disposition while reducing their liability.[12] These constructs go back to legal forms of feudal family estates and stewardship, such as the trusts in common law, and had been targets of the civil law reforms accompanying the emergence of capitalism. Yet, capitalists only used these new legal forms to expand markets to achieve full alienability of a maximum number of assets. With alienability assured, they could move on to create forms of "property" according to their needs.

I use the term "capitalist" here mainly for rhetorical purposes. Analytically, the precise term in the Weberian sense would be the distinct group of "investors," whereas the term "capitalist" also includes the entrepreneurs.[13] If we define the latter as individuals who do not only pursue profit but also a project, such as launching a new technology, one conspicuous observation is that often entrepreneurs, such as the paradigmatic family business founder, aim at full control via private "property," even often accepting full personal liability. In contrast, investors display another paradoxical stance. On the one hand, they want to reduce risks by limiting their liability, favoring opaque ***property*** arrangements different from private "property." At the same time, they strongly prefer full liability of those actors who receive their investment, which is most salient in the relationship between lender and borrower. Moreover, they also prefer clear assignments of ***property***. So, there are two forces, one favoring clarity of ***property***, the other its opacity.

Therefore, to understand ***property***, it is essential to recognize the deep relationship between finance and property in modern capitalism, which is obscured in the understanding of private "property" in the legal and philosophical field, which, however, also shapes the ideology of ***property*** in modern economics.[14] Modern economics stresses the clarity of property rights, but investors prefer

12 Pistor 2019. Historically, limited liability was not universally favored by entrepreneurs but by newly emerging investors operating in the capital market; Ireland 2010.

13 Investors were a distinct type of agent emerging in the 19th century;Preda 2005.

14 Historically, this contradiction played out with full force in the early history of the United States, when some founding fathers, in particular Washington, were deeply engaged in financial operation of land colonization, while settlers simply aimed at occupying land. This led into conflicts, if land was assigned via government fiat as financial asset to be sold to future proprietors, while settlers already claimed possession, Lockean style; Goetzmann 2017, 388 ff.

opacity in practice; as the Chinese proverb says, you catch fish in muddled water. One task of this chapter is to develop a conceptual frame that can deal with these complexities.

Property, agency, and institutional action

Property, freedom, and violence

Our starting point is the relationship between ***property*** and agency, which we have already established in the previous chapter. This relationship stays at the center of the tradition of German idealism on which I build, especially Hegel.[15] Hegel's philosophy allows us to dissect the uneasy marriage of economics and "property" in a productive way. However, we will not follow his approach literally but only as an essential inspiration. In this sense, the approach is Hegelian, or, dogmatically speaking, neo-Hegelian.[16]

One red thread linking most philosophical contributions to ***property*** is that ***property*** is a material condition of freedom, since freedom must express itself in actions that necessarily engage external objects. It defines this formally as delineating the domains of freedom that different individuals must mutually respect. This implies that ***property*** must be a universally valid category if we accept the idea of individual freedom. ***Property*** combines negative and positive freedom. First, ***property*** excludes others from interfering with my choices, and second, I have nothing to choose from without ***property***. This notion of ***property*** is not economic in the narrow sense, although it refers materially to scarce goods. Scarcity matters conceptually because only if a good is scarce are people interested in appropriating it, even if others control it. This leads us back to our discussion of theft.

15 My discussion is deeply influenced by Jakob Blumenfeld's magisterial work; Blumenfeld 2024. Hegel's notion of ***property*** is mostly discussed in the context of the Philosophy of Right, Hegel 2009, §§ 41-71. In this view, Hegel is recognized as the creator of the German term *Privateigentum*. However, as Schnädelbach explains in detail, different from the Anglosaxon theories of ***property***, which Hegel fully absorbed, Hegel did not believe that *Privateigentum* is a sufficient condition for freedom; Schnädelbach 2000, 205 ff.

16 My Neo-Hegelian view is developed in Herrmann-Pillath and Boldyrev 2014.

Theft is a central theme in Hegel's thinking about ***property***.[17] Hegel starts with possession and argues that claiming possession of a good can always mean theft if that excludes others with similar intentions. Once possession is claimed, theft not only materially deprives others of the good but also invalidates their claim. Hegel approaches this constellation from an analytical level: Theft is an unlimited expression of freedom that formally and materially invalidates the freedom of others. Hence, theft leads to conflict, which is not just a struggle over the good but a struggle over recognition or lack of recognition. ***Property*** means recognizing the possession claim.

To some extent, this is a Hobbesian view, but Hegel adds the dimension of the person and her freedom. Unlike the anglophone philosophical tradition, individual freedom is not seen as a precondition of social interaction but only emerges from struggle. This means that freedom results from recognition of the other, and the same applies to ***property***. Different from possession, ***property*** is only possible by being recognized. In considering civil society, Hegel lifts this argument on an even more abstract level in relation to money and exchange. Money is a medium of abstraction, thus eventually constituting ***property*** as a right in exchange, effectively implying the *erga omnes* transition we discussed in the previous chapter.

As we see, Hegel covers many aspects that we extracted from the analysis of the language of ***property***. His view departs from economics even though he explicitly refers to the economy and receives many insights from the Political Economy of his time.[18] In modern economics, few approaches come close to his view on ***property*** and struggle; notably, Douglass North, in his later works, co-authored with Wallis and Weingast.[19] This departs radically from his earlier New Institutional Economics approach in explaining institutional evolution, particularly ***property***, due to violent struggles over control of resources. Hence, throughout most of human history, ***property*** regimes do not reflect economic forces of efficiency but the role of ***property*** arrangements in pacifying society, though by violent means controlled by a ***property*** holding group that had concluded a peace treaty among themselves and enforced their ***property*** on all others.[20] Like Hegel, North and co-authors argue that ***property*** only transcends this constellation in a society

17 Blumenfeld 2024, 194 ff. Blumenfeld's account differs from the mainstream interpretation (e.g. Ritter 2004) since he looks at Hegel's oeuvre in toto. Then, a similar tension emerges as in the juxtaposition between the *Phenomenology of Spirit* and the later works. The *Philosophy of Right* analyzes a historical state that is already manifest due to the unfolding of Spirit, whereas the *Phenomenology* explores the historical struggle of its emergence, both societal and individual. The focus on theft belongs to the latter.

18 The state of Hegel scholarship on this point is summarized in Herrmann-Pillath and Boldyrev 2014, 21 ff. Important contributions include Waszek 1988 and Priddat 1990.

19 North, Wallis, and Weingast 2009.

20 This view receives abundant empirical support in Widerquist and McCall, 2021.

following the rule of law and constitutional constraints on power. Under such a regime, further ***property*** evolutions will reflect the economic forces of efficiency.

Hegel would not endorse the latter conclusion. On the one hand, Hegel clearly assigns ***property*** to the level of civil society, which corresponds to North's rule of law regime. Yet, Hegel goes beyond in diagnosing dysfunctional distributional consequences of a civil society that is not embedded in ethical life, which he defines by the fundamental institutions of family, corporations, and the state. This represents a dialectical move from concrete (struggle) to abstract (civil society) back to concrete on the higher level of ethical life.[21] This corresponds to a view of freedom that goes beyond negative freedom in emphasizing the role of institutions in ethical life to provide the conditions of positive freedom.[22]

The tradition of German idealism partly anticipates what today is labelled liberal or progressive ***property*** in the anglophone discourse.[23] ***Property*** is not an individual right but is bound to recognition in the community and hence inherently includes obligations, especially ethical ones. This also transpired in the previous chapter: Most culturally diverse forms of *property* define this as a right assigned to an individual and tied with obligations to the community that recognizes this right. Radically different from the Lockean tradition, ***property*** is not a given or "natural" individual right but is an institution through which societal governance is enacted. Most importantly, this also means that ***property*** cannot be reduced to the contingent historical outcomes of past struggles.[24]

In seeing ***property*** as an institutional medium of pacifying society, it is not mainly contextualized in the economy, even though its objects are economic goods. Most economic theories of ***property*** commit the error of concluding from the latter that ***property*** is contextualized in the economy or, even narrower, markets. Furthermore, even if we consider its pacifying role in the first place, pacification is not necessarily peaceful because it often means violent suppression of resistance against appropriation.

Property and embodiment

Hegel's philosophy also suggests moving to a deeper analysis of ***property*** as constituting the conditions for agency. Following the detailed elaboration by Basso

21 Pippin 2008.

22 Neuhouser 2008.

23 Dagan 2021, Alexander et al. 2009.

24 An extreme version of the opposite view is Nozick's theory of ***property*** as historically evolved entitlements which current legal orders can only protect and thereby sustain; Nozick 2013, 150ff

and Herrmann-Pillath, I approach ***property*** in the two movements of outward and inward embodiment.[25] I do not explore the entire embodiment framework here, though, only focusing on what is needed to understand ***property*** as an institution. The gist of the argument is shown in Figure 3.1.[26] Hegel approaches the mind as a complex totality with different "moments", which he calls "spirit" or in our context, more specifically, "objective spirit." That means the spirit as mind is not "inside" the individual but is an assemblage of the subject, objects, and other subjects. Outward embodiment refers to Hegelian "expressivism," that is, the mind is only real in expressing itself in the world and creating objects, such as linguistic utterances or labor.[27] Vice versa, these objects become inwardly embodied, shaping the mind; for example, writing down an idea changes my thinking.[28] Finally, this interaction between the mind and the world includes the recognition by others in a fundamental way, for instance, since the meaning of my utterances is constituted by their collective understanding.[29] In sum, mind as spirit is not an internal given for human interaction with the world. Still, it is an emerging and evolving process engaging the individual and the world and is, in this sense, "objective."

25 Basso and Herrmann-Pillath 2024. These tightly coupled movements correspond to Sartre's analysis of appropriation, which we explored in the introduction.

26 The original version is in Herrmann-Pillath and Boldyrev 2014. The diagram is the modified version of Basso and Herrmann-Pillath.

27 Expressivism is a core concept in Charles Taylor's interpretation of Hegel, Taylor 1975.

28 This view is well developed in modern cognitive sciences, see, for example, Menary 2007.

29 This critical point has been made by many 20th century thinkers, foremostly, Wittgenstein in his argument of the impossibility of a private language Wittgenstein 2009, Candlish and Wrisley 2019.

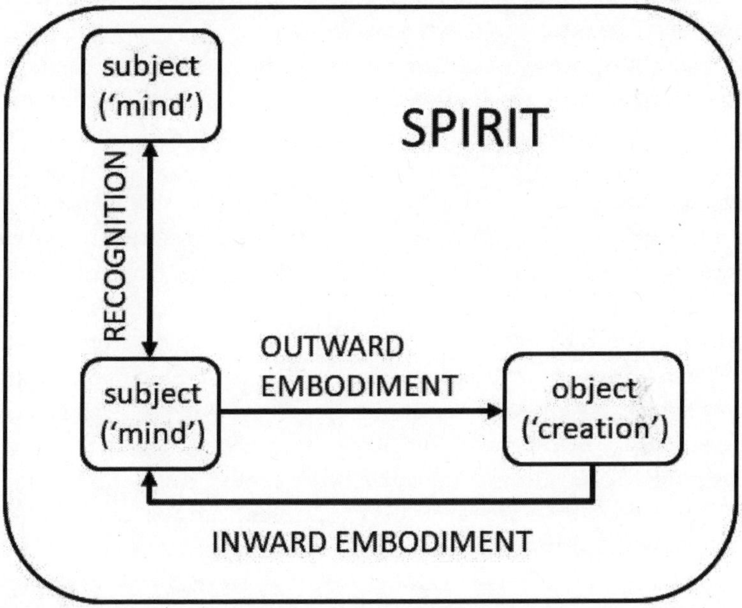

Figure 3.1: Hegel's notion of objective spirit
Source: own diagram (based on Basso and Herrmann-Pillath 2024)

Hegel's concept of institutions as incorporations of objective spirit must be seen against this background of two movements of embodiment. For Hegel, institutions are a "second nature." This means, on the one hand, institutions are internalized, which Basso and Herrmann-Pillath render as an "inward embodiment." For example, the institution of money becomes internalized if we adopt a calculating stance towards social interactions, such as weighing mutual gifts in terms of monetary balances and not, say, appreciating them in terms of expressive meaning. On the other hand, outward embodiment means that the institution is essential in creating our capacities of action, resulting in material manifestations. For example, if I own my car, I can adorn it with my personal items or change its design according to my taste. Inward and outward embodiment continuously play together: Acquiring the car as my own creates psychological ownership, which motivates my expressive action, such that eventually, my feeling of ownership is further enhanced. We add the Hegelian dimension of recognition: If my *property* becomes highly personalized, others will strengthen their stance of recognizing this as my own. In other words, we institutionalize ourselves, and we are being institutionalized in the recognition by others. We can approach this as the primordial form of institutionalization, which is independent of developed forms in human societies, such as the law.[30]

The Hegelian view implies that ***property*** is constitutive of human agency. Hegel develops this in terms of the relationship between humans and nature, such that ***property*** means establishing human dominance over nature to enable human action. We come back to this point in Chapter 5. Here, we look at the implications on the concrete level of single objects of ***property***. The role of ***property*** in creating agency corresponds to recent developments in research on material agency, which argue that agency is not a property of individuals but emerges in assemblages of bodies and artefacts.[31] This refers to Merleau-Ponty's famous example of the blind person's stick, which becomes a part of the body as seeing the world. This kind of inward embodiment of material artefacts is well recognized in the brain sciences today, with brain structures assimilating objects even across sensory domains, and corresponds to theories of extended cognition, which claim that artefacts like the laptop become constituents of our cognitive system, now including the brain and the computer.[32] These views move beyond possession as a mere power of disposition, maintaining the clear separation between subject and object of ***property***. In distributed agency, this distinction implodes and transforms into what Barad calls intra-action.[33] Subject and object merge and constitute a new agential entity.

Clearly, such a transition can only happen if the material entity is durable in relation to the flow of actions. On non-durable items, we can only express ***property*** as referring to a type of action that is my personal characteristic. Yet, we notice the closeness to the etymology of ***property***. If I eat bananas three times a day, I can claim this habit as my own, but I cannot go to the grocery and claim the bananas there as my own because of my habit. The habit is embodied, but not the banana. This is different if I wear a watch evoking precious memories of my grandmother. The watch has become part of my personal identity. If I lose it, my claims are based on both my formal "property," and this embodied relationship. Embodiment is implied in the legal construct of "subjective value" that can be invoked in cases such as the division of a family estate during an inheritance dispute court proceeding.[34]

30 Interestingly, this view combines two seminal theories of ***property***, Locke and Hume. Locke emphasized outward embodiment in his ideas of labor creating primordial property. Hume emphasizes the role of recognition, even in a fundamental cognitive sense, as ***property*** is seen by others as belonging to a person; on the latter, see Schlicht 2018.

31 Malafouris 2013.

32 Clark 2011.

33 Barad 2007. We referred this view to Sartre in the introduction.

34 Serkin 2016, 94 ff.

Even though embodiment is not referred to in mainstream economic and legal theories of property, it is essential in many ways. An important example is intellectual "property," which builds on the idea that ideas express individual creativity. This corresponds to the view that ideas are outwardly embodied and materialize in entities physically separate from the creator. This raises the interesting question of whether a legal person can own intellectual "property," which was initially denied, obviously referring to embodiment implicitly.[35] However, one argument in assigning intellectual "property" to organizations was that if the inventor is a company member, this company also provided the conditions for her creative agency. This agency is, therefore, embodied in assemblages of the material structure of the company. Hence, one can regard the company as the creative agent.

IPR is also a paradigmatic case for inward embodiment. When IPRs are institutionalized as "property" and hence become more tradable on markets, this can drastically change the motivation for creative action, even dampening creativity. This is well established in psychological theories on intrinsic motivation: The stronger the extrinsic incentives, the weaker intrinsic motivation can become.[36]

Embodiment is also at the core of one of the most influential theories of property, John Locke's. Hegel and others also received this by relating the claim to ***property*** to labor invested. This means, literally, that labor incorporates an object, such as the land, into the tiller. The young Marx also grounds his notion of alienation on embodiment since if the worker is expropriated of the product of her labor, this breaks this embodied connection, amounting to physical harm and violent theft, though legally legitimized by the construct of wage labor.

To summarize, the essential result of considering ***property*** as embodied is that the notion is independent of external forms of institutionalization, such as the law. ***Property*** is an emergent aspect of humans' agency as social beings and is, as such, a human universal.

The Aoki-Bourdieu model

The dialectic of inward and outward embodiment constitutes an essential phenomenon of institutions, which is performativity. Following the approach developed by John Searle, we can say that institutions create a social ontology via socially recognized cognitive transformations.[37] The formula of the so-called status function describes this as "X counts as Y in context C," for example, treating a

35 Boldrin and Levine 2008.

36 This is an example of performative mechanisms in incentivization; Herrmann-Pillath 2016.

37 Searle 1995, Searle 2011.

piece of paper *X* as "money" *Y* in the context *C* of market exchange. The transition from possession to ***property*** is a similar kind of transformation, although on a higher level of abstraction. In the case of money, this transformation mainly applies to a small set of objects, such as a national currency. In the case of ***property***, the transformation creates a vast range of objects defined over anything that can be treated as ***property***, as we discussed in the previous chapter as the reflexivity of "property." In addition, as we have seen, ***property*** may take different forms, and "property" is the form that also involves the assignment of monetary value. This is salient when considering land: Land is a complex natural entity transformed into an "estate" via the "property" transformation that renders it an abstract cartographic object with clearly demarcated boundaries and which has a monetary value on the real estate market.[38] For the status of this object, it does not matter whether the proprietor changes the physical nature of the land, although this can affect its value on the market. Similarly, any object attains a distinct form when transformed into ***property***.

In this view, the context is crucial: The market context drives the cognitive transformation into "property." This fundamental distinction between the market context and non-market context has been inhering many historical changes in ***property***, such as when, in the Roman provinces, the combination of Imperial ***property*** and leaseholds resulted in a vibrant market of land that the Imperial surveyors had registered.[39] On the other hand, Indigenous claims on land are contextualized in a radically different way, though similar to the early Roman ritual treatment of Italian land, especially sacred land such as city walls. Hence, according to Searle, various forms of ***property*** create different agential powers, such as different degrees of how far actors can trade land via markets. This manifests the performative functions of institutions.

The cognitive transformation of objects is semiotic as it relates them to certain signs that indicate their status as ***property***, such as a land deed. Searle's emphasis on language as a foundation of institutions applies with a vengeance on ***property***. However, we should refer not only to language but also to all kinds of semiotic mediation.[40] For example, a boundary marker is a sign of ***property*** and may not

38 Vanuxem 2022, 37 ff. The critical transformative role of land surveying and cadasters has been emphasized in various contexts, such as Roman agrarian history, Weber 2014, or colonial dispossession; Bhandar 2018.

39 The interesting point is that the Imperial land as occupied land only became tradable in the form of leasehold which assigned prices to land without having the full status of ***property*** in the original Roman territories. Via this transformation, land gradually assumed a special status of "property." The cognitive complexity of this historical transformation was debated among Roman lawyers in terms of terminological ambiguities regarding so-called *duplex dominium*, Giglio 2018.

40 Rose 2019, 267 ff.

primarily have the purpose of physically blocking access to an estate. These two functions must be neatly separated: Even if the fence is broken, it still is a sign of ***property***. However, as the famous case of the neighborhood with broken windows shows, these signs can change people's attitudes dramatically since the broken window can invite theft and trespassing concerning that building and everywhere in the neighborhood.[41] This is evidence of the embodiment of the dialectics and the performativity of signs expressed in behavioral changes.

In economics, few theorists pay attention to this critical role of semiotic mediation.[42] One exception is Aoki's theory of public representation.[43] Aoki argues that institutions are constituted by public representations that induce behavior that reproduces the institution. We can distinguish between two levels: the level of the individual and the group. On the group level, institutions are stabilized or altered via the interactions between group members who follow the institution. This includes strategic interactions triggered by individual self-interest (such as incentives and sanctions driving looting) and all forces of conformity, such as imitation. One result of these interactions is public representations, such as broken windows, which result from a growing number of burglaries and vandalism. These broken windows trigger embodied, individual evaluative stances, such as certain emotions or biases. These stances generate behavior that, on the population level, works out probabilistically, such as raising the probability of burglary.

Many lines of causality connect the individual and the population level. A critical one is cognitive *Gestalt* effects, as in the broken window paradigm.[44] That means there is a general cognitive bias towards creating patterns from partial information, which differs from simple imitation in possibly enhancing specific trends that are not yet statistically salient. The levels are connected via critical mass effects and frequency-dependent mechanisms.[45] Someone who would usually not dare to paint graffiti on a private home may have a *Gestalt* perception of a neighborhood where this is usually done and may observe a growing frequency of such events. He has a personal preference for acting similarly if a certain threshold in these frequencies is transgressed. Once he decides to do his own graffiti, this may trigger similar responses from others.

---

41 Ranasinghe 2019. The "broken windows theory" had a tremendous impact on policing strategies in the US but has faced growing criticism.

42 However, there is much evidence in game theory and its application that linguistic representation of outcomes matters for behavior, Capraro, Halpern, and Perc 2024.

43 Aoki 2001, Aoki 2011, Herrmann-Pillath 2017, Takizawa 2017.

44 Schlicht 2018.

45 Kuran 1997.

The interaction between semiosis, behavior, and population level patterns can be interpreted using Bourdieu's habitus and symbolic capital concepts.[46] This view also dovetails with Weber's notion of order, although this is purely cognitivist and sidelines emotions or embodiment in general. We summarize the basic model of institution in Figure 3.2 that results from a fusion of Aoki and Bourdieu.[47] We follow Max Weber in approaching institutions as a form of action, hence institutional action.[48] Weberian appropriation, when enacted in an order, is such an action resulting in ***property***. However, in the Aoki-Bourdieu model, this is not a reified institution, but firstly, reflects a steady state in interactions between individuals (upper part of the diagram), which Aoki conceptualized as strategic games, compatible with Weber's view on struggle. Bourdieu, here close to Searle's notion of context, posits that these interactions are specific to social fields.[49] This is very significant when we discuss ***property***: In the social field of a rural village, land is a different thing than the same land in the field of real estate market dealing with land, say, of that village which is close to a suburban area.

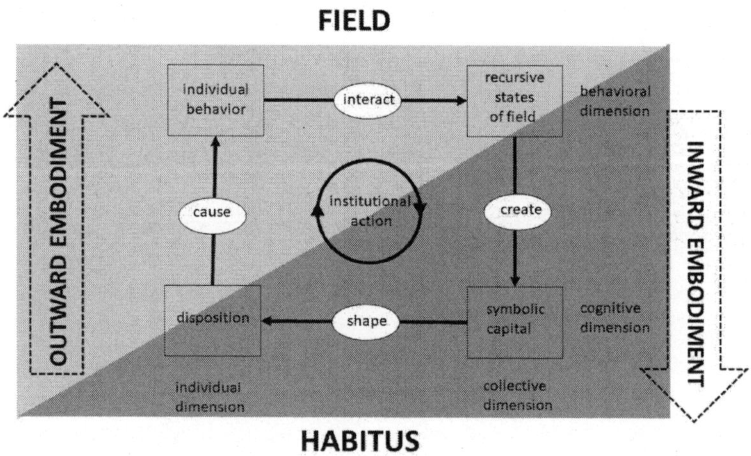

Figure 3.2: The Aoki-Bourdieu model of institution
Source: own diagram (based on Basso and Herrmann-Pillath 2024)

46 Bourdieu 2019b.

47 For the details of this fusion, the reader may consult Basso and Herrmann-Pillath 2024.

48 I have developed this argument in various forms, rejecting the reification of institutions and treating them as an aspect of behaviors, for example, the notion of "institutionally guided behavioral patterns" in Herrmann-Pillath 2013.

49 Bourdieu 2019a. Other authors have also proposed the concept of field, notably Fligstein and McAdam 2012.

For these field-specific interactions, symbolic media and signs are constitutive. Aoki calls these public representations, Bourdieu symbolic capital. This captures the semiotic dimension of ***property*** and refers to a wide range of phenomena, including the law. The interactions and symbolic media are collective-level phenomena which connect with the individual level via inward embodiment. This is what Bourdieu refers to as habitus. Habitus creates dispositions to action, as in the broken windows example. On the population level, these dispositions play out in terms of statistical patterns, such as frequencies of burglary, with outward embodiment as the fundamental process.

Habitus and symbolic capital refer to long-run outcomes of institutional evolution. Take, for example, the rise of the sharing economy and the development regarding car usage.[50] The car represents a complex and rich set of symbolic capital manifest in a semiotic pool that conveys meanings of cars, such as status goods, convenient tools for transport, or technological sophistication. In the past, this merged into generating strong behavioral stances favoring car ownership, such as young people aspiring to acquire their first car as a symbol of independence and freedom. This was a distinct form of car-related habitus. Today, this stance has been weakening considerably, and car sharing offers new ways to relate to cars without "property." This may eventually cause a reconfiguration of symbolic capital centered on cars that will accompany new forms of habitus. Yet, as we have seen when overviewing Sartre's concept of appropriation, even in the case of car sharing, elementary forms of appropriation take place, such as driving the car in one's own way or temporarily adorning it with some items, such as a protective charm fixed at the rear mirror.

One important conclusion from this analysis is that the law cannot exclusively define ***property***. As in Weber's approach, institutions are regularities in actions, and law is only one specific semiotic mode in motivating and sustaining actions. This is another way to state the performativity of institutions. This can be taken literally in the context of the judicial process, as law only becomes binding via court decisions. For example, in Germany, the legal status of tenants has been shaped mainly by court decisions that protect their rights, eventually leading to the transformation of rented flats into a form of ***property***. On the other hand, as long as courts do not get involved in resolving conflicts, actual ***property*** practices can diverge widely from the law.[51] This may even result in conditions of legal pluralism, such as the coexistence of formal and customary law.

Equipped with the methodological work of this section, we will now turn to developing our new approach to *property*, the theory of havings. We will do this

---

50 Henning 2023.
51 Ellickson 1994.

in two steps. In the next section, we clarify the meaning of the three most common terms used to describe ***property***: possession, ownership, and property. We will continue using these terms in our theory of havings, referring to structural outcomes of actions of having, which, unlike Max Weber, we do not confine to appropriation.

Getting names right: Resetting the standard language of *property*

Confucius famously said that to reinstate proper order in society, it is necessary to get names right (*zheng ming*). This is certainly true for ***property***. Hence, our aim is not to supersede the existing language of ***property***, which would be highly impractical, but to clarify its meanings and reinstate it in the larger context of the new language of havings. We begin with possession since this concept is widely used across all human societies and often simply means "having" something.

Possession

A theory of ***property*** must start with possession as its primordial form. The critical question is whether possession is just a physical state of factually occupying or seizing an object or whether other constitutive elements must be included, notably expressing the intention to possess and recognizing possession as *property*.[52] As we will see, these distinctions are crucial for developing a notion of non-human ***property*** in Chapter 5. These distinctions also mark divergent approaches to possession in the civil law and common law domains, with the former tending to see possession as a physical fact and the latter as a right. This goes back to the long shadow of feudal law in common law: *seisin* in feudal law is close to the modern conception of possession as a right, not just a physical state.

In 19th-century jurisprudence, there was a famous dispute over possession, with one side claiming that physical seizure is sufficient and the other requiring "anima," hence the intention to possess.[53] This offers another way to justify Locke's theory. We could interpret labor as an expression of possession independent from making the linguistic claim insofar as someone who spends effort would not rationally do so if she did not intend to possess the object. In other words, we would not treat the physical fact of changing the soil as establishing possession but treat

52 Rose 2019.

53 Emerich 2017. The protagonists where the famous legal scholars von Savigny and Jhering.

the effort as a sign claiming possession.[54] This differs from the embodiment explanation but refers to the recognition in the sense that spending labor calls for the recognition of possession from others. Considering the observations of the previous chapter, almost all societies approach possession in this way as primary evidence of ***property***.

The debate over *animus* in possession shows that we cannot simply equate possession with sheer physical control. This transpires in research on young children compared with chimpanzees.[55] Human children develop a sense of assignment beyond simple appropriation in recognizing possession of others, including as a third party and in the absence of the possessor, and they respect signs of possession left by someone absent. In comparison, chimpanzees appropriate what they can get when the possessor is out of sight.

There is also the important phenomenon of the endowment effect.[56] This effect means that people display a wedge between their valuation of an object when they are possessors or not, so that in barter games, the reservation prices of sellers and buyers differ when the same people are assigned to these roles, in turn, leading to a less-than-optimal volume of trades. Behavioral economists have often maintained that the endowment effect is grounded in generic loss aversion.[57] However, further experimental research has shown that the effect results from the physical assignment of an object to a person. Merely assigning a right to possess does not suffice. Moreover, in hunter-gatherer groups, the endowment effect is more pronounced the closer the groups live to a market, hence an environment with stronger forms of institutionalization of exchange.[58] This reveals that the awareness of the possibility of alienation determines the strength of the effect. On the other hand, since the earliest series of experiments, researchers noticed that the endowment effect vanishes once people see themselves as engaging in a series of trades, hence perceiving possession as only transient.[59] This observation suggests that assignments differ in the degree of how far they are experienced as creating an embodied relationship with an object, and it also shows that possession is a performative phenomenon that is itself an institutional action of ***property***.

Therefore, we can approach possession as an embodied sign of ***property*** in the Aoki Bourdieu model. This has important implications as there can be a broader range of signs that express possession as a claim with *animus*. An important ex-

54 Nozick criticized Locke, arguing that even throwing tomato juice into the sea would establish Lockean ownership since that is an effort to change the chemical composition of the sea Nozick 2013, 175.

55 Tomasello 2019, 265 ff.

56 Thaler 2016, 12 ff.

57 Gintis 2007.

58 Apicella et al. 2014.

59 Kahneman 2012, 297 f.

ample that we have already mentioned is when some lawyers suggest interpreting Indigenous claims on the homeland as possession, which would undermine their case if they did not live there for a long time.[60] However, this is only one, though powerful, sign of possession; other signs may also justify their claims, such as demonstrating communication of claims, hence *animus*, over the same period. Another aspect of this is that today, possession is also related to incorporeal rights, such as intellectual "property." Here, physical seizure does not make sense but certainly signals that claim possession. This perspective would also allow for flexibility in conceptualizing such forms of *property* which are mostly seen as "property." For example, in the case of intellectual "property," a trust structure could be imagined where the holder of the "property" only has rights to the benefits but cannot interfere with the possession, such as anyone being allowed to copy Mickey Mouse in any creative way, hence claiming possession, but paying rent to the proprietor of the copyright.

In many societies, possession is the fundamental form of ***property*** and relates to a form different from the modern Western understanding. In principle, there are those forms of ***property*** that relate to the market and hence are economical in the narrow sense and those ones that define social status and reflect Arendt's distinction between wealth and ***property***. In the latter case, possession can obtain considerable institutional strength and is often an element in defining legal pluralism in the sense that possession is governed by customary law and "property" by hegemonic state law. We have already mentioned the case of Imperial China, where permanent tenancy was a widespread phenomenon, even across generations. The *property* was related to the status of the taxpaying social elite, including even lineage trusts as formal proprietors, so this ***property*** was not individualized. The trust managers were stewards. Economically, the peasants were the effective possessors close to full control of all specific powers of disposition. In addition, giving up possession in case of economic straits was often realized with the right to redeem land even in the next generation. This amounts to a sort of strong ***property*** that even overcomes alienation. To some extent, the alienated land would be a pawn, with the pawn still assigned to the original possessor.

Possession appears close to Weber's notion of a legitimate power of disposition if we free ourselves from the established legal meanings. Then, as Weber also argues, this can include all powers of disposition allocated and assigned within organizations of any kind. This would extend possession beyond what is conventionally treated as ***property*** and refers to a wide variety of institutions, such as sinecures or the powers of a CEO. However, there is a distinction between the role or position and the particular incumbent: Possession becomes ***property*** when the

60 McNeil 2017.

incumbent controls access to the position *together* with the position. A sinecure may become a heritable right of a family. A modern CEO does not have these powers. This shows the relevance of Max Weber's narrow definition of *Eigentum*: If a modern CEO had the right to bequeath her position to a child, that would transform the position into her *Eigentum*. Possession can also be even stronger than ***property*** when, in certain arrangements, such as the common law trust, the proprietor has no right to possess in the sense of direct physical control but only receives benefits from the underlying asset.

Considering these complex constellations, one way to distinguish between possession and dispositional powers is in the temporal dimension, also involving the distinction between physical state and right. Power of disposition is manifest in any form of controlling a valuable good, even only momentarily. If it persists over a longer time span, the question is whether this becomes a right that does not depend on appropriation but mainly on recognition. Again, the semiotic dimension of ***property*** comes to the fore.

Ownership

Consider a thief: Many legal settings recognize his possession unless a stronger claim on the ***property*** is proven, which shows the strength of possession as a sign of ***property***. At the same time, we also noticed that there are different grades of possession in terms of the strength of the embodied relationship. The question is whether this relationship can take a form that transcends possession.

In his famous critique of Kant's conception of marriage as a civil contract, Hegel argued that the relationship between husband and wife is mutual belonging.[61] Its contractual form is widespread in human societies, mainly in establishing male control over the female. In many cases, this means that the husband establishes possession of the wife and her various services to the degree that the wife's own right to possession and ***property*** is severely curtailed. These constellations are very different from conceptions of the marital relationship as grounding in love, mutual recognition, and care. In such a relationship, sharing reigns instead of possession, even when recognizing specific claims, such as spaces for privacy. Mutual belonging may also establish exclusivity to the extent that, in some legal settings, a husband can claim compensation from his wife's lover for damaging the flow of benefits from his wife.[62] In this case, mutual belonging would

61 Hegel 2009, § 161.

62 https://www.economist.com/united-states/2023/06/29/in-north-carolina-a-jilted-husband-can-sue-his-wifes-lover, last access May 24, 2024.

also suggest a form of ***property***, manifesting in the exclusivity established by an expectation of marital fidelity.

The Roman conception of *dominium* does not know a relationship of belonging between subjects and objects of ***property***. When animals are treated as things, this gap is also visible, as there are two very different forms of enacting the human ***property*** of animals. One form is exploiting them as a resource and completely ignoring their sentience, for example, treating pigs in factory farming in a way that does not respect their needs and natural ways of life. The other is treating them as pets and literal family members, often expressing deep care and maintaining intensive mutual relationships, as in the case of dogs. Dogs are an interesting case since dogs also stay in mutual relationships with humans without being subject to ***property***. A telling example is street dogs in India who form close alliances with humans in urban areas, often associating human families with dog lineages over generations.[63] The humans and the dogs co-habit in a relationship of mutual belonging, also including reciprocal exchange of benefits, such as dogs getting access to food provided by the humans and, in turn, acting as sentinels for the human group.

As we have seen in Chapter 2, the idea of mutual belonging is dominant in Indigenous conceptions of ***property***. Partly, this follows from their distinct spirituality. The Western conceptions of nature, including both animate and inanimate objects, define a speciesist difference between humans and all the rest, denying the soul to animated beings in the Cartesian reduction of the body to a machine. This is clearly a cultural form of spirituality, which we will discuss in detail in Chapter 5. At this point, we diagnose that this separation between humans and all other nature leaves the question unanswered of where the next boundary could be drawn between animate and inanimate objects.[64] This boundary does not exist in Indigenous spirituality since nature is seen as part and parcel of a world governed and permeated by spiritual entities.[65] The critical point is that this totality encompasses distinct living beings and inanimate objects, which are seen as elements in larger spiritual assemblages. As I argue in Chapter 5, this view can be translated into a semiotic reconstruction of ecosystems.

As we have seen in the previous chapter, Indigenous spirituality transforms all objects into relational objects since humans always relate to spiritual entities, and no objects can be considered abstracted from these relationships.[66] For example, a hunter does not simply kill and appropriate a prey, but the prey and its spirit ne-

63 Ragavan and Srivastava 2020.
64 Povinelli 2016.
65 Sahlins 2023.
66 Trosper 2022.

gotiate the kill with the hunter and even agree, provided that the hunter conducts the appropriate ritual acts of recognition. The paradigmatic case of this relationality is land. Land is appropriated in various forms, such as hunting grounds, to regulate the behavior of humans and their relationships. But at the same time, the land and the humans belong to each other, even in the sense that the land incorporates people. The relationship of belonging is bidirectional.[67]

If we consider the conditions of Western disenchantment of the world, apparently, there is no place for this kind of relationship. However, our analysis of embodiment suggests otherwise, and this is familiar in the modern lifeworld. The critical question is whether we can diagnose a generic reciprocal relationship between people and things. This is the mode of care, in the specific sense that a thing embodies affordances of care. For example, a classic car's proprietor feels obliged to take care of it, keep it clean, look for all necessary repairs, and take the car to meetings with other aficionados where cars meet their "fellows." Care typically affords enormous investments of time and money. This also sustains the dialectics on the inward and outward embodiment since this investment enhances the identification of the possessor with the object.[68]

Therefore, we can distinguish between two forms of possession depending on whether possession also implies this relationship of care and identity. The poverty of our language of ***property*** does not allow for conceptual separation of these two forms, which seems necessary, for example, to adequately deal with Indigenous claims on the land. As shown in Figure 3.3, these forms are subordinative possession, exemplified in Roman *dominium*, and identifying possession, which establishes a relational form of ***property***.

Therefore, following relevant proposals in the literature on the ***property***, I suggest distinguishing relational ***property*** from other forms. However, the term ***property*** is still problematic, and therefore, I suggest exploiting the English distinction between *ownership* and *property*.[69] This is also problematic since, in some influential uses, ownership is regarded as the most potent form of "property."[70] As we have seen, ownership translates the equivalent to absolute "property" in civil law, whereas ***property*** refers to the "bundle of rights" view in common law. However, there is another linguistic strand outside legal uses where ownership refers to a

67 Lieber and Rynkiewich (2007) show for Oceania that these ideas are rooted in what they call a "Lamarckian" worldview, hence a prescientific belief, namely that people, even in the fetal stage, receive environmental impacts that continue throughout their lives, making them a part of the place where they live. See also Chao 2022.

68 In the introduction we discussed the conditions in Amazonia, where care in the form of feeding is an appropriate action.

69 This is a view often taken by anthropologists, for instance, Brightman, Fausto, and Grotti 2016.

70 Honoré 1961.

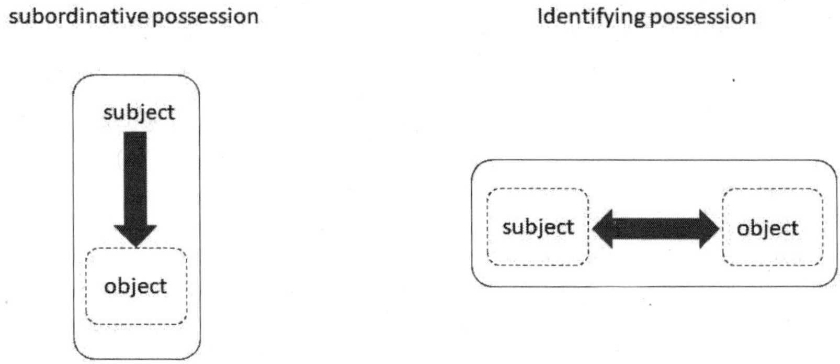

Figure 3.3: Two forms of possession
Source: author's diagram

special relationship between a subject and an object. For example, we may speak of the "ownership" that students have in their university as something desirable without implicating that they are proprietors.[71] We mean that the students feel they belong to the university, actively contribute, and may even maintain the relationship as alumni for a lifetime. As we see, this kind of ownership combines rights with obligations of care.

Accordingly, I define ownership as relational ***property*** to be distinguished from possession: Possession, though also strongly embodied, does not entail the commitment and obligation to care. An important case of ownership is, therefore, stewardship, which is typically implicated in English translations of Indigenous notions of relating to land. Stewardship is possession with a strong obligation to care. At first sight, this is often caring for other humans, such as stewardship of families. But even then, the receiver of the care is vicariously the object, such as the estate, since, after all, future generations do not yet exist. In Islamic notions of ***property*** all ***property*** is stewardship in place of Allah as the ultimate proprietor.

One essential form of ***property*** that combines possession and ownership is the commons, although this includes many variants, some of which thin out the ownership aspect. The reason is that there is a difference between a formal commons as a cooperative open to all kinds of members and a commons grounded in a strong sense of community belonging.[72] What is shared between both is that the community of the commons is the holder of the ultimate ***property***, whereas

71 This often classified as "pychological ownership;" Dawkins et al. 2017.
72 Federici and Linebaugh 2019.

members only have distinct rights of possession. For example, a forest is a village commons, and the villagers have rights to logging and hunting.

Such a general construct can take many different forms. The members of a commons have ownership if the commons is inalienable and if membership is bound to sharing an identity, which can be kinship, living in a village for generations, or a shared mission, such as an eco-community. Still, this leaves much leeway on how possession is organized. Despite shared ownership, individual rights may be exclusive and even encompass sublease by contract.[73] Typically, many commons prohibit the latter, but a formal cooperative might even allow for that. The sensitive point is that contracting out possession implies that individuals use the commons without being owners, hence without the accompanying commitments to care. Such commitments must be defined contractually and do not follow from ownership.

If we take care as a litmus test for distinguishing between ownership and possession, there are many phenomena we can account for, such as the relationship between a tenant and a flat. A tenant may have legally protected rights of possession, so the landlord cannot arbitrarily cease the lease at any time. However, this relationship can be further strengthened if the tenant invests care in her flat, such as adding valuable fixed items or embellishing the balcony in a way that she cannot simply take them along when moving out. However, contrary to Locke, she might invest as much as she likes; this will not transform the lease into "property." What is becoming stronger is her ownership of the flat. This may not count in a legal dispute over cancelling the lease contract if this is justified by law. The only way to consider it is by asking the next tenant to take these items over for a price, which, however, will not reflect the subjective value of the original tenant.

Property

Against the background of the previous two sections, we can now define "property." The critical difference between the former two and "property" is abstraction, disembodiment, and embeddedness in markets mediated by money. Accordingly, the "property" has a value measured in monetary units. Ownership is literally priceless, and possession can be assessed in monetary terms, though not necessarily. The stronger the monetary aspect in possession, the closer this relationship comes to "property." For example, as in the commons, members' rights approach "property" if they become alienable via the market and are priced, for example, when there is a lease contract between a member and a non-member.

73 Schlager and Ostrom 1992.

This example also shows that the legal distinction between "property" and contract is partly misleading.[74] We can grasp this when analyzing "property" as assetification.[75] The semiotic operation of "property" turns any kind of object into an asset, whether corporeal or not. Hence, a financial claim that is not "property" in the strict sense, since it does not work *erga omnes*, becomes an asset if it becomes itself an object of "property." In other words, assetification follows from the reflexivity of ***property***.

This is also critical when considering the distinction between possession and "property." "Property" is possession assetificated. Normally, "property" is not seen as a financial asset, and I use the term in a wider sense here, even though this clearly follows from the relationship between "property" and wealth as *Vermögen*. *Vermögen* is "property" in the sense defined now. This is also clear from the fact that all kinds of objects that can be traded on markets and have a price are considered a part of *Vermögen* (this is Weber's view, as seen in Chapter 2). If an object cannot be alienated, this is not *Vermögen*. So, we would count this as possession or ownership. For example, if in a commons, the individual possession would be tradable on markets, these would constitute the wealth of the commons in the aggregate, say the aggregate value of rights of logging. But the forest is not wealth if it cannot be alienated. As has been argued in the context of environmental issues, this even applies to the level of entire countries: A less developed country may have large natural resources that could be assessed as "nature capital" and become part of national wealth.[76] However, the difficulty is how this pecuniary assessment can be implemented independently from just considering commodity prices, which would assume the alienation of these natural resources.

There is a performative dimension here as the differential treatment of "property" may crowd out the non-property relations. For example, members of the commons may collectively fall into the trap of the tragedy of the commons if they only follow market incentives and start to ignore the obligations to care following from ownership.[77] Assetified logging rights result in long-term destruction of the forest. Therefore, the community may regulate market transactions, such as imposing caps. This is only one example of the detrimental behavioral impact of any measurement linking performance with measured outcomes, because this directs attention away from what cannot be measured.

74 Wolff 2020.

75 In economic sociology the term "assetization" is used, Tellmann 2022. We differ from that in employing a wider meaning for "assetification," following Herrmann-Pillath and Hederer 2023. Assetization focuses on financial markets, whereas I refer to assets as all kinds of goods that are evaluated in terms of flows of monetary income generated, such as regarding a good as a pawn.

76 Bateman and Mace 2020.

77 For historical examples, see Hübner 2020.

We have already referred to pawn shops in the 19th century, where "property" dominated even small-scale possession.[78] People even pawned minor objects of daily life, such as their coats for church attendance on Monday to get through the week, and then redeemed before Sunday when the week's salary was available. Therefore, all personal items became assets and hence "property." This was decoupled by linking loans with regular income flows in the modern banking sector, and today, most personal items are, therefore, no more assets. So, my kitchen utensils would count as possessions but not "property." Suppose I refer to the family silverware inherited from my parents that I intend to hand over to the next generation. In that case, its status is ambivalent in that it certainly counts as ownership but still would be valuable as wealth, even traded on markets. I may consider it a backup for rainy days, but nay, avoid selling it, only using it as a pawn.

In sum, a critical insight of our discussion is the fundamental difference between ownership and "property." From now on, we will skip the quotation marks for "property" and move to our new terminology of havings in the next section. Ideal-typically, ownership is inalienable having, and property alienable having. This is even salient when considering objects that count as both: My beloved old car is alienable, hence my property. But my feelings of ownership constitute it as partly inalienable, grasped legally in the notion of subjective value.

Beyond *property*: modes of having

Action modes and structural modes of having

We will now present a synopsis and further development of our discussion of ***property***. Obviously, we face a problem: Our language does not give us a generic term that covers all the distinct forms of relating a subject and object unless we use ***property*** in bold italics, as done so far. But this creates confusion with "property." Therefore, I suggest the generic term of "having."[79] In German, we can refer to a full set of terms that relate to the verb *haben*, such as *Habe* similar to the English *belongings* or *Haben* in *Soll und Haben* used in accounting. These terms appear antiquated but are still in use. In English, I introduce a neologism, "Havings" as noun corresponding to the verb "to have." From now on, we use havings for ***property***. Other terminological distinctions follow. In English, we can handily differentiate

78 Woloson 2012.

79 In English, there is the alternative of *holding* and *holdings*, e.g. Nozick 2013, 150. However, this is not congruent with other languages, even in the European context; Aikhenvald 2012.

possessor, owner, and proprietor, whereas in German, we have *Besitzer* for possession and *Eigentümer* for property, but no immediately available term for ownership. We might suggest *Eigner* here, as this relates to the root *eigen* as in *eigentümlich*. But this is partly a semantic neologism, even though *Eigner* is in use.

We can distinguish between three actions of having and three structural outcomes, that is, havings, of these actions, or "action modes" and "structural modes." We have seen in the previous discussion that the notion of appropriation, though critical, does not cover all aspects of the institutional action of having since it only focuses on the agent to which the having belongs. Having is recognized by the other actors in a community. Hence, having has the aspects of appropriation, recognition and assignment, and forms of havings are possession, ownership or property, the latter in the previous sense of "property." Unlike appropriation, the actions of recognition and assignment do not presuppose intentional action by the appropriating actor. Recognition is an action taken by another party. The assignment may rely on the actor, such as when a king assigns the land to himself, but even in these cases, this is legitimate only if it is justified with reference to another party, such as God, who did this assignment. Recognition and assignment are not necessarily converging, as different groups need not recognize an assignment.

These distinctions help analyze complex historical developments such as the colonization of the Americas. For example, the French emperor assigned the conquered regions' people and land to the crown, even recognizing the native rights to land by incorporating them as new subjects of the Empire. Intruding settlers appropriated the land forcefully, thus failing to recognize the rights of the natives.[80] In the United States, reassigning the land to the new sovereign resulted in legalizing appropriation by settlers.[81]

We can describe and analyze having in these two dimensions of action modes and structural modes, with examples, in table 3.1. However, the table should not be read in an exclusive way as far as the modes are concerned since all can apply simultaneously (see discussion below). We present pure cases here only for illustration. For example, and importantly, appropriation alone cannot fully reflect property as understood in modern societies, but also requires recognition, especially legally, but also in society, such as when it comes to property and inequality.

We can render the table in a more accessible graphical version. Here, we put the Weberian concept of the power of disposition at the center: Havings result in a specific individual power of disposition, an essential aspect of agential power. Whereas having and havings highlight the individual perspective, the notion of

80 Greer 2017.
81 Cai, Murtazashvili, and Murtazashvili 2020.

Structural modes		havings		
Action modes		**possession**	**ownership**	**property**
having	appropriation	1	2	3
	recognition	4	5	6
	assignment	7	8	9

Table 3.1: Modes of having
Source: own data

power is essentially relational.[82] We can specify a particular form of dispositional power by highlighting the modes dominating the relationship between individual and the other actors in a group, organization or wider society. One important consequence of this view is that we eschew the term "rights" when referring to having, which is universally associated with property, such as in "property rights." Even if we refer to property in the new terminology, the corresponding notion would be "property powers." Rights are a specific institutional form of assigning havings.

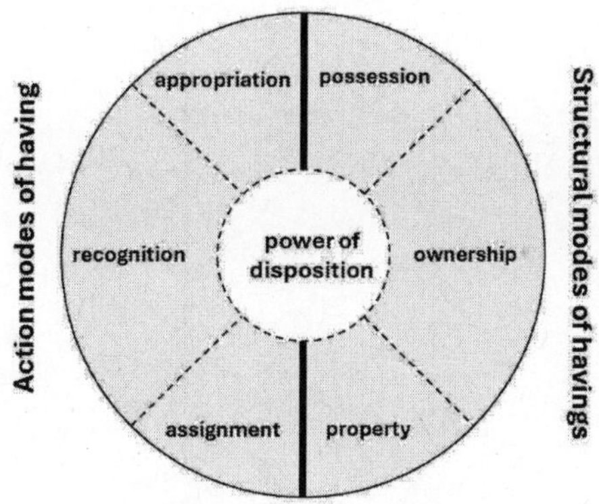

Figure 3.4: Modes of having as determinants of dispositional power
Source: author's diagram

1. A pure act of appropriation resulting in possession is theft, lacking both recognition and assignment (Figure 3.5). The thief can also sell the stolen goods, which are a form of property, without recognition.

82 This approach is informed by Coleman's classical definition of power, which is congenial to an economic point of view: "The power of an actor resides in his control of valuable events. The value of an event lies in the interests powerful actors have in that event." Coleman 1990, 133.

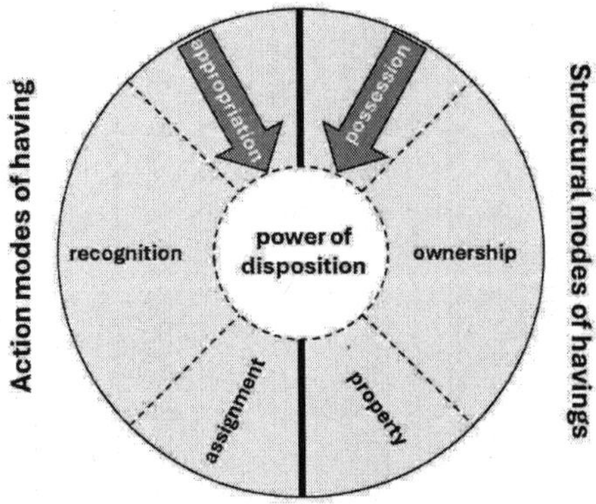

Figure 3.5: Theft
Source: author's diagram

2. Appropriation with ownership is the Lockean model of appropriating a free object by spending labor on it, such as picking up a stone and painting it as a piece of art for decorating the home (Figure 3.6). If sold, the object becomes legitimate property.

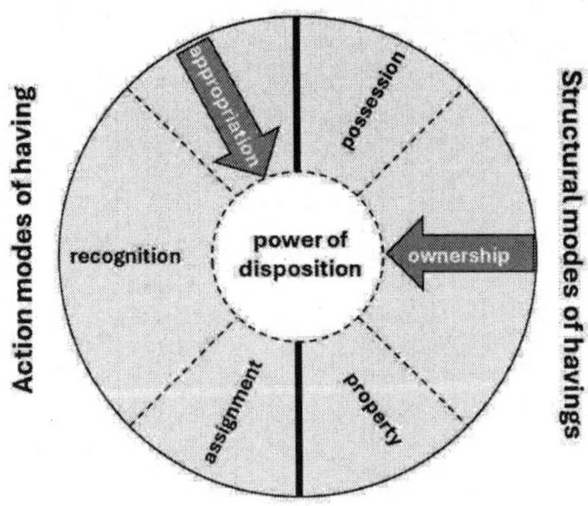

Figure 3.6: Lockean having
Source: author's diagram

3. Appropriation with property is buying a drug illegally on the black market: There is a contractual relationship, but this lacks legal recognition (Figure 3.7).

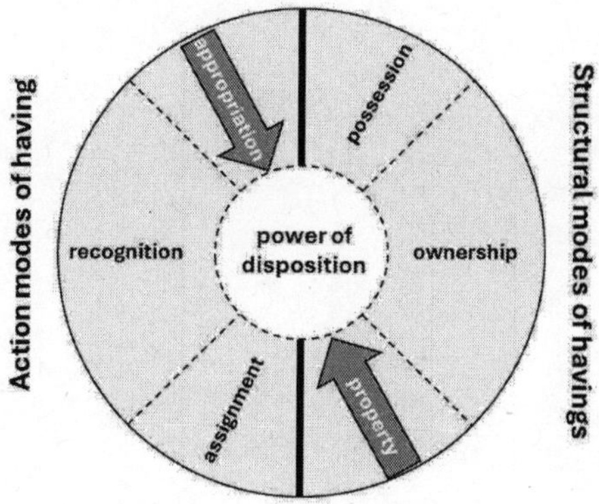

Figure 3.7: Illegal property
Source: author's diagram

4. Having by recognition results in possession if others respect my physical power of disposition, such as the seat at a conference table over several days: We might regard this constellation as consensual havings (Figure 3.8). However, the seat was neither assigned to me nor do I appropriate it formally (although I might leave my papers there overnight). The position in a queue is recognized, but mostly I cannot sell it (even though there are indirect means when individuals wait on behalf of others and receive a fee).

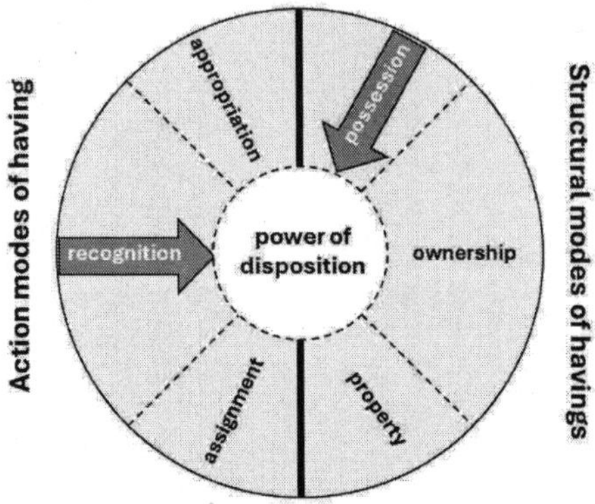

Figure 3.8: Consensual havings
Source: author's diagram

5. Recognized ownership is manifest if others respect my individual style of clothing and do not imitate me: The displays of my identity belong to me (Figure 3.9). Hence, we can speak of recognized havings. Since I did not register a copyright for the design, I do not appropriate my personal style.

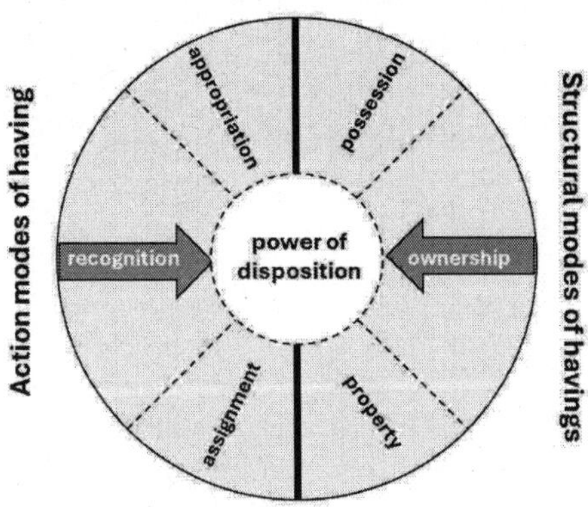

Figure 3.9: Identity havings
Source: author's diagram

6. Property is recognized if colleagues respect a marketable invention by someone who has not yet filed a patent (Figure 3.10). There are transitory forms such as when a musician earns income from life concerts, since her unique performing style is assetificated though not legally protected.

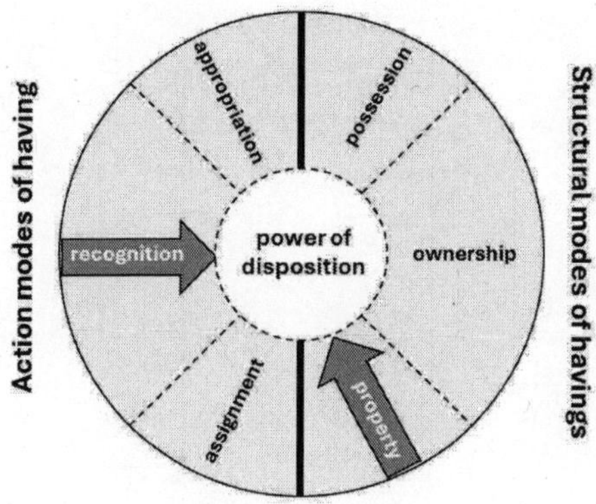

Figure 3.10: Recognized assets
Source: author's diagram

7. The eldest son is assigned the deceased person's house by custom, even though the law might prescribe equal inheritance among children (Figure 3.11).

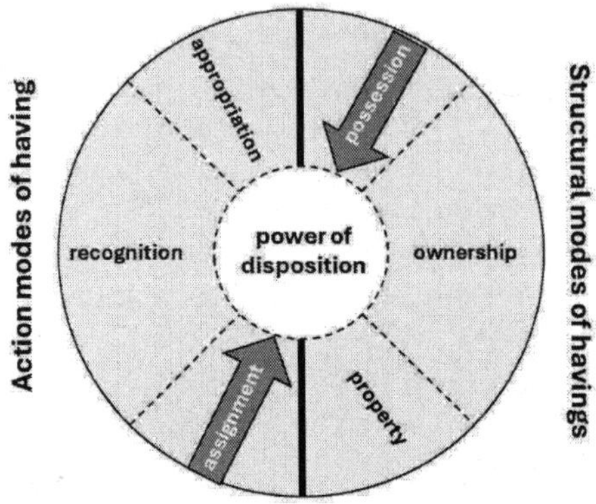

Figure 3.11: Customary inheritance
Source: author's diagram

8. A priest is assigned certain sacred objects that manifest his role in religious ceremonies. Other important cases include entitlements that are strictly bound to individual actors, such as pensions (Figure 3.12).

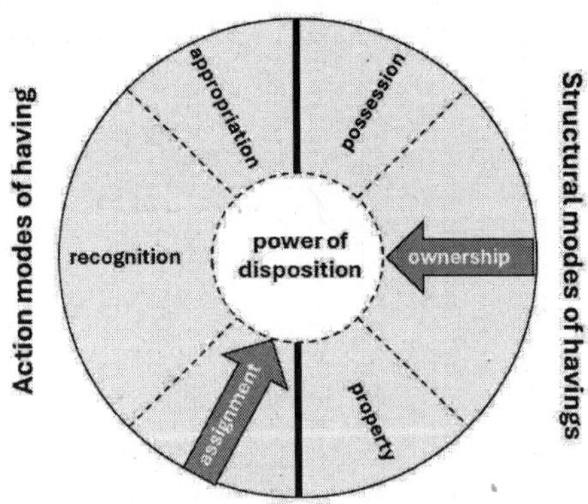

Figure 3.12: Entitlements
Source: author's diagram

9. A person suffering damage is assigned a right to financial compensation (Figure 3.12). In this specific sense, tort law establishes havings, which is different from conventional views about separating legal domains.

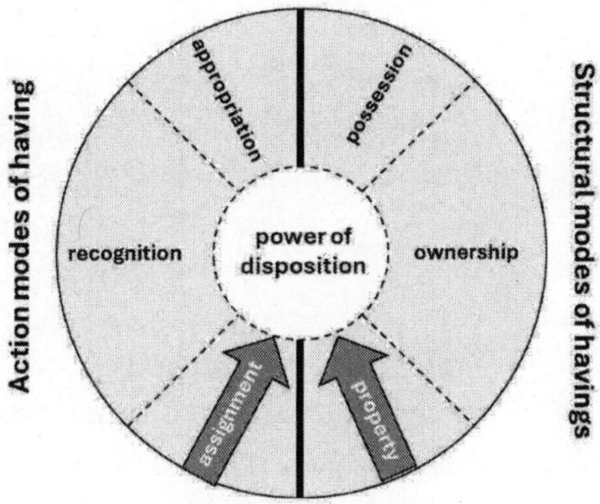

Figure 3.13: Compensation claims
Source: author's diagram

The cases presented are pure cases and ideal-typical. Mostly, the modes mix, such as if I buy a car at a dealer, this is an act of appropriation which is legally recognized as a sale and is registered with the authorities assigning a car plate to me, identifying me as the proprietor. Luxury car producers offer many choices for individualizing even a new car, constituting ownership. Leasing a car is appropriation via possession and property but leaves the car assigned to the dealer, with full legal recognition of these two distinct roles in having the car.

These distinctions are essential to differentiate between cases, such as when possession results from an act of appropriation or an act of assignment. For example, as we have seen in Islamic law, inheritance is a matter of assignment, and the heirs do not need to appropriate the inheritance. In civil law, there may be disputes over the inheritance, so acts of appropriation are necessary. Still, even if the matter is decided in the courts, the result may lack recognition in the community to which heirs belong. In situations of legal pluralism, inheritance often violates legal norms relating to gender, so women cannot appropriate property lacking recognition and assignment unless they go to court.

Compared to the standard approach to property rights in economics, the theory of havings allows for much richer contextualization. The triad of *usus, fructus* and *abusus* stemming from Roman times only refers to the dimension of appropriation and is even shallower, as in the new view, this only describes different powers of disposition, and only in the dimension of appropriation, and even ignoring ownership. From another angle, these powers can, in turn, become objects of having, such as the right to *fructus* being assetified and legally recognized. The standard approach also cannot deal with the broader social meaning of having, such as defining social status. However, as we argue in the economic context, we do not analyze these broader meanings but rather how they affect the modes of having. For example, status goods often define habitus and symbolic capital, implying that someone may be restricted in appropriating such goods even if the person has the financial means. This is expressed in a lack of recognition or as refusal of assignment. Traditional societies often had dress and consumption codes that only gradually eroded under the impact of capitalist expansion. But such constraints persist. For example, a green activist sociology professor may have the financial means to appropriate a Porsche but faces a lack of recognition if he does so, as this violates assignments of classes of objects to social identities. Here, we might distinguish between the object, i.e., the car, and a right to appropriate it, which is not assigned to certain people. In a caste society, such restrictions are explicit.

Embeddedness of structural modes of having

Most standard economic analysis focuses on the action mode of appropriation. We can examine the intersections of the structural modes in relation to appropriation in more detail. We saw that the three structural modes are not mutually exclusive but can stay in tension.

In Figure 3.14, area 1 represents the strongest form of havings in the structural mode of appropriation, which combines ownership, possession, and property. This is the case of a family estate where a family member lives and has the full rights to alienation. In practice, this means that the proprietor may not be constrained to using the estate as collateral for taking loans invested in his business. However, he still has solid emotional bindings to the estate and would avoid selling it at almost any price. Yet, no binding legal claim of heirs to the property exists that would contain alienation. If this constellation emerges from a legally valid testament, the full structure is shown in figure 3.15: The heir is a Blackstonian proprietor without appropriation. This is remarkable because it vindicates recent views that inheritance is the origin of private property.[83]

83 Harke 2020 ; Vinzent 2024.

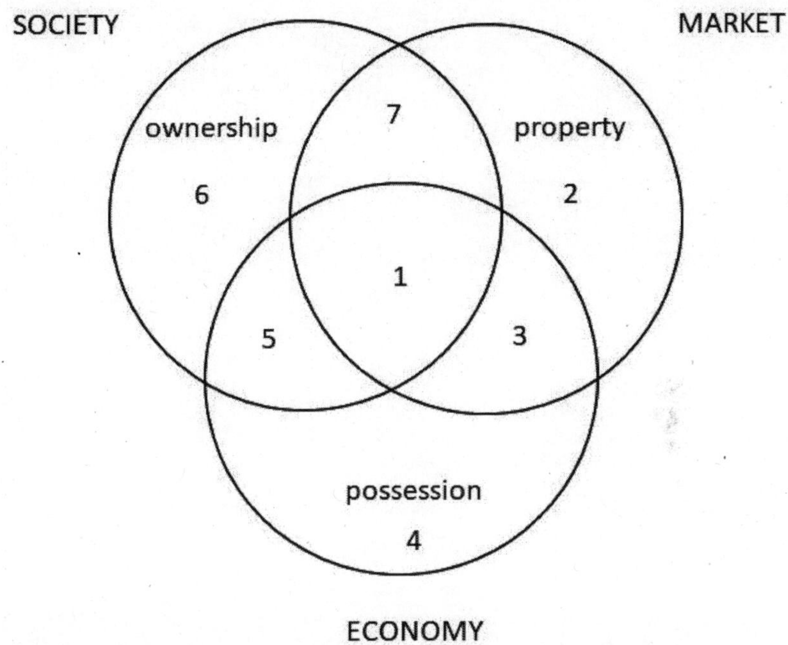

Figure 3.14: The interaction of structural modes as embedded in society, market and economy
Source: author's diagram

Compare this with area 5: This is the example of a traditional family business that does not go public because the family regards the business as inalienable (Figure 3.16). Legally, their ownership is property, but in our theoretical framework, there is a fundamental difference between the two structural modes. This is directly relevant to business practice. For example, in accounting, the family business might not value its assets at market prices but at historical costs. In Germany, this resulted in the construction of hidden reserves, as the actual wealth of the company may not be visible in the public accounts. However, it can be estimated by various means, such as taking the market prices of the various parts of the assets (such as the factory premises). As for the current owners, they may see themselves as stewards of the family business, which means that their having is mainly in the modes of assignment within the family and recognition in the local and business community.

The case of pure ownership (6) is the common law trust where owners are blocked from exerting possession and cannot alienate the trust's assets. In this

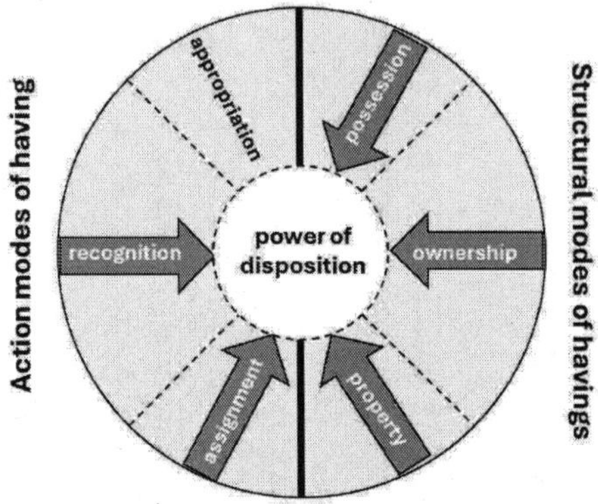

Figure 3.15: Blackstonian proprietor without appropriation
Source: author's diagram

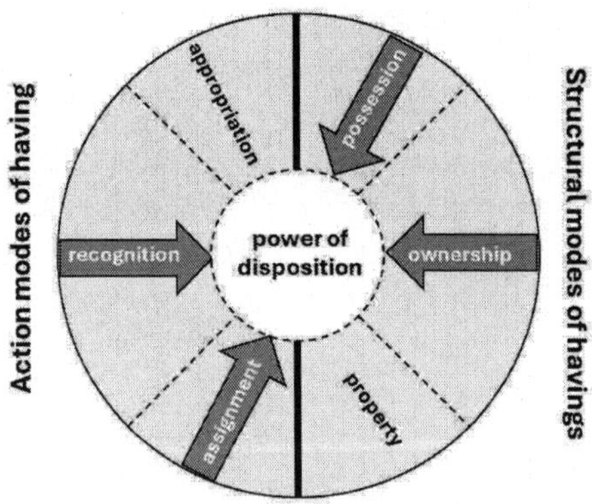

Figure 3.16: Traditional family business
Source: author's diagram

case, we would need to draft different diagrams of modes of having for the different individuals related to the trust, the legal proprietors and the trustees. I leave this task to the reader. Similarly, the community in a commons is the owner, whereas the individuals are the possessors. If the community has a collective decision procedure and action concerning certain elements of the commons, such as irrigation systems, this constellation switches to case 5. Area 7 is the case in which, for example, the owner of a family estate has rented this out to someone else and is also a proprietor in the civil law sense.

Area 4 is the case of a manager who manages a factory representing the owners, such as with statutory authority, which would preclude selling the factory in toto (Figure 3.17). Many variants exist in history and across societies, such as lineage trust managers in China. As mentioned, it is important to distinguish this from the mere control of powers of disposition assigned to all kinds of managerial positions. A possessing manager also has strong rights vis-à-vis proprietors, especially in large publicly listed companies. A key challenge of corporate governance is that legally, the top executive obtains possession via assignment and recognition but may abuse her powers to appropriate the company, that is, pursuing her own agenda independent from legal proprietors.

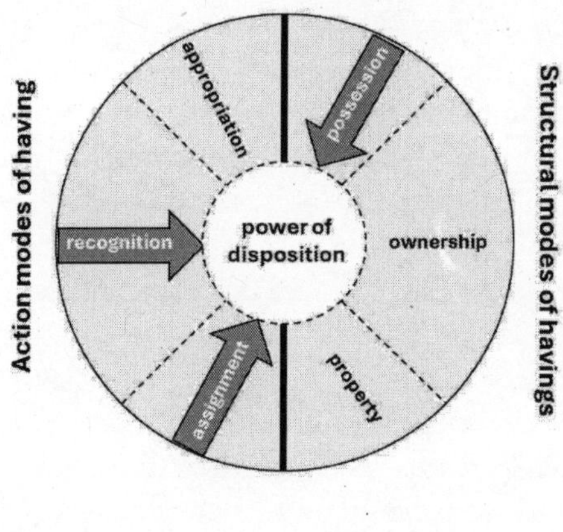

Figure 3.17: CEO of a listed company
Source: author's diagram

In case 3, we can locate managers who are proprietors without personal attachment to the business. This includes the extreme cases when a company's property is only held for selling after restructuring the business, as in many private equity funds. In comparison, an entrepreneur with a mission tends to area 1. Case 2 is a publicly listed company shareholder who only considers the value of the shares when deciding whether to have shares and may even switch havings in a very short time (Figure 3.17).

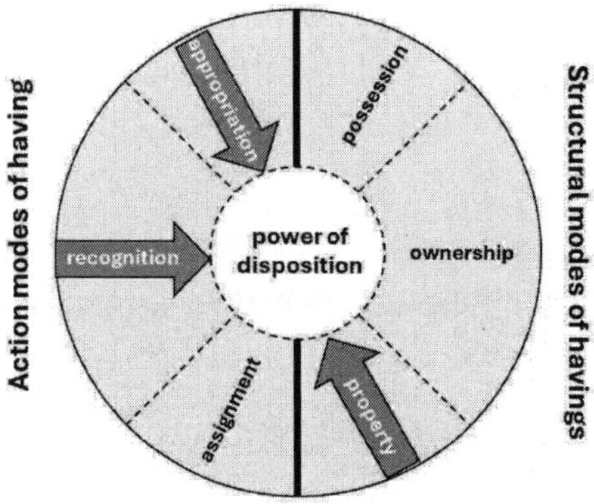

Figure 3.18: Shareholder
Source: author's diagram

All these examples show that the distinction between property and ownership is often visible when the person who has the object is willing to incur costs as measured by market prices to hold it. In the case of the shareholder, these may be those who accept holding shares even in the face of massive losses because they are confident that the business will succeed in the long run and identify with the company's mission. An interesting empirical illustration of this difference is the rich literature on "socio-emotional wealth" in family business, which shows that family business owners (in my parlance) appreciate non-pecuniary values in having the business, which becomes visible if, for example, they invest in historical premises even though there is no direct economic benefit, or if they contribute exceptionally large sponsorship money to the local community where the headquarter is located since the founding times.[84]

In Figure 3.14, I have also indicated that the structural modes differ regarding embeddedness. Following Karl Polanyi's seminal work, embeddedness is widely

84 Berrone, Cruz, and Gomez-Mejia 2012, Swab et al. 2020.

used in understanding social constraints on appropriation.[85] Our new framework allows for dissecting embeddedness analytically in the modes of recognition and assignment. Seeing ownership as related to society means that in a Polanyian sense, the having of the object mainly serves social functions, such as expressing one's identity or defining status, which relates to the modes of recognition and assignment. Different from Polanyi, I distinguish between economy and market. This is necessary because possession is not necessarily related to the market (think of a subsistence farmer) but is still about controlling economically useful resources. This differs from explicitly referring property to markets in the sense of alienability and monetary measurement.

We have already presented several examples of how a given structural mode can result from different modes of action. One important point is that the structural modes can become media of appropriation, which implicitly connects the two dimensions of modes in the sense of reflexivity. This is obvious when it comes to possession: Possession can result from seizure; hence, it is also appropriation, considered an action. Theft is the most direct form of this action mode. Ownership, as in the example of Indigenous claims, becomes a form of appropriation if the claim is grounded on tradition, history or spiritual meanings, which, however, strongly depends on the other modes, such as sacred enactments of assignments by spiritual powers in the past. The expropriative appropriation of Indigenous land worked both via possession and property, as in claiming land via rights in the early United States. In this case, there was even a conflict between the two modes, as the property owners backed by the state rejected the claims of settlers who just acquired land by possession without paying for the sovereign land rights.

The latter observation is important to recognize that appropriation by property does not necessarily mean establishing private property. One example is herding, such as nomads or early ranchers.[86] In these cases, the animals are private property, but the herders claim the land to be open access to their benefit. This claim is vicariously made by roaming the animals and effectively means that the open-access resource is appropriated since farmers may be displaced. The herders appropriate the animals in the first place, and they are symbolic media claiming possession of the land. This observation generalizes that the appropriation of benefits may not require private property, an insight that Weber already elaborated on in arguing that the openness of social groups may be a condition for appropriating a benefit. This is also visible in the competition between open access and proprietary regimes in software.

85 Polanyi 2001.
86 For the case of North America in colonial times, see Greer 2017, 259 f.

Therefore, the various forms of state, collective, and public ownership discussed in economics may fall under property as a form of appropriation. State ownership is appropriation by a group of possessors who claim benefits, a phenomenon familiar to resource-rich countries.[87] Natural resources are often assigned to "the people" as a collective. This does legally prevent individual appropriation: For example, if "the people" legally own the gold resources, wildcat mining is illegal appropriation resulting in possession by individual miners, which, however, is not recognized beyond their community. Legally, possession and property are assigned to the government, representing the people. However, this often results in another form of illegal appropriation if corrupt officials appropriate possession and property. The latter may not be recognized legally, but if the resources are sold beyond the country's borders, international law recognizes these as property, thus enabling frictionless market exchange.

Private property plays an essential role in market exchange and the distinct form of appropriation by exchange mediated by money. We already observed that in this context, the *erga omnes* view matters to safeguard the reliability of the contractual relationship. However, "private" does not mean "personal" in the sense of natural persons. This leads to confusion about distinguishing between private property and property. In the framework established here, private property becomes obsolete since all other forms of property in the economics distinction can be property, such as those familiar with so-called state capitalism. "Private" is too coarse to distinguish the empirically diverse forms of having. At a closer look, "private" is a form of assignment, like the other terms, such as state-owned. One important historical episode that made that clear was the post socialist transformation after 1989, when managers of state-owned companies often became the new proprietors of companies, a process labelled "insider privatization."[88] In theory, the political transformation was about reassigning havings from state to private. In practice, the managers already had appropriated companies as possession, which was also partly recognized in society. Accordingly, the reassignment was biased towards the insiders. The case of China that we discuss in the next chapter shows the complexity of such transformations.

Another perspective on the pitfalls of the private property concept is the debate over "liberal" forms of property.[89] As mentioned previously, even the original Code Civil notion of absolute property recognized its societal embeddedness in laws and regulations expressing public interests. Hence, what is essential about the "private" is already covered by the term property as used in this chapter.

87 Wenar 2017.
88 Peters 2023.
89 Dagan 2021.

Conclusion

The legal theory of common law prescribes a "numerus clausus" for property; that is, it limits legal choices to a fixed list of alternatives. The theory of havings represents the opposite pole: Having and havings circumscribe a rich ecology of economic life and how powers of disposition are allocated and evolve. We have developed a more parsimonious conceptual framework to grasp this richness.

The reader may point out that this theory has a major weakness compared to the established economics account: I do not present hypotheses about what determines the realized forms of havings, akin to the economics of property rights relying on conceptual tools such as transaction costs. Indeed, the approach seems descriptive in the first place. I agree. I follow Max Weber's view that these realized forms are outcomes of social struggle, not of narrow economic forces independent of the interests, passions and visions of actors who strive to obtain powers of disposition to realize their desired ways of life. Methodologically, this means that the explanation is mainly the task of the historical sciences and hence a multidisciplinary endeavor.

However, the concepts I have suggested point beyond their meanings towards sets of explanatory tools that can be mobilized in such historical explanations. For example, the action mode of recognition invites the consideration of ideological developments and the rise of new worldviews, perhaps explored in religious studies, or the action mode of appropriation would include the aspect of how technology enables such actions, which is a standard topic in economics. Similarly, property may be conducive to economic analysis since market actors employ economics performatively. In comparison, ownership is best understood from the perspectives of sociology or psychology. Ultimately, all these contributions must be combined to understand a particular status quo of havings in society. In the next chapter, I demonstrate this for a Chinese case.

Chapter 4: Methodological case study – Havings, culture, and urban development in Shenzhen

Introduction

We continue elaborating our new view on havings, demonstrating its descriptive and analytical value: Our empirical case study is China, specifically the megacity of Shenzhen, which experienced extremely rapid economic growth after 1978 and is today one of the most advanced urban settlements in China, embedded into the Greater Bay region together with Hong Kong and other megacities, and the home of many high-tech companies leading in China and globally. We will not go into the details of this development here since I have dealt with it in a series of publications since 2019, including a book-length treatment.[1] We will only focus on what is conventionally called land ownership, now labelling as "land havings." My aim is to demonstrate the methodological powers of the new theory of havings.

China is important since the literature on economic property rights has long highlighted the strangeness of its so-called property rights regime in the sense of opaqueness, complexity, and misfit with standard prescriptions, viewed from the common understanding of capitalism and socialism.[2] These observations are tensioned with the strong record of economic growth over four decades. Ill-defined and insecure property rights are typically considered recipes for stalled economic development. This led some researchers to conclude that perhaps unclear assignments may have advantages, at least at certain stages of development and transition to the market.[3] I will argue that these debates miss essential aspects of the action and structural modes of having. One reason is that the discussion meanders in a white area between the standard structural categories of state, col-

1 Herrmann-Pillath, Guo, and Feng 2021. For a comprehensive overview of Shenzhen development until the 2010s, see O'Donnell, Wong, and Bach 2017.

2 The edited volume Kennedy and Stiglitz 2013 has various contributions highlighting these views. The tension between established economic theory and Chinese practice is also salient when dealing with havings in Imperial China, Ocko 2004.

3 Ho 2013.

lective, and private property and the micro-level of property rights as defined by *usus*, *fructus*, and *abusus*. The analytical categories of having fill this blind spot. The upshot of my argument is that the Weberian struggle over powers of disposition unfolds in this white area, and stable allocations emerge.

We begin by examining the two socialist categories, state and collective ownership. They play an essential role in our case study since the Chinese constitution assigns land to two categories of proprietors: the state in the urban areas and the collectives in the rural areas.[4] There is no private property of land in China. When the special economic zone Shenzhen was established, the land was mainly agrarian, which required nationalization of collective land because rural land was legally constrained to mainly agricultural uses. With the continued spatial expansion, the areas surrounding the SEZ were also transformed into state ownership. However, this straightforward narrative fails to account for the diversity of modes of land havings in contemporary Shenzhen.

Basic institutions of having in Chinese socialism

State ownership as a multiplicity of having

The rich literature on state ownership in China has very early diagnosed principled differences between the Chinese case and other socialist countries, especially the Soviet Union.[5] These differences account for many of the distinctive features of the Chinese transition to a market economy after 1978, shaping the transformation of Shenzhen's rural regions. In most socialist countries, state ownership went hand in hand with centralized economic planning. In China, Maoist ideology pushed the decentralization of planning and managing state-owned assets. We can conceptualize this in terms of the action and structural modes of having.

The Chinese model involved relatively strong rights of possession of various government entities on different levels, such as the county or the province, distinct from the central government. Possession resulted from assignment in the first place, which is also the expression of the ultimate political power of the central government. For example, in the 1970s, even large SOEs were assigned to

4 For a comprehensive overview of land law in China, see Qiao and Upham 2017.

5 The key contribution was Granick's 1990, which defined the "regional property rights" approach, which I fully developed and applied in various contributions in the 1990s, building on the synthesis in Herrmann-Pillath's 1991. This synthesis integrated corresponding Chinese contributions, such as Fan Gang's.

low-level administrations, which were recentralized in 1980. One specific result of such assignments was that within the same territory, state havings include many different possessors, such as the municipality or SOEs of different administrative levels, including central government, the military, and others.[6] In other words, the "state" as the subject of havings is a highly diversified structure where the various constituents could enjoy distinct rights of possession. This implies that a municipality does not necessarily have full regulatory power over all state actors in its territory.

Apart from assignments, there are several ways of appropriating objects. The most important one is investment. That means if a particular state actor invests in an object such as an SOE, this is a means to establish claims on it. There is no legal prescription here, but such claims are mostly being recognized by the different government entities, including the central government, to some extent. With the gradual transformation of SOEs into shareholding companies, another form of appropriation uses the resulting form of property in M&A procedures, meaning standard shareholder voting rights allocations.[7] Government entities can also appropriate assets via the capital market if shares are traded. This is important in the context of land since this allows for the appropriation of land even via a market-type transactions among state actors. In more recent times, one institutional form of appropriation via property is land use rights, which are legally different from property and, therefore, allow transfer of state havings to non-state actors. A land use right is a legal form of possession in the first place, but if it becomes tradable, it takes the form of quasi-property. Meanwhile, state ownership implies that the ultimate owner of all state havings remains the central government. This is consistent with Imperial China, where all land was assigned to the Emperor. That means state havings in China manifest a complex multiplicity of forms, with an assignment to the central government; yet there are various forms of possession, with some even transformed into the property of non-central actors.

As a result, state havings are described today as "hybrid" since state actors can have assets in many ways.[8] For example, this includes the property of private companies via minority shareholdings. Since the government acts as an influential stakeholder simultaneously, and the CCP party cell in a private company has effective means of enforcing opinions, a minority shareholding can imply relatively strong possession of the government even though the legal form of the company is the property of a non-state actor.

6 Hsing 2006 speaks of a multiplicity of "socialist land masters."
7 There are many complex varieties; for an overview, see Li 2020.
8 Bruton et al. 2015 discuss the Chinese case in a global context.

At the same time, the government itself cannot be treated as a monolithic actor, as we have seen. This reveals strong performative effects in institutional actions since appropriation, recognition, and assignment are contextualized and continuously reshuffle distributed agential powers, constituting actors via weakening or strengthening their positions. For example, many lower-level governments retreated from having smaller-scale SOEs because they were not profitable and were draining social resources. However, this does not mean they gave up all possessions in the successor companies, if any. On the other hand, a large SOE can have several possessors. This was dubbed "regional property rights" in the literature of the 1990s, which referred to the layered structure of jurisdictions, which, however, is further complicated by the additional matrix that relates each actor both to a territorial jurisdiction and to a line authority, such as, for example, a specialized ministry for communication technology. Although these complex structures have been streamlined over the years, a paradoxical result of further marketization and modernization of corporate governance is that public shareholding SOEs reproduce this structure in the composition of the various shareholders, which can be different state actors, and today even including non-state actors. Another complication is that critical decisions are ultimately taken by the CCP, especially regarding top executives. Therefore, the CCP should be considered a possessor of independent status.[9]

The latter observation reflects the nature of the Chinese body politic as a "party-state," also stated in the constitution.[10] This raises the question of whether the category of state havings is partly misleading since the top decision-makers are almost exclusively party members within the government and other state-related organizations.[11] The CCP also creates porous boundaries among all state actors, even if these may have formal rights of autonomy since party members are subject to party leadership beyond the organization's boundaries (*nomenklatura* system). This constellation creates tensions between the modes of recognition and assignment. Beyond a specific assignment of possessions, the recognized power of disposition may be allocated differently according to party authority. The critical phenomenon is the direct control over the actors who exert powers of disposition via the control of the *nomenklatura*.[12]

9 I develop this view in detail in Herrmann-Pillath 2017a; compare Blanchette 2020.

10 In most economics literature about China, this fact is ignored, even by experts (contrary to the views of Chinese lawyers, Jiang 2010). For example, in her otherwise highly informative book, Jin compares the "Western" with the "Chinese" market economy in terms of the different roles of government, thus conflating government and party; K. Jin 2023. In Herrmann-Pillath 2017a I have argued systematically that there are two different types of networks of actors who control companies, private and party.

11 J. Wang 2014, X. Jin et al. 2022.

12 Beck and Brødsgaard 2022.

Collectives in rural society

According to the Chinese constitution, Chinese villages are self-governed. The collectives own rural land. However, the meaning of "collective" is open to interpretation since there is a distinction between hamlets, villages, larger administrative villages, and even townships that goes back to pre-1949 terminology.[13] Many administrative functions have been transferred to the township level in recent decades. This also implies that elected village cadres are less influential than township officials.[14] These trends go back to the Maoist period when the rural areas were organized as People's communes. These communes distinguished production teams and production brigades as lower levels of commune administration. The commune administration was mainly on the township level, and the brigade corresponded to the village. When the communes were abolished in the early 1980s, these terms were restored, thus also marking the historical continuity of spatial structures. For example, contrary to the slogan "from fisher village to megacity," historically, Shenzhen was a market town that played an essential role in regional trade with the British colony Hong Kong, and there were hundreds of villages in the county that today is Shenzhen.

The historical background is important because land assignments stay in continuity even with the conditions before 1949.[15] In South China, a large share of land was controlled by lineage estates, which we already discussed in previous chapters, and tilled by permanent tenants. After the communist revolution, the feudal landholders were expropriated. Even though this meant that the "evil gentry" was often physically exterminated, the critical transformation in havings was less the expropriation of individual landlords but of the lineage estates in which the gentry occupied the leadership position. In this constellation, the distinction between possession and ownership is informative, as leadership implies possession, but not ownership, which rests with the lineage, that is, the larger local kinship group, which included the poor members of the lineage.

However, the lineage land was not redistributed to the individual tillers since, after a few years, the collectivization process started. There was an intermediate stage where many landholdings, such as fruit orchards or ponds, were transformed into cooperatives, with villagers as shareholders. Interestingly, these models were like lineage estates, where individuals and lineage branches held shares, including specific projects such as investing in establishing a new local market. These cooperatives were soon disbanded, and collectivization quickly

13 Ho 2001.

14 Schubert and Ahlers 2012.

15 Potter and Potter 1990 and Chan et al. 2009 are key contributions that reveal these continuities.

moved to establishing the People's communes. However, this did not mean that the land assignments were radically changed, apart from the brief "Great Leap Forward" period when the communes were organized like military units. Assignments were not about the land in the first place but about the labor, that is, which team would till which land. Since the villages were not resettled, this implied that most of the families that lived in a particular place before 1949 continued to work on the same land. There were many disputes and tensions in the villages about allocating work tasks because the assigned land also determined labor productivity and, hence, work point allocation, the way the product was collectively allocated.[16]

In other words, the modes of assignment and possession played together in complex ways, and the socialist formal institutions did not adequately reflect the real structures of havings. Partly, assignments were determined by the topography of the settlements, which in turn reflected social structures that had been radically attacked since 1949. Assignments were mediated via the organization of labor and resulted in a pattern of possessions, which was reinforced by labor investment. In the Shenzhen area, many villages were single-lineage villages. That means the settlement structure often reflected the internal division of lineages into branches with closer relatives. When the production teams were formed, these often reproduced these divisions. Consequently, the social structure of the village partly continued to manifest in the assignments of labor and land.

This can also be interpreted as implicit recognition of traditional land havings in a different linguistic frame of socialism (signs in the Aoki-Bourdieu model). In a nutshell, in single-lineage villages, the socialist collectives operated like lineage estates, in which, theoretically, the individual households could work like tenants. This model had already emerged in the early 1960s but was denounced by radical Maoists. Yet, the transition from implicit possession via labor organization towards possession by assignment was easily orchestrated, as happened after 1978. With the new "responsibility system" in the countryside, farmers became quasi-tenants of the socialist agricultural organization.[17]

After the demise of the People's communes, the rural areas underwent the first wave of reforms that delegated production tasks to single households while allowing them the freedom to use assigned land for growing other crops and agricultural activities, such as raising pigs. This system was gradually expanded, resulting in the long-term assignment of land to households, becoming like the old permanent tenancy system. The critical difference is that the collective remains the ultimate owner of the land. However, considering the congruence of administra-

16 Madsen 1984 is a thick account of these conflicts.

17 This transition has been described by many scholars. For a textbook-style overview, see Naughton 2018.

tive divisions with social structure, this often implies that the village is the owner, and the village corresponds to a lineage. Therefore, there is a direct continuity between land havings before 1949 and today, with the only difference being that the local elites have been radically transformed, or, in this sense, how village and lineage leaders were recruited. In Maoist times, this led to many conflicts and tensions, as old elites often could reinstate their positions, having been recognized as leaders over generations. After 1978, the economic dynamic also engendered many changes in leadership structures, with entrepreneurs becoming influential, often having a party background.

Finally, an essential aspect of rural land havings was that all farmers had a right to a plot for their homestead, including a small space for raising vegetables for their own consumption. These plots assumed critical significance in the urbanization of the rural areas in the Greater Bay region.

Urbanization and transformation of havings

The case of Shenzhen involves the transformation of rural land into urban land. This is necessary because Chinese law tightly circumscribes agricultural land use for other uses to safeguard China's capacity for food self-sufficiency. Often, this means that villagers may obtain other land in compensation if they continue to work in agriculture. The transformation is nationalization in legal form since only state-owned land can be used for non-agricultural purposes such as industry. There are legal prescriptions for compensation, which, however, do not consider the increased value of the land in these new uses; they only consider the loss of agricultural income for the farmers. Hence, land issues often stay at the heart of corruption, triggering rural unrest.[18]

Nationalized land can be used in any way depending on the municipal zoning regulations and urban development plan. The essential distinction between land ownership as property and land use rights as possession corresponds to rural conditions in the sense of long-term land leases. That means an entity may acquire land use rights as a tenant over a more extended period, such as 40 years for residential uses. For example, a developer may acquire these rights and build a new residential area with a shopping mall and pay fees to the municipal government or even a lump sum, akin to buying the rights. According to Chinese law, the buildings are not subject to state ownership but are considered private property. Accordingly, developers can sell real estate on the market without government interference. This distinction between the two types of property is important as the

18 Tao 2023 is the most comprehensive analysis of these developments.

property of the building implies the appropriation of the land to some extent, depending on the recognition of possession. This works similarly to the mechanism in state ownership in general, as mentioned previously, namely that investment may result in recognized possession of the investing actor, even if this deviates from the formal assignment,

These constructs have played a critical role in China over the past three decades in funding municipal expenditures, often also involving complex financial arrangements with so-called local government investment vehicles.[19] In such cases, the local government could activate land simultaneously in two ways. First, land use rights, aka land possession, are allocated to various parties to earn income, and second, land ownership is used as collateral for those investment vehicles to borrow money from banks. We can also speak of the financialization of government budgets that grounds in the distinct structure of land havings.[20] A necessary consequence has become salient recently: Land has acquired a market value since declining prices for real estate also create downward pressure on the prices of land use rights and, hence, the implicit value of land. This affects the value of the collateral and, via the lower income from land use rights, local governments' budget. Via land havings, real estate finance and government budget are tightly connected.

The transformation of rural land in Shenzhen was comprehensive in that in 2004, all rural areas in the jurisdictions were transformed into urban areas, with the necessary consequence that all rural citizens attained the status of urban citizens. The entire rural land became state-owned and controlled by the municipality. However, even in the first stage, this did not imply that villagers had lost control of the land.

In the area of Shenzhen, there were more than 300 native villages, many of them single-lineage villages. When the special economic zone was created, the villages in that area and its close neighborhood developed a distinct response to the opportunities offered by this economic revolution.[21] This started with the initiative of farmers who realized that the massive inflow of migrant workers created a demand for cheap accommodation. Villagers started adding stories to their houses and soon moved out since they could afford pricier housing, becoming absentee landlords. Collectively, the villagers realized that they could use their village land for similar purposes and accompanying infrastructure. The phenomenon of "urban villages" emerged from these initiatives. Most urban villages have a native village as a core and are located on originally rural land.

19 Feng, Wu, and Zhang 2022.
20 Pan, Zhang, and Wu 2021.
21 D. W. D. Wang 2016 is a comprehensive account of these transformations.

They count as "communities" *shequ* today, the lowest level of the administrative hierarchy, but often refer to themselves as "village" (*cun*). Soon, at least 50 per cent of the Shenzhen population lived in these settlements.

A critical institutional feature of urban villages is that the land on which they were built was still under the control of the native villages. Native villagers took the step to transfer their land from the village as an administrative unit to newly established cooperative organizations with different labels. However, after a few years, they converged on the organizational form of "shareholding cooperative companies," which were also recognized by specific administrative regulations.[22] However, Chinese company law does not recognize such entities as a distinct legal form. In this sense, we can diagnose the performative emergence of an institutional and organizational form from actions centering on land havings. As rural areas were not yet nationalized, these SCCs controlled the collective land. After nationalization, they often retained control of the land use rights. As said, this partly operates via appropriation by investment.

Unlike many other cities in China, villagers in Shenzhen could resist expropriation because they were closely knit kinship groups and could strike a deal with the municipality.[23] Within a few years, millions of migrant workers flocked into Shenzhen, creating a massive demand for residential construction. However, migrants cannot afford high rents unless they receive high wages. Villagers offered such accommodation, thus contributing to keeping wages low and the international competitiveness of Shenzhen manufacturing high. Moreover, low wages also kept the costs of infrastructure construction low. The municipality watched these developments with mixed feelings, as the urban villages were not built according to legal standards, were messy, and, in the early years, also hotspots of crime and prostitution. However, the municipality did not have the financial means to offer public housing at subsidized prices. Hence, the deal emerged that the SCC would continue developing urban villages but would morph from a quasi-business entity to a parafiscal organization that fulfilled most functions of lower-level urban administration, such as public security, waste management, or even schooling.[24] In compensation, the SCC would retain and manage the land use rights for the municipality.

The latter arrangement had the vital implication that in later stages of development, the SCC became partners in renovating and redeveloping the urban vil-

22 For an overview, see Cheng et al. 2024.

23 The picture is more variegated at a closer look, both within Shenzhen and comparing with urban villages in other places. Developments are highly contextualized and situated in local political economy, hence Weberian struggle. For example, Wong 2015, Kan 2019.

24 Po 2012.

lages. This is often accompanied by finally relinquishing control of land use rights; however, this follows lucrative deals with the developers endorsed by the municipality. In such cases, most of the rights are sold to the developers, with the proceeds going to the SCC and partly to the villagers, either as a share of those profits or as their share of the original homestead. Such deals could involve complex side agreements, for example, giving villagers special purchase conditions for acquiring upscale apartments in the newly built residential areas.[25] At the same time, the municipality extended and strengthened its formal grassroots-level administration, gradually reducing the parafiscal roles of the SCC. In sum, the villagers lost property and often even possession. Yet, they retained ownership, to which we now turn.

Havings and recognition in the medium of ritual

SCC as lineage organization

We will now look at the structure of havings in more detail. The SCC is the critical actor in the complex structure of land havings in urban villages.[26] The SCC is a legal person that controls property of two different kinds: real estate in the form of buildings and other construction and land use rights. The villagers own the SCC itself. We can speak of ownership here as the original kinship relations in the villages define the SCC.

Initially, the shares of the SCC were assigned to the villagers based on households, hence, the male household heads. Facing demographic changes and demands for recognizing legal prescriptions for equal treatment of women, this was interpreted as a claim based on the original household registration of the individual members. However, the shares cannot be regarded as property since they cannot be traded and have no price. Also, because inheritance is constrained, outmarrying women may lose their claims if they change registration. Often, a criterion is whether individuals continue to work and contribute to the community in the broadest sense. Further, the total number of shares has been frozen, so newly-born members do not receive fresh shares. This effectively stabilizes the household as the owner of shares and, hence, the SCC.

25 For a detailed case study, see Herrmann-Pillath et al. 2024.

26 The following discussion is mostly based on own research in Shenzhen, as published in Herrmann-Pillath, Guo, and Feng 2021, Cheng, Herrmann-Pillath, and Li 2022, Cheng et al. 202, Herrmann-Pillath et al. 2024.

Hence, the shareholding arrangement in the SCC reflects the structure of the lineage to a large extent, even implying that the original subdivision of the lineage is reproduced, which was implicit in the production team assignments of the People's communes. Specific projects of the SCC may be assigned to groups representing the original teams. These historical linkages are explicitly invoked, such as in village museums, which display the old team leaders.

However, another element in SCC ownership relates to the distinct form of collective shares, meaning that the SCC holds its own shares. Hence, there is a twist in the corporate governance structure since the supervisory board also includes representatives of the SCC as a distinct entity, similar to executives in endowments and trusts. Today, these individuals are mostly party members. In many cases, the CEOs of SCC have several "hats:" Apart from being CEOs, they may be village leaders, heads of the lineage, and Party secretaries. Beyond these roles, they are often independent entrepreneurs. This creates a complex picture of having an SCC. There are cases where the role of the CEO is powerful and bolstered by the dominance of his relatives in other leadership positions. Hence, these individuals almost appropriate an SCC as possessors. However, at the same time, they must follow the party line in their decisions so that we cannot simply speak of individual appropriation. Via party membership of leaders, the SCC is only semi-autonomous.[27] In general, the municipality also pushes opening the SCC to external shareholders, but apparently, villagers resist the following dilution of their ownership.

The hybridization of kinship and organization is salient in rituals that display SCC identities. One important example is the New Year celebration when the dividends are distributed. As in historical lineage estates, this includes a ritual of feasting with the "common pot," where all villagers join and eat from a shared pot with a mix of valuable food, in the past, mainly fatty pork.[28] This food sharing symbolizes the sharing of economic benefits in the SCC. Lineages and lineage culture are critical in permeating Shenzhen's land ownership despite the complete transformation into state havings. The material manifestation is the cultural square and the ancestral hall, which represent the center of the original ritual space of a village.

We can analyze the previous account in terms of the action and structural modes of having for the different types of actors. The individual villagers (Figure 4.1) have ownership by recognition and assignment but do not have property or

27 The party's role is increasingly converging to the SOE pattern elucidated previously, reflecting the general trend of party expansion on the grassroots level; Cai, Liu, and Jiang 2023.

28 On this peculiar dining ritual, see J. L. Watson 1987. Watson studied the New Territories. On the more recent conditions in Shenzhen, see Guo and Herrmann-Pillath 2019b.

even possession of the SCC. They are also blocked from appropriating it, as the only channel would be via the shareholder assembly.

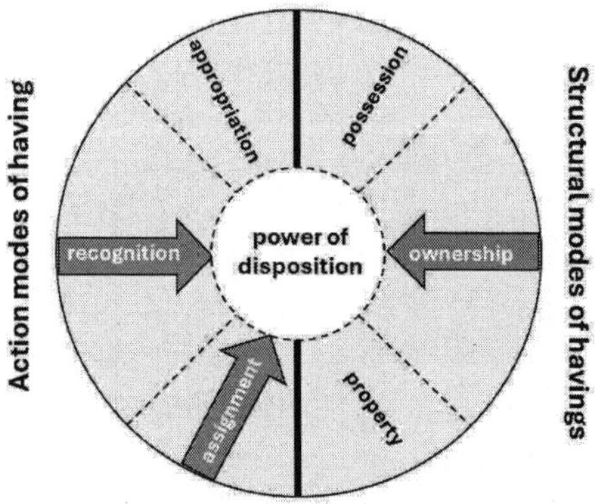

Figure 4.1: Villagers' having of SCC
Source: author's diagram

In contrast, the villager leaders, with their different hats, may play different roles depending on the local context. There are cases where they have full powers of disposition in terms of action modes, including individual appropriation (which may be denounced as "corruption" among villagers), but do not have property, which is legally with the SCC itself as a corporate entity. Naked appropriation may even lack recognition, as shown in Figure 4.2.1. In contrast, responsible leaders accountable to the villagers do not appropriate the SCC and share ownership with the community (Figure 4.2.2).

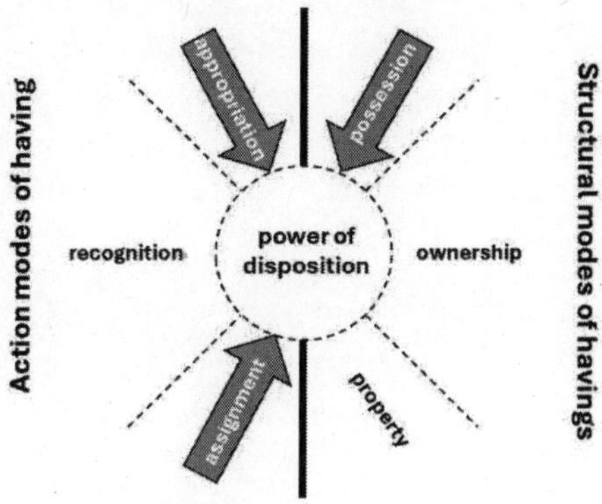

Figure 4.2.1: SCC leaders: corrupt
Source: author's diagram

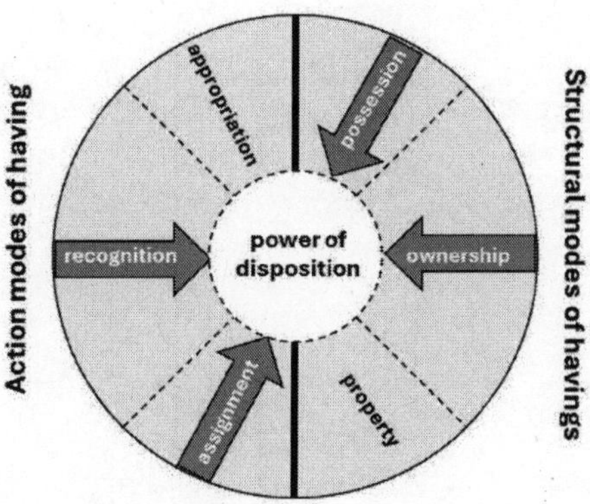

Figure 4.2.2: SCC leaders: responsible
Source: author's diagram

The government can also play different roles. If we focus on land here as a major asset of the SCC, only the government has property. This is different from buildings, where the SCC can also have property. In many cases, different from Shenzhen, the government appropriates the land, including the land use rights. I show the case (figure 4.3) where this does not happen. The government leaves land use rights to the SCC, hence possession.

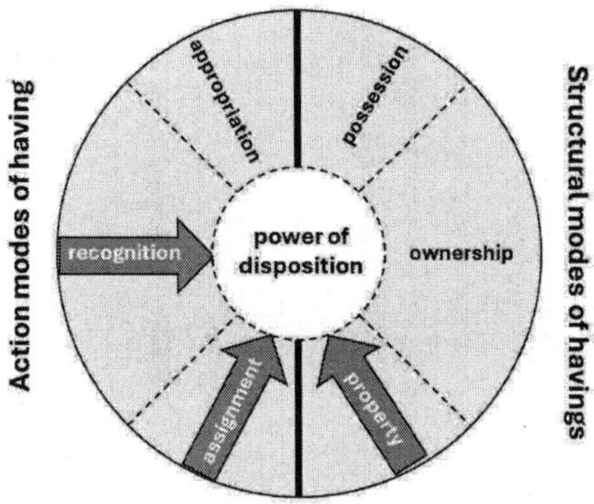

Figure 4.3: Government and SCC
Source: author's diagram

In sum, we see the modes of having and havings interplay in a complex and contextualized form. To understand these constellations, we need to go beyond economic factors. A critical issue is the nature of the land as being performed in different framings of property and ownership.

Ritual space and ownership

The notion of ritual space is critical for understanding the relationship between possession, ownership, and property of land. Following earlier work, I define the ritual space as the territory owned by the village as the "ancestors' land," a concept like the Indigenous notion of the homeland. The background is the history of migration in China, especially in the Song dynasty when many Han Chinese fled from the North to the South, facing the Mongol invasion. Via various routes and waves, settlers arrived in the area of today's Shenzhen. The first settlers are identified in the historical records and the lineage genealogies. There are important cases where settlers belonged to a larger surname group and shared a genealogy that traces back to earlier times. For example, several villages in Shenzhen originated with the family named Huang and consider the same high ancestor as their origin, even though the lineages are separated, starting with the first settler arriving in this area.[29]

As a result of further economic development, population growth, and the violent conflicts over land in the area (Hakka wars), a differentiated social structure emerged in the 19th century, with some lineages becoming more powerful landlords, though mainly via lineage holdings.[30] Lineage estates were crucial for securing the social status of local lineages as a collective good and, therefore, were not simply appropriated by single individuals or families. For example, lineage estates funded schools accessible for all lineage children to nurture a maximum number of talents who might eventually succeed in Imperial examinations and achieve high officialdom. Lineages also established local markets and supported infrastructure development for their gain, such as building bridges with toll gates.

Rituals were paramount in maintaining lineage solidarity and identity, such as the dragon boat races that pitted villages against each other. Concerning land, ownership, distinct from possession, was embodied in the ritual space. In contemporary Shenzhen, we can observe its manifestations in line with historical conditions. The traditional village was dotted with temples, steles, pagodas, and tombs that delineated its land, with the ancestral hall and a main temple at the centre.[31] These locations were determined by *fengshui* (Chinese geomancy) procedures by which the flows of cosmic forces were identified. Both define the location of all these ritual artefacts and can be influenced by them. In modern Shenzhen, the "cultural square" is a widespread urban assemblage that stays in this tradition: This is a public square with the ancestral hall and a temple used for leisure and entertainment and ritual activities such as lion dances. The cultural square of Xiasha village in downtown Shenzhen hosts mega events such as a 10,000-table "common pot" where Huang from all over the world gather to cement the solidarity and cooperation in this large surname group interpreted as kinship rooted in a common ancestor.

Two cases typically represent the ritual space as almost ideal. This is because they are in the Bao'an district, which urbanized later and had more space to include ritual concerns in urban development.

---

29 For a special study of the Huang, see Guo and Herrmann-Pillath 2019a.

30 Classical contributions are R. S. Watson 2007, Siu 1989, Faure 2007.

31 Lagerwey 2010.

The first case is Fenghuang village aka *shequ*.[32] The Wen lineage's ritual space is spanned by the central square with an ancestral hall and temple, which is also the location of a neighborhood office and other cultural facilities, most importantly, the "old village," renovated as a tourist site; the other pole is a newly built temple complex on the premises of the old village temple on the hills. This place is interesting as it is a natural reserve that is wholly state-owned, yet the SCC has obtained rights to build and manage this temple complex for religious and leisure uses. Since religious meanings are sensitive and therefore oblique, only knowledgeable observers recognize the ritual significance. For example, there is a vegetarian restaurant near the temple complex with the only parking space on top of the hill. This space is minimal and only accessible with a special permit. All other visitors must climb the hill via stairs marked by auspicious Chinese characters. The ritual work is the effort spent (which is considerable in subtropical climates). The two poles of the ritual space are in viewing distance, and the connection is regularly enacted via processions connecting the places, such as when villagers hold a traditional wedding.

My other example is Shanghe village, which is another Huang village.[33] This case is fascinating as it involves a negotiation about transforming ritual space. This transformation became necessary because, at the turn of the millennium, the municipality built a vast central park on the land belonging to the village where the cemetery was located (Bao'an Park). In principle, the CCP explicitly refuses to recognize the ritual meanings of cemeteries and often even adopts an aggressive stance in demolishing cemeteries to render the land useful for economic purposes. In this case, another solution was found.[34] The municipality agreed with the village to relocate the cemetery to the hills, which originally belonged to the village as forest commons (a *feng shui* forest). Not far away, there is another sacred location on the hills, a Daoist temple managed by the SCC, and, as in the Fenghuang case, it is a registered religious temple with a sitting priest. The other pole of the ritual space is the central square with an ancestral hall and temple near the SCC's headquarters.

The Shanghe case directly reveals the importance of the ritual space for the land havings. With the land expropriation for the park, the municipality fully reclaims the land, and even the ritual space has been annulled in that area. Hence, property is clearly with the government. However, within the original boundaries of the village, the ritual space has been reinstated, thus manifesting ownership of the villagers. However, villagers did not have property in the land surrounding

32 This case is extensively documented in Herrmann-Pillath, Guo, and Feng 2021.

33 Herrmann-Pillath et al. 2024.

34 For an interesting comparison, see Trémon 2015.

the cemetery, which is partly also a natural resource. The government arranged another form of compensation as a new and large luxury condominium, Xicheng villas, was developed. Here, villagers were assigned land use rights, only to hand them over to the developers at a price. So, apparently, villagers lost all property. At the same time, a side agreement was reached that gave villagers special rights to make their first purchase. Many Huang families moved to this place to set up three-generation families. Again, the indicator is indirect but substantial: A birth clinic is almost exclusively for Huang clients on top of the hills. This luxury resort allows women and newborns to follow traditional rules of postnatal ritual. In other words, despite giving up all property for profit, the possession of land and villas is embedded in ownership manifest in the ritual space.

In sum, we see how ownership mediated by ritual practices determines the allocation of claims on havings among various groups. The villagers deploy different means to keep control of their land even though they do not hold any property title individually. As a collective, the SCC represents their rights, but even it does not have property rights in the strict sense. Recognition and assignment are critical modes for the current allocation. Assignments partly persist from Maoist times, and ritual practices can be seen as articulating the pertinent claims on possession. We can even diagnose ritual practices as forms of appropriation. At the same time, the municipal government expresses recognition in various forms. One follows the implicit rules in state ownership to recognize investment by particular actors as justifying claims of possession, and the other endorses ritual practices as important elements of public life in Shenzhen.

Modes of having and real estate in Shenzhen

Basic structure of havings

The continuity of lineages over many centuries suggests the possibility that regarding land havings, via village customs, a particular habitus is reproduced: the materiality of land becomes a sign in the sense of the Aoki-Bourdieu model. This has also been observed in the New Territories of Hong Kong, even suggesting resemblances with the conditions in mainland China today.[35] After the communist riots of the 1960s, the British administration gave many privileges to the lineages in the New Territories, which had proven to be reliable partners in countering the

35 J. L. Watson 2004.

riots, keen to protect their traditions and well aware of the ferocious attacks on tradition during the Cultural Revolution unfolding a few kilometers away across the border. These privileges included rights such as building larger houses than in other Hong Kong districts, thus making the land even more valuable. At the same time, traditional estates and tombs continued to enjoy special legal protection.[36] The increasing value of land created strong incentives even for the younger generation lineage members to partake in traditional activities since this is necessary to confirm and sustain their claims on the land. This mutual reinforcement of ritual and land havings motivated even émigrés to keep contact with their native places.

Therefore, it is worthwhile to briefly glance over the conditions in the New Territories in the early 20th century.[37] One crucial aspect is the interaction between Chinese customary law and the British administration of what had become Crown land after 1898. The New Territories were part of the historical Bao'an county to which the area of Shenzhen belonged. The critical historical fact about land havings in this area is that most land did not belong to single owners, but at least to two, often several, and that this mainly involved lineages and lineage trusts. The customary system of having was conceptualized in the distinction between "skin" and "bone" of land, with the latter referring to full legal ownership manifest in paying the land tax. In contrast, the "skin" (land surface) might be the object of complex forms of legitimate possession, including perpetual.[38] In contrast, the British authorities required the clear assignment of land to only one proprietor. This was implemented via a systematic cadastral survey and precise identification of owners while establishing strict legal standards on how a tenancy contract differs from property.[39] The latter targeted the widespread practice of permanent tenancy.

The British aimed at transforming traditional havings into property, pursuing goals similar to the transformation unfolding in Europe in the previous centuries, such as enhancing the alienability of land and easing its use as collateral. However, their enforcement of unequivocal property followed Imperial precedent in a significant way, namely identifying the taxpayer as proprietor.[40] The other possessors would be downgraded legally, meaning their claims would no longer have property status. As we had seen earlier, before the British intervention, these claims amounted to property in many ways, including the right of inheritance. This pattern reveals a fundamental difference between the Imperial and the British notion of property. In Imperial China, the taxpaying proprietor differed

36 Nissim 2016, 127 ff.

37 Hase 2013.

38 Kroker 1958.

39 The British followed the general approach to colonial dispossession as analyzed by Bhandar 2018.

40 Osborne 2004.

from the non-taxpaying possessor and quasi-proprietor in that it was less in the economic functions of the claims but in recognition of the social status as belonging to the landowning elite, the gentry. Hence, we diagnose the difference between what I call "statist" and "contractual property" (Figure 4.4). Before the British intervention, there were no registers in the New Territories because the Imperial government had frozen land registers centuries ago to relieve the population's tax burden. Hence, whether the land was registered depended largely on those who had land and wanted to get official recognition from the Imperial state. This difference was expressed in the distinction between the "bone" and the "skin" of the land.

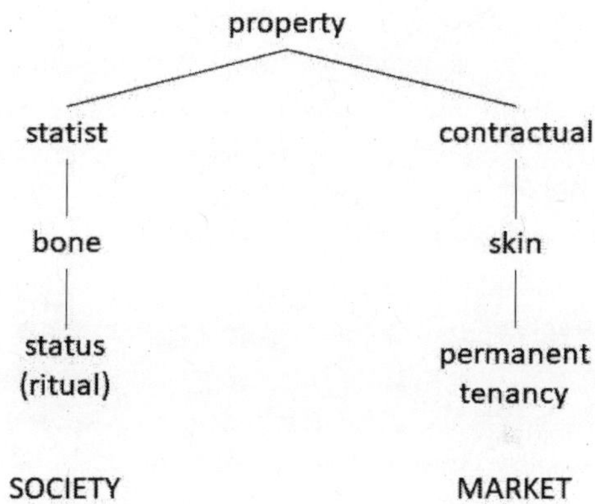

Figure 4.4: Statist and contractual property in Imperial China
Source: author's diagram

The "bone" versus "skin" duality reflects a form of property which defines an essential divergence from Western conceptions.[41] Owning the "bone" as statist property was not embedded into the market context but embodied the social status of a group to which the proprietor belonged, such as the wealthy and powerful clans in the Greater Bay Area. In contrast, owning the "skin" did not involve a property title but a contractual relation embedded into the market, which was recognized as legitimizing possession in the community, such as permanent tenancy. Insofar as statist property relates to social status, it is part and parcel of the body politic of the Imperial state (manifest in the complementary right to take part in Imperial

41 Mazumdar 2001.

examinations). In contrast, contractual possession is embedded into the market. Remarkably, this inverts the Polanyian assumptions about social embeddedness and markets as opposites.[42] Socially embedded contractual possession scaffolds market transactions, whereas state-enforced legal rights obtain this function in Western capitalism. Accordingly, we diagnose two different concepts of statist property, reflecting two fundamentally different forms of statehood.[43]

What is the role of ownership? Ownership is not congruent with property and often refers to transactions not mediated via markets. In Imperial China, this applied to land that accrued to the owner via inheritance: the owner as possessor was factually seen as steward of the family line and, therefore, would be tightly constrained in exerting his rights on the market. For example, when selling land, close relatives had the explicit right to veto and exercise a right of first refusal. As elaborated in the previous chapter, ownership refers to a specific type of relationship with the object owned, which we diagnose as the object constituting the owner's identity, whereas property always implies the possibility of alienating the relationship via a market transaction. By implication, ownership is mainly based on recognizing the owner's status in a specific community.

Figures 4.5.1 and 4.5.2 summarize the two scenarios for the permanent tenant and an individual absentee landlord (which is different from a manager of a lineage estate). The regular tenant's case features a strong role of possession and ownership, the latter mostly resulting from assignment, that is, inheritance. Inheritance can be mediated via the lineage if the tenant leases the land from the lineage trust. The absentee landlord neither claims possession nor ownership, and his property is recognized by the government.

Let us now turn to the conditions in Shenzhen today. As we saw, the law prescribes the fundamental distinction between land and land use rights. At the same time, in the urban villages, another significant factor that is not universally present in China is ownership by the lineages. If we look at the three structural modes of havings regarding the action mode of appropriation, we get a picture that differs from our model of Chapter 3 (Figure 4.6). The reason is that land use rights stay at the center of the market. Hence, it is possession that is embedded into the market, not property. Property is state-owned and, therefore, does not seem amenable to markets: This was the conventional assumption in combining state ownership with central planning of the economy. Accordingly, we see property as embedded in the economy. For example, China's government has much stronger eminent domain rights than liberal market economies. However, as we

42 Myers 1982; Pomeranz 2008.

43 The Chinese view on property reflects the view of markets as statecraft, established two millennia ago and continuing until today: Zanasi 2020, Herrmann-Pillath and Zhao 2023.

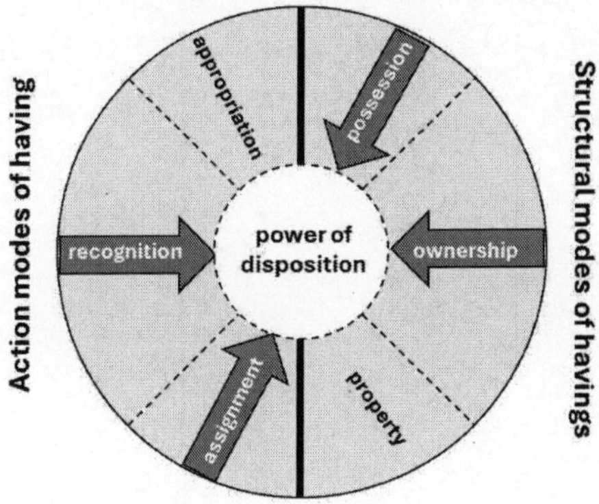

Figure 4.5.1: Tenant in Imperial China
Source: author's diagram

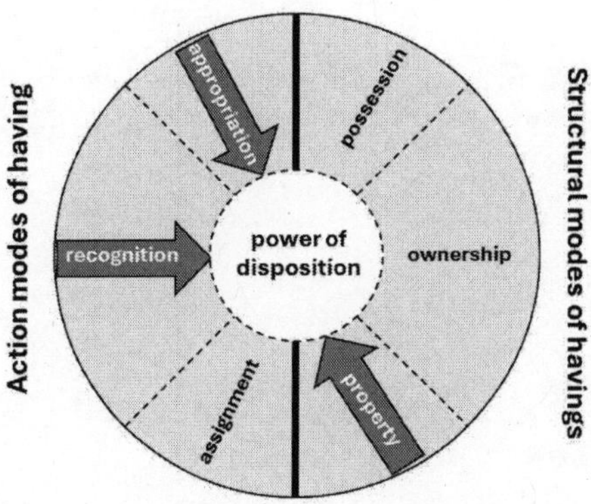

Figure 4.5.2: Landlord in Imperial China
Source: author's diagram

saw, the construction of land use rights also allows for the marketization of state-owned land, with the government also obtaining a role as a player in the real estate market. We can speak of the financialization of statist property.

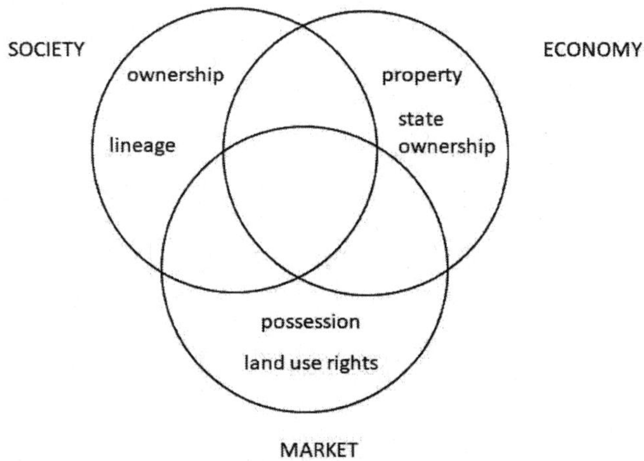

Figure 4.6: Structural modes of havings and embeddedness in Shenzhen
Source: author's diagram

We can further detail this analysis by examining how actors are constituted in this constellation of structural modes and embedding domains, represented by the numbers (Figure 4.7).

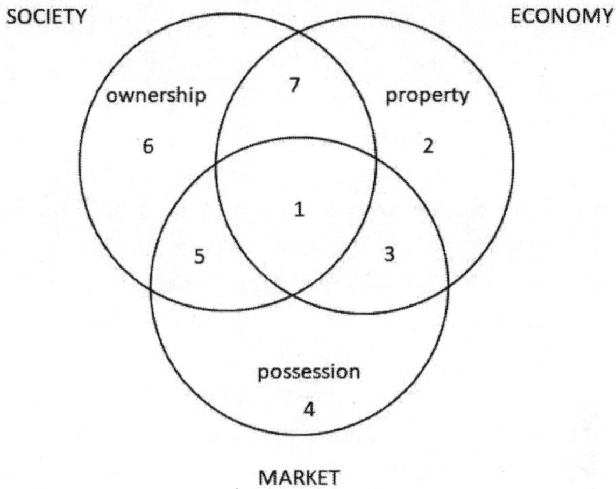

Figure 4.7: Modes of appropriation and types of agencies in Shenzhen real estate (see main text)
Source: author's diagram

1. Strictly speaking, this category does not exist in Shenzhen since private property of land is legally prohibited. However, there is the case of individual farmer plots. The individual families originally appropriated these plots. Even though all the rural land was nationalized, the plots remain indirectly and individually appropriated via the buildings that former farmers have, in the sense of property. Only when a developer buys the land use rights (possession) and also buys the building is this category hollowed out because the building no longer embodies individual appropriation of land. In addition, farmers are owners only via their status as lineage members. That means the SCC is the party that negotiates with the developer over the sale of land use rights. This constellation reveals the importance of also considering other modes of having. The villagers were assigned rights to plots during the period of collectivization and may hold these rights even over generations. This assignment has no legal status after nationalization. However, it is still being recognized in the real estate market practices, which bolsters the effect of the incorporation of claims via the buildings.

2. As we have seen in Chapter 3, this category is very important in capitalist economies as it refers to all kinds of proprietors, such as financial institutions, who invest in property titles such as shares only for trading. In Shenzhen, this is limited as far as land is concerned. However, there is the case of "speculation" in the real estate market, that is, the buying and selling of buildings, which indirectly

also implies the control of the land use rights. Moreover, as said, the government can be seen as a proprietor in this sense, without engaging directly in the market, apart from the actions of selling land use rights. The land is unequivocally assigned to the state, which leaves some ambiguity about which state agency is the one who represents the state, which matters in urban planning, such as in the case of conflicting views of district planners and municipal planners or even provincial-level administration concerning the future development of the Greater Bay area. Hence, their assignments are a political process in the first place. Recognition has a role to play, especially when recognizing the claims of SCCs. By assigning land use rights to SCCs, their property is recognized implicitly; however, they are subject to the same political process, given their parafiscal status.

3. In this case, the proprietor is also the manager. Yet, the company has no ownership relation with the object, as it is only market oriented. In Shenzhen, one important example is that SCCs establish separate real estate companies as wholly owned subsidiaries that can operate in a market logic, such as when acquiring property elsewhere. This is highly significant as these companies are legally the property of the SCC as a legal entity, meaning they are no longer held by villagers as shareholders. This allows a shift in possession towards the leadership elite of SCC. We can diagnose this as operating in the mode of appropriation. There are sometimes conflicts with villagers over such measures, as they see their assignments diluted. At the same time, authorities may express recognition because this allows them to proceed with urban development projects more smoothly.

4. This is the case of an agent that acts on behalf of proprietors and owners. For example, an SCC may invest in real estate and maintain land use rights, but it may conclude a service contract with a developer and maintain an arms-length relationship with management afterwards. One consequence of this constellation can be that developers may also stay in close contact with higher-level administrations, thus even sidelining the SCC. This can be analysed as a recognition shift, resulting in reduced parafiscal roles and powers of SCC.

5. Here, the owner is not the proprietor of a title that allows the trade of the object on markets. This is the case when villagers live on the village territory and are owners of the land since they are shareholders of the SCC, with the shares being excluded from markets. However, they are not proprietors of the land. The SCCs that possess land use rights after nationalization might trade them, but they usually do not because this would dilute lineage ownership. This is a question of assignments: In terms of assignments, villagers are owners, but they are not possessors.

6. These owners neither possess an object nor have a legal title that would allow trading it on markets. The typical case is a villager who emigrated but would still be regarded as a member of the village community (hence, would enjoy rights of

inheritance). As said, ritual is an essential medium of such assignments, which obtains appropriative functions: Active participation in rituals implies a claim that the assignment is valid.

7. This is the case when villagers move out of their native territory after redevelopment. Still, the SCC retains the land use rights and agrees with a developer about managing the project after completion. The territory is regarded as ancestral land, which explains why land use rights are kept under SCC control ("absentee ownership").

We will now examine how these various actors create specific patterns and practices in the real estate market in Shenzhen together. The litmus test is the so-called market for "small property."

"Small property" in the Shenzhen real estate market

A peculiar phenomenon in the Shenzhen real estate market is the so-called "small property."[44] Small property emerged as a spontaneous extra-legal contractual form of trading real estate without the land use rights, resulting in a bifurcation of the market into two segments, one the formal market based on clearly defined property arrangements grounded in state ownership of land and user rights be developers, and the other the market without full legal recognition of the contracts because of ill-defined land havings (hence, "small").[45] Given the formal institutions of land ownership in China, no sale of real estate including the land, is legal. There is a wide scope for conflicts: For example, someone buying an apartment might be dispossessed if the underlying transfer of land rights were invalid, even without being aware of this. However, the courts recognize possession. For example, if a small property is pledged, and the possessor of the pledge claims possession, that would not be recognized because there is no title, and hence the pledge is illegal. On the other hand, the original contract that constituted possession is indirectly valid by legally recognizing past possession.[46]

Millions of transactions on the small property market have been successfully concluded in the past three decades, even though no valid title was transferred. The numbers are astounding: In 2020, close to 50 per cent of all housing units in Shenzhen were small property, more than 5 million units without legal property titles, compared to only about 1.9 million units of "commercial housing" with legal titles (other units include factory dormitories or social housing). Demand

44 For an excellent in-depth study, see Qiao 2018.

45 Lai et al. 2017.

46 Qiao 2018, 161 ff.

remains strong since small property housing is traded at a discount compared to commercial housing (which is also explained by quality differences, not just legal risks). The market is highly liquid and operates smoothly.

We overview the structure of the small property market in the two stages of development, the first until the mid-2010s and the second until today.[47] In the first stage (Figure 4.8), we focus on the constellation where villagers possess buildings and sell residential units to buyers who do not earn a legal property title. That is, the small property transaction is a contractual transfer of possession. However, the individual villagers are not possessors of the land on which those units are built. With the nationalization of land, the proprietor is the municipality, which leaves the actual possession of land use rights to the SCC. This act is not simply by administrative fiat but recognizes the ownership of the SCC. Ownership of the SCC matters crucially for the small property market as the SCC is a guarantor for the single transaction, with the individual villagers being its members. This function is at least implicit in the transaction because the SCC has a substantial interest in sustaining the small property market, thus representing a shared interest of all villagers.

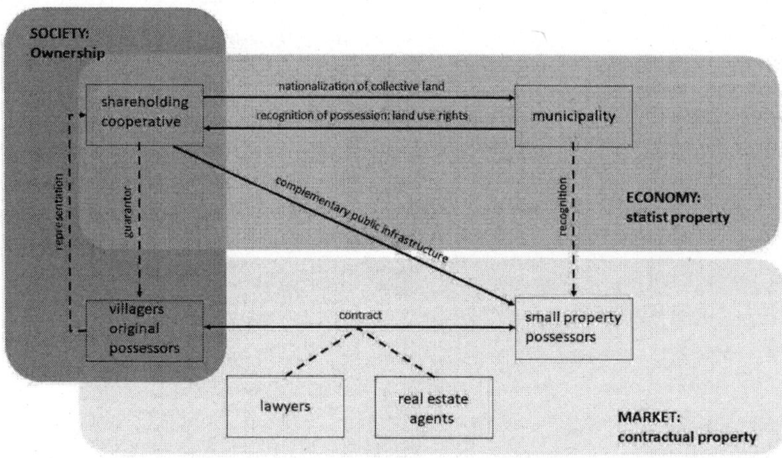

Figure 4.8: First stage of small property development
Source: author's diagram

The small property contract replicates the customary law structure of witnesses and middlemen in contractual possession. The witness is a lawyer who

47 In more detail, see Lai, Wang, and Lok 2017 and Lai, Chan, and Choy 2017.

factually operates as a notary without formal legal validity. Yet, the contract drafted and sealed by the lawyer witnesses that the two parties have agreed on a deal and its terms. The lawyers assume a position of trustworthiness because they depend on keeping a professional reputation and staying in the market. The middleman is primarily the SCC since in the urban villages, even private partners of a deal are SCC members, that is, native villagers. As we saw in the Fenghuang case, in contracts with third parties, the legal partner is the subbranch, whereas the SCC, as such, is a guarantor. This is explicitly recognized in many contract templates of small property transactions, where the SCC confirms the unit's status and registers the contract. In affirming its moral authority as a lineage, the SCC is a guarantor of the trustworthiness even of an individual villager acting as a private agent. Since the community has an interest and the moral obligation to develop its long-term wealth, trust is a crucial asset and is bound to the community.[48] One crucial cultural marker is the emphasis on century-old local traditions, as epitomized in the lineage rules (*jia xun*) setting standards of morality for all members.

Another important observation is that small property transactions are regarded to be legally valid if they are conducted among the members of the village community. This reflects that the underlying ownership relation is still framed in terms of the collective, reminiscent of the "bone" and "skin" distinction: Transactions within the village do not affect the "bone." This interpretation is vindicated by the observation that small property holders may obtain a legal title if the unit becomes a part of a redevelopment project. This defines stage two in the evolution of the small property market (figure 4.9).

In the second stage, the developers emerge as critical actors, manifesting the transition of statist property towards formal marketization. In this structure, the government delegates project planning and implementation to the developers while maintaining governmental control of urban design via approval and monitoring. However, the government does not reclaim ownership from the SCCs; the latter act as the developer's partners, who receive land use rights from the SCC as actual possessors.[49] The developer offers formal property claims to buyers of residential units. This includes recognition of small properties. Suppose a small property building is demolished during the redevelopment of urban villages. In that case, the original possessors of the small property may get compensation, such as a price discount for transferring a new unit with a formal property title to them. That means the original contractual possession based on the transaction

48 Tong et al. 2021.
49 Lai et al. 2023.

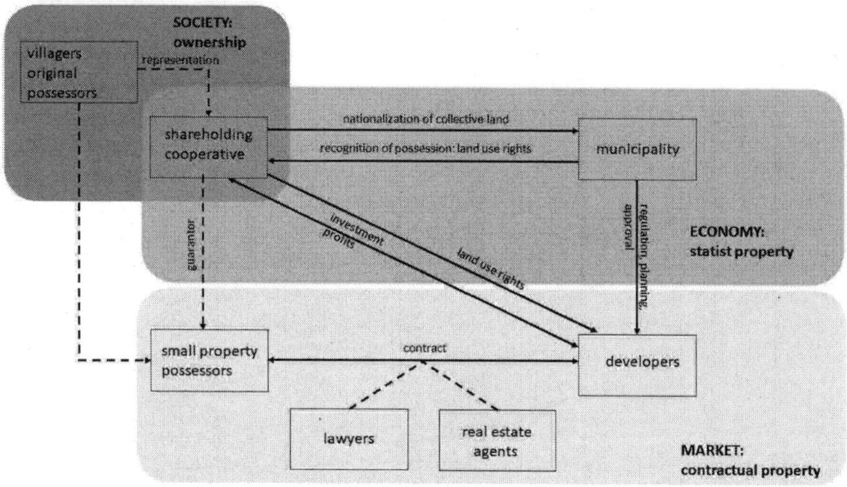

Figure 4.9: Second stage of small property development
Source: author's diagram

between villagers and buyers is transformed into a relationship between the developer and proprietor of an apartment in the new unit.

Ownership no longer matters for sustaining the real estate transaction in this new structure. However, ownership remains recognized in the government, developer, and SCC triangle. Therefore, a paradox emerges in this new form of appropriation: State having enables marketization with formal recognition of non-state property.

A final, though important observation is that the distinction between small property and commercial housing also relates to the differentiation of Shenzhen inhabitants according to household registration *hukou*. This reveals another aspect of statist property. In principle, individuals without *hukou* can also buy commercial housing but must fulfil more stringent conditions than non-*hukou* holders. That means appropriating the more valuable commercial housing is also a marker of social status reminiscent of Imperial China.

Conclusion

The case of Shenzhen shows that the standard concept of "institution" cannot grasp the complex realities of actions of having and their resulting structures of havings. This is even the case if we add the distinction between formal and informal institutions often invoked by institutional economists to explain divergences between formal law and economic realities. In both variants, institutions appear as external determinants of economic phenomena. In contrast, the Aoki-Bourdieu model shows how institutions emerge endogenously by the actions of individuals interacting in what Weber has referred to as "struggle." Further, the Shenzhen case demonstrates that the standard taxonomy of property in economics fails even descriptively: Even though Chinese law concurs with them in distinguishing categories such as private versus state property, we cannot understand practices of having on the ground.

The Aoki-Bourdieu model concurs with economics in approaching the Weberian struggle in terms of strategic interactions between various actors, which is amenable to game theoretic analysis.[50] However, it goes beyond this regarding symbolic capital or signs as endogenously evolving and becoming critical determinants of strategic behavior. Ritual spaces are material manifestations of symbolic capital, and they influence the dispositions and capabilities for action, most importantly, in our case, villagers' collective actions in claiming their havings.[51] The struggle over havings is not only about appropriation but also about recognition and assignment. Even if the government appropriates the land, it may still recognize ownership of villagers and assign land use rights to them: The latter are signs of ownership, not property,

This analysis suggests we cannot easily generalize to different cases, which is well documented in field research. Local contexts matter, and structural outcomes differ. Convergence of outcomes mostly results from a powerful actor enforcing outcomes, mainly the government. We observed this in the history of commons in early modern Europe, and it is salient in China today.

50 For the small property case, see Qiao 2018.
51 A seminal study is Tsai 2007.

Chapter 5: Normative case study – More-than-human having

Beyond the Rights of Nature

This chapter explores the normative consequences of our new theory of having. We concentrate on the simple but radical question of whether we should expand the domain of having to non-humans. In one respect, this is a moot question, as we already do: Legal persons can be subjects of property, and they are only represented by humans, such as the CEOs of listed companies.[1] There is a rich world of human-created non-human entities which are recognized as proprietors. This thinking emerged in the Middle Ages canonical law, reflecting arcane legal debates such as whether the community still owned a monastery once the last monk had passed away. One influential interpretation conceived the buildings as embodying the continuity of the community.[2] Hence, our question needs specification, namely whether we should recognize other species as potential holders of havings. At first sight, this might be resolved by treating each individual living non-human as a legal person: This would imply that there must also be a human representative.[3] As we have seen in Chapter 2, in Indigenous thought, the idea is that a spirit owns each living being. Our question goes further in asking whether other living beings can be treated at par with humans as natural persons with the capacity and the right to have. This includes the radical question of whether other species can express and enact having without human representation.

Conventional thinking denies that right to other species, rooted in the traditions of Abrahamitic religions that treat nature as owned by God, who left it to the use of humans who act as stewards.[4] This created a deep cleavage between humans and nature, making nature an object of human action without autonomous

1 Searle (1995) treats the "free-standing corporation" as an emergent element of social ontology, not merely a linguistic construct.

2 Thomas 2011, 207 ff.

3 There is a small but insightful literature on this question, for example, Hadley 2015, Deckha 2021

4 Vinzent 2024.

agency. The climax of this thinking was Cartesian philosophy, which profoundly shaped Western science in distinguishing between mind (aka soul) and body, with bodies seen as mere mechanisms or machines. Other species only have bodies and are just mechanisms without sentiency or agency. As such, they cannot have havings. More specifically, this refers to the critical role of language in defining humanity since Aristotle. Property and interaction in the property mode require language; therefore, other species cannot make claims or negotiate over property. Does this also mean they cannot claim havings?

This view ties up with the idea maintained in most of human history that some humans may not count as holders of havings, thus reducing them to mere animals. Property has often been seen as separating the domains of civilized humans with superior mental capacities from others who are merely subject to the control of the former. By implication, inferior humans can become the property of superior people, as in the case of appropriating other humans as slaves, denying property to Indigenous people, or subjecting women to male power.[5] Accordingly, we can also present the argument of this chapter as simply continuing with the human rights movement that tore down these distinctions within the human domain, now moving on to other species.[6]

It is important to distinguish my argument from the general case for the Rights of Nature.[7] Rights of Nature include a broader range of rights than rights to having, like human rights, in which a right to having may be only one specific right. However, rights of nature may not necessarily include rights to having insofar as nature is not necessarily individualized. This difference is well-known from animal rights debates:[8] For example, the Rights of Nature may allow humans to intervene, say, against an invading species, which is seen as destabilizing or even destroying an ecosystem. If animals have individual rights, eradicating such an invasive species may be seen as violating their individual rights to life. Rights of havings are such individual rights, just as in the human case. Interestingly, this would suggest a different solution to the issue of invasive alien species: If we treated the incumbent species as having the resources of their habitat, the invasive alien species would commit theft, which would call for policing.

A Right of Nature may mean to lift existing regulations of nature protection to a constitutional status. For example, a law on natural reserves is implemented via regulatory measures that can be changed according to policy preferences. If, say,

5 Möllers 2024. The independent agency of those "subhuman" beings was hence seen as threatening and demonic, manifest in phenomena such as the late medieval witch-hunts, Federici 2021.

6 Singer and Harari 2023.

7 Boyd 2017, Knauß 2018, Chapron, Epstein, and López-Bao 2019.

8 Hadley 2015, 7.

a valuable mineral resource is discovered, the government may decide to change policy and withdraw the status of a natural reserve to a particular territory. Today, this may be alleviated by regulations on ecocompensation, such as creating a natural reserve somewhere else.[9] In contrast, if this regime becomes protected as a constitutional right, this policy change would be much more constrained, as the natural reserve would be constitutionally protected. Yet, ecocompensation may still be judged to conform to the Constitution. The situation is radically different in the case of recognizing the havings of other species. First, in the nature reserve, all living entities would have rights as proprietors of the land, so a policy change would require applying eminent domain with adequate compensation.[10] This is open to be challenged at the courts and raises questions about adequate compensation. For example, we cannot pay the birds to let them buy nesting places elsewhere. Second, even more radically, the idea of a nature reserve becomes meaningless since all territory is at least co-owned by other species (even downtown urban areas).[11] As we will see, more-than-human having implies enforcing a regime of multi-species co-habitation on humans.

In this sense, especially regarding the economy, assigning havings to other species has many more consequences than a general Right of Nature. The setting is the same as in the case of European colonization if we consider land. The land was declared *terra nullius* as no havings of indigenous people were recognized. Similarly, nature *in toto* is treated as *terra nullius* and, hence, can be freely appropriated by humans. Hence, the first question is how far we must recognize existing havings of other species, beyond ourselves assigning these to them. This radically transcends the Hegelian view on property we took as a beacon in Chapter 3. For Hegel, the exclusive right to property, or havings in our new terminology, defines humanity in terms of freedom. Only humans can be free; therefore, other species would be excluded from Hegelian property. Therefore, the question of havings has the radical dimension of discarding an anthropocentric metaphysics and opting for a biocentric ontology of life.[12]

In this chapter, I focus on land as having because this is the universal resource that all life needs if we include water, that is, treat land as the surface of planet Earth. This notion of the surface is not the same as the abstraction of mapping but relates to the idea that all life on Earth ultimately relies on sunlight that ar-

9 Gastineau, Mossay, and Taugourdeau 2021, Wang et al. 2022.

10 Bradshaw 2020, 55 ff.

11 This fact is salient in the recent initiatives of "rewilding" cities; Apfelbeck et al. 2020, World Economic Forum 2022.

12 Modern philosophers often maintain the view of German idealism in regard to freedom as the essence of being human, even when arguing in favor of nature's property; Wesche 2023.

rives at the surface and is processed by plant photosynthesis.[13] Heterotroph organisms rely on plants and add spatial complexity to this system via their forms of mobility and interaction. However, their living would ultimately be constrained by the net primary production of a particular area that results from photosynthesis. This measure is also employed to assess the human appropriation of nature, as the claim on the surface reduces the photosynthetic productivity of an area. On the other hand, land is also a critical resource in the human economy. Moreover, land has been the theme in many controversies over property, with many economists arguing that this should be exempt from private property. Therefore, land is a topic that is highly suggestive when discussing recognizing havings of non-human living beings.

Debunking speciesism in possession

The starting point, quite obviously, is possession. This ties up with the reverse argument of naturalizing human havings. This means interpreting the territoriality of other species as a proto-property without the accompanying human institutions.[14] The argument works in both directions, naturalizing human property and rendering territoriality in economic terms as a property right. This view can be grounded in simple game-theoretic models that have been aptly dubbed the "strategy of bourgeois:" In a conflict over a resource, an incumbent and an attacker may fight, however, at a cost to both.[15] Since the capacities may be uncertain, one winning strategy for both is to respect the incumbent's rights to the territory, provided that the incumbent signals a readiness to fight. This means that fights are often ritualized within a species without actual fatal damage. We can modify such scenarios by assuming that the incumbent is more willing to fight, perhaps motivated by an endowment effect. The upshot is that claims to territories, though always disputed, are generally recognized in a state of nature. This is a regime of mutually recognized possession.

In terms of the powers of disposition framework, natural possession can therefore be defined in the basic modes of recognition and possession, with appropriation most salient in efforts to overcoming an incumbents' resistance against invaders (Figure 5.1). However, can we treat possession as a "right?" This

13 This is reflected in various approaches to measuring the human impact on planet Earth, such as HANPP (human appropriation of net primary production); Krausmann et al. 2013; Jenkins et al. 2020.

14 Bradshaw 2020, 45 ff.

15 Gintis 2007.

depends on how we judge animal communication compared to human language. Obviously, if possession is also recognized by humans, this becomes a right. Hence, some forms of nature protection, such as blocking humans from disturbing nesting sites of birds, can be considered as recognizing animal havings. This enacts the assignment mode: Humans assign possession to an animal, such as the nesting site, to a protected bird.

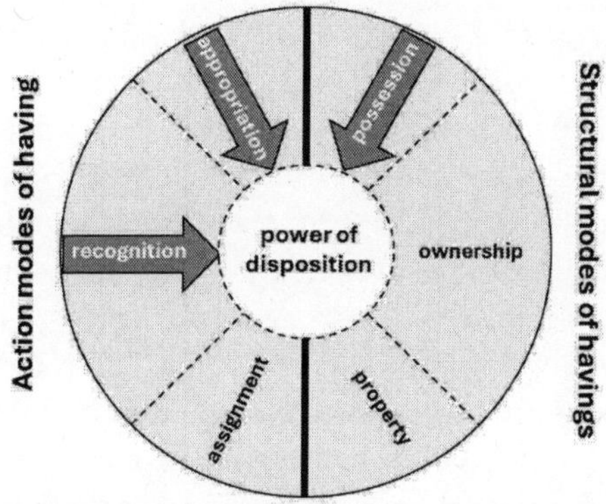

Figure 5.1: Possession in nature
Source: author's diagram

Considering whether natural possession can and must be recognized by humans, it is helpful to go back to the debate over *animus* in 19th-century jurisprudence that we already met in Chapter 3. According to the opinion that possession is merely indicated by factual use and occupation, it is straightforward to recognize possession of all other species: The earthworm possesses the piece of soil where it dwells. Immediately, we see that this would imply that regarding one surface area, millions of living beings possess this, below, on and above the surface. We can say that all members of an ecosystem co-possess the surface.

This raises the question of whether we only include living entities as possessors. This is an important issue since the Rights of Nature are often interpreted as implicating the rights of non-living natural entities, such as mountains and rivers.[16] Such extensions are problematic because they even widen the net to include all physical structures on Earth. Singling out a specific river and no other

16 The Cyrus R. Vance Center 2020.

structures seems arbitrary and is primarily grounded in certain human beliefs about spiritual meanings.[17] However, if we treat the ecosystem as a system of co-possessors, we only need to consider distributed agency in including non-living entities, though in relation to all other living entities, including humans. For example, salmons possess a spawning ground; hence, the river is also constitutive of their agency, so we can include it in the system of co-possession.[18] The same applies to humans, including their spirituality. In sum, we regard the ecosystem as an assemblage of living and non-living entities. Still, drawing the line between the living and the non-living entities remains a critical issue in specifying the structure of havings, since we cannot reduce the land to an abstract mapping.[19] The non-living entities often play a crucial role in defining the boundaries of ecosystems or structuring the accessibility of specific resources.

The notion of possession also motivates rethinking Locke's reasoning. This employs a speciesist definition of labor in treating only human labor as a source of property. Labor is linked to the notion of human personhood and the related idea of intentionality. However, we can also treat labor as a physical process driven by elementary forms of autonomous agency (often denoted as "work").[20] An autonomous agency is universally defined as a system which employs physical labor to sustain its capacity to generate labor. All forms of goal-directed behavior count as an autonomous agency, including the simplest bacteria. Hence, Locke's argument also applies to the earthworm that spends physical labor and transforms the soil for its benefit and even for the tiller's benefit. Consequently, there is no difference between the tiller's Lockean claim on the land, based on his labor, and recognizing the earthworm's claim to possession: Tiller and earthworm are co-possessors of the land because they both transform the soil by expending physical work in a goal-directed process to sustain their ways of living.

Locke's speciesism may be defended along the *animus* school of thought: The earthworm does not express its claim. This means that physical occupation and labor do not suffice to establish possession. However, *animus* is implied in communication, even in the simple Hawk-and-dove game where signalling establishes incumbents' claims. Animal territoriality is rich in all kinds of communication that may not act *erga omnes*, but at least towards con-specific rivals (after all, *erga omnes* also addresses humans only). This is *animus* in possession, even without human forms of intentionality. In fact, the reach of this argument is broad as it may include all kinds of chemical signals, such as pheromones. In this case, the hu-

17 Wesche 2023, 188 ff.

18 White 2001 is a fascinating case study of such issues.

19 Povinelli 2016.

20 Kauffman 2000, Kolchinsky and Wolpert 2018.

man / non-human borderline may be drawn, depending on whether the signals are intentionally sent or if they are just left without intention. These are tricky questions, but we may conclude that even if we restrict the reach of *animus* to intentional signalling, this will legitimize possession for many other species. The Lockean tiller must share possession with them.

However, we must raise doubts about this interpretation of possession. There are different interpretations of territorial behaviour.[21] The discussion so far suggests the interpretation in terms of exclusive claims, in the sense of human property. But this is highly misleading since animal territoriality is not exclusive, cross-species anyway, but even intra-species. Interpreting animal behavior as "bourgeois" human-like is grossly misinterpreting animal signalling. For example, dogs leave scent markers to indicate their presence but not to exclude others. The scent markers are a form of messaging and storytelling, hence much more complex than mere territorial marking.[22] The same applies to birdsong, which allows for many forms of conviviality, even intra-species (for example, there are forms of hospitality). This would imply that evolution has fostered the emergence of regimes of co-possession as co-habitation, which are embodied in the species-specific signalling systems. Comparing territoriality with human exclusive property is utterly misleading. Hence, we must also discard naturalistic property explanations as staying in continuity with non-human behavior. Exclusive property is a recent cultural creation independent of any biological roots.[23]

The triad of modes of having can grasp these differences. The previous argument suggests that animal signalling does not necessarily imply the appropriative mode, as game theory assumes. We can interpret birdsong as a conversation about assignments and their recognition. An animal assigns a territory recognized by others, but it does not appropriate the territory, only certain benefits that accrue from staying there, such as food resources. There are different forms of possession, such as more exclusive ones directed at valuable items in the territory and more inclusive ones, such as recognizing co-possession.

21 Despret 2019.
22 Gibson (2021, 106 ff) is an extensive discussion about the deep flaws in equating territory with property.
23 Widerquist and McCall (2021, 188 ff) agree.

Evolutionary ownership

We can further develop this view in considering ownership. The argument on animal territoriality as a system of communication that signals co-habitation in the ecosystem could also be interpreted in terms of ownership. The conventional assumption on human possession is that the human alters the object, such as the land, and therefore appropriates it without changing her own nature. However, a strand in property debates also supposes that property has a transformative effect on its holder.[24] This is salient in the civilizing aspects of property, which, for example, is seen as fostering attitudes of tending to or handling the property adequately. The Hegelian view radicalizes these ideas in stating that without property, the individual cannot adequately express herself and thereby transform herself spiritually. The question is whether we can interpret more-than-human having along Hegelian lines. If this can be shown, we can extend the notion of ownership to other species.

This is a complex question that I cannot fully deal with here. The key is how we interpret evolution, as often the argument is made that non-human behavior is genetically determined due to selection.[25] In contrast, human behavior is mainly shaped by culture, which implies a fundamental difference regarding having as a cultural practice. However, the argument of selection also goes the other way around as it is radically externalist: If the environment determines the properties of an organism, this will count as ownership in the sense that the organism's identity is determined by what the organism disposes of.[26] The relationship between organism and environment is fundamentally bi-directional: The organism disposes of environmental resources for its survival, and these resources also constitute the environment that selects the organism.[27] In other words, we cannot just consider this relationship at a certain point when both appear to be fixed and unrelated beyond the appropriative actions of the organism. In the evolutionary dimension, this must be reversed, even in the sense that the organism is "owned" by the environment. This corresponds to the Hegelian view that the transformative effects of property are developmental since the spirit unfolds through time.

24 John Stuart Mill was a famous advocate, see Möllers 2024.

25 My position is systematically developed in Herrmann-Pillath 2013 and overviewed in Herrmann-Pillath and Hederer 2023.

26 This reversal of perspectives has been one of the critical issues in the philosophy of biology over the past decades; classics include Oyama 2000. These debates have been motivated by the question of how the notion of biological information makes sense across supposed divides such as nature versus culture.

27 This has been elaborated in theories of niche construction, Odling-Smee, Laland, and Feldman 2003. Niche construction theory has also been extended to human culture; Spengler 2021; Kendal, Tehrani, and Odling-Smee 2011.

However, I do not further pursue this line here as this would still tend towards naïve Darwinian selectionism. If we follow genuinely interactionist paradigms such as Evodevo and co-evolutionary theories of non-genetic inheritance, the Hegelian interpretation becomes even stronger. Clear cases include the evolution of animal cultures, such as distinguishing between the genetic capacity for birdsong or nest-building and the cultural tradition of specific expressions in bird populations assigned to a specific territory. In these cases, we can speak of ownership in the same sense as Indigenous conceptions of land ownership, that is, as a relational phenomenon. The cultural tradition of birdsong expresses the mutual belonging of organisms and land. Against the Hegelian claim that only humans can be free, this mutual belonging includes the freedom of agency in creating cultures of belonging.[28]

A crucial point is that all organisms relate to land via their relationship with all other organisms living there. In the ecosystem, even the top predators have evolved in a way that sustains the entire community. Here, the topic of invasive alien species is highly relevant since they are unrelated to all the other species in the ecosystem and fall back on a simple appropriative mode akin to theft. Again, the evolutionary trajectory is what counts: Since the aliens are not part of the shared evolutionary history of the community, they act in a dysfunctional way, even to the extent of destroying the community. In contrast, this reveals that the ecosystem members have ownership of the land, which translates into a multiplicity of territories. In a sense, the invasive alien species aggressively monopolizes the territory, whereas the community manifests the coexistence of many territories in one spatial segment. This is the essence of cohabitation.[29]

This argument is also of great significance for human property. Colonization of non-European territories was always accompanied by humans carrying invasive alien species, such as rats or bacteria. For the colonizers, the *terra nullius* of North America seemed to be a reality, facing the thin population density. However, this was only the consequence of disastrous epidemics carried over by the colonists, even themselves, a tiny group initially. But the invasive alien species spread rapidly, advancing the forward march of the humans. Hence, humans and non-humans were both invasive alien species drastically affecting the human-shaped ecosystems of North America, also via indirect effects since humans acted as top predators before the Europeans arrived. With the elimination of a large share of the native population, their regulatory ecological functions also crumbled. Accordingly, we can interpret Indigenous land ownership in the same evo-

28 Prum 2017. An influential approach to integrating evolution and culture is Jablonka, Lamb, and Zeligowski 2014.

29 Vanuxem 2022, 63 ff.

lutionary framework as non-human ownership: Territory and human ways of life were mutually adapted and sustained the larger ecosystems. This synergy was destroyed by human colonization and the invasive alien species accompanying the humans.[30]

This discussion concludes that we can even speak of mutual ownership in the ecosystem, along the lines of the Hegelian idea of marriage, that is, a relationship of belonging. Even the top predator is not the ultimate holder of the ecosystem but is also "owned" by the prey in that its actions contribute to the ecosystem's healthy functioning and sustain the prey population. The predator that kills a prey possesses it, which is embedded in the larger system of mutual belongings mediated via the ecosystem. In this sense, as in Figure 5.2, we can now conceptualize more-than-human having as being constituted by the structural modes of possession and ownership. Recognition is the dominant mode, now including multispecies cultures. Appropriation is regulated by recognition mechanisms and becomes dysfunctional in the case of invasive alien species.

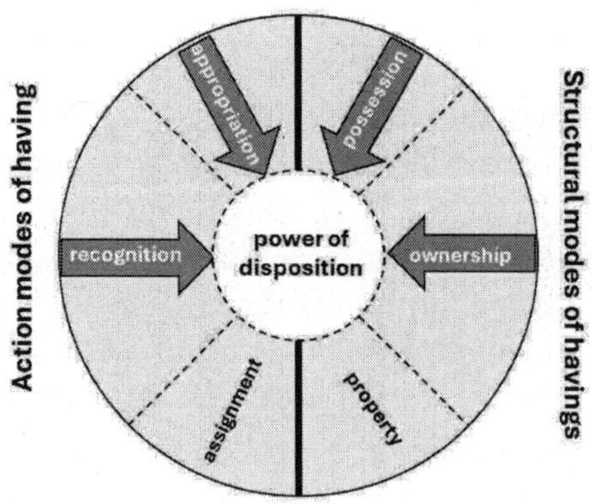

Figure 5.2: Ecosystem having
Source: author's diagram

In conclusion, we may argue that the ultimate subject of ownership is not the individual organism but the ecosystem. This view corresponds to the analysis of

30 In a fascinating study of West Papua, Chao (2022) shows how the oil palm plantations can be interpreted as invading assemblages of humans and palms that jointly destroy the local ecosystems of human-non-human co-habitation, implying that the invasive plant has agency of its own. Indeed, this is how the Indigenous people perceive the oil palm in their spirituality.

the commons. In the commons, the community is the owner, and members have possession rights. This generalizes another aspect of the Hegelian view, in this case, and German idealism in general, namely, that the community creates havings that sustain the community. This deep connection between havings and community becomes only visible when we consider the processes in time that led to such a constellation, which is history in the case of humans specifically, and evolution for all living beings.

4. More-than-human property

So far, the debate on animal havings has chiefly considered property in the conventional meaning.[31] This would imply that living beings may hold property titles, which requires recognizing them as legal subjects. This question has been widely discussed in the broader context of whether animals have individual rights.[32] Considering the cases of humans deemed incapable of exerting rights, such as very young children, the general view is that lack of capacity does not mean that these persons are denied the rights but that a caretaker exerts these rights until maturity. The only criterion for having rights would be that the individuals have a certain status defined by sentience and a capacity for autonomous action. Sentience is essential for judging whether denying a right involves suffering since having a right can be seen as a form of protecting an individual from harm.[33] Autonomy means that a right gives a secure space for action. These two understandings have much in common with negative and positive freedom ideas. Negative freedom means that someone else cannot interfere with my life, such that I suffer restriction, damage or another negative effect. Positive freedom is about my capacity to take autonomous action.

Until today, the notion of freedom has often been normatively restricted to humans. However, if we substitute this notion with the conceptual pair of sentience and autonomy, we can expand its reach considerably. The animal rights literature has thoroughly explored the issue of sentience, as this defines the capacity for suffering. The critical question is whether suffering must be considered an internal state defined by feelings and presupposes a sort of consciousness, at least in emergent forms. This revives the Cartesian distinction between mind and matter since nociceptive behavior would be excluded from sentience as it is seen as a

---

31 Hadley 2015, Bradshaw 2020.

32 Deckha 2021.

33 Singer and Harari 2023, 5 ff. Then argument was first formulated by Bentham.

mere mechanic reaction. Nociceptive behavior is universal since evolution selects all behaviors that avoid damage. In contrast, sentience is about *feeling* pain. Even if one accepts this distinction, the domain of sentience has been expanding considerably in recent decades.[34]

The dimension of autonomy shows a similar conceptual quandary. We have already noticed that from the general physical point of view, all living systems are autonomous agents. They endogenously generate goals, maintain boundaries to the environment, and determine actions within certain degrees of freedom to sustain and reproduce. Hence, we meet the same problem: freedom refers to some distinct human quality of reflection and higher-level consciousness that would distinguish this from autonomy in general. Research has been advancing speedily in this field and has recognized forms of consciousness that are different from humans but still have similar behavioral expressions.[35] For example, octopuses are curious and playful and make jokes with humans. Yet, almost certainly, their inner world is alien to ours.[36] In other words, we need to distinguish between human forms of consciousness and non-human forms, which undermines any case of human exceptionality.

The upshot of this brief discussion of a very complex field is that the distinction between humans and non-humans can certainly not be made in a principled way and depends on normative judgements of empirical data, which are constantly changing, but clearly show a direction, which is expanding the "human-likeness" to ever wider circles. For our argument, this means that we should avoid any border-drawing propositions if we aim at generalization. However, the apparent consequence is practically problematic as it would mean that barring future progress of science, we must recognize the status of legal beings to all forms of life.

This differs from many positions in the literature on animal property, mainly concentrating on higher animals such as mammals. But this reproduces speciesism within the non-human domain. If we accept the more comprehensive view, this has discomforting consequences for humans. The most significant is that a fundamental philosophical belief is shattered, namely that our body belongs to us.[37] If we accept the scientific fact that humans are holobionts, that is, that the body is at the same time the host of many other species, foremostly in the gut, then we must conclude that the body is co-possessed by those other species: The intestinal tract is the "land" possessed by the bacteria living in it, technically a holobiome.[38] Interestingly, this restates aspects of Indigenous spirituality in

34 Godfrey-Smith 2020.
35 Andrews and Monsó 2021; Bridle 2022.
36 Godfrey-Smith 2017.
37 Waldron 2023.
38 Yong 2017.

which humans connect with spirits, and after all, the word "possession" also refers to being "possessed" by spirits. Today, we know that our states of consciousness depend very much on the life inside the gut, as recognized in the term "gut feelings," without knowing the facts behind it. Even the notion of personhood is, therefore, an ecological construct. "We" are not just "us" but also "them" inside us.

We can add the essential role of the immune system in defining and protecting the boundary between the holobiont and the environment, in this case, specifically, any other entities that would aim at appropriating the body. This is analytically similar to invasive alien species in ecosystems, as a virus infecting a body invades the holobiont as having an inner ecosystem, the holobiome. We discussed the case of eradicating native populations by the colonists' introduction of unknown disease carriers. There is a match between the outer ecosystem and the inner immune system, and the immune systems of native people could not withstand the invasion of alien germs.

Moreover, another related discussion is about the relationship between free will and the brain.[39] Suppose neuroscience shows that our action is determined mainly by neurobiological processes that unfold before we are conscious of our decisions. In that case, this may lead to the conclusion that "we" do not own ourselves in the sense of the autonomous moral and mental domain in which we perceive ourselves as free actors. We also cannot simply identify the brain as the alternative locus, in the sense that the brain owns us, as the boundaries between brain and body are ill-defined.[40] After all, many holobiont processes affect the brain. On the other hand, if we ask for the ultimate source of our sense of identity, many scholars suggest that these emerge from socialization and acculturation, thus deeply embedding our individuality in sociality to the degree that contra our internal complexity, our feeling of being a unified actor is the consequence of being externally assigned as such.[41] There is a highly significant parallel to the discussion of property in relation to the community: Our status as an individual and free actor does not express our inner nature but is assigned to us in relation to the social system for which this status is critical to organize cooperation and coexistence.

This discussion shows the way out of the analytical dilemmas we have encountered. Suppose even the human person cannot be considered a unified actor but an ecological assemblage. In that case, this implies that we can generalize the treatment of ecological assemblages as the primordial forms of legal subjects in the theory of havings.

---

39 For a comprehensive discussion, see the contributions in Ross et al. 2007.

40 Jasanoff 2018.

41 Bogdan 2010; Damasio 2010. Zawidzki 2013 refers to this process as "mindshaping."

Here, the distinction between the modes of having is productive. Consider the relationship between the bacteria in the intestinal tract and what we experience as our personal identity. In learning about my nature as a holobiont, I can recognize these bacteria as co-possessing what I experience as my body. However, this does not necessarily mean that I also recognize them as having the car I drive. Humans agree with me in assigning possession of the car to me as a holobiont, thus transforming myself into a legal subject. I would immediately stop being capable of any action if I started to figure out how I could agree with the co-possessors of my body about my actions. Yet, I could recognize ownership of the holobiont that I am as different from property of the legal subject I am assigned to.

This is a Hegelian perspective in that the individual is now conceptualized as an emergent entity where two movements play together. The original Hegelian view only recognized the interaction between the individual and the social environment, in the sense that individual freedom cannot be taken as a given but only emerges in a community; hence, it is an emergent property of this interaction. The Hegelian view is ecological, in other words. We can now add the deconstruction of the individual as holobiont. The result is dismantling the long tradition of possessive individualism in Western thought, with the ecological self as the locus of distributed agency of having.[42] This is salient if we return to considering the modes of havings in relation to the mode of appropriation. That means we ask how individuals are being appropriated and thereby constituted as agents of havings.

Let us detail this argument in terms of modes of havings (Figure 5.3).

1. This area defines the classical notion of the person as a legal subject. The person owns herself, and this is also implied by being the subject of property. Moreover, the person is also in complete control of herself; that is, she possesses herself. This is the free person. However, we can introduce modifications according to the action modes of having. As said, the legal subject is effectively emerging from assignment and recognition by society, which differs from the idea of natural rights. Similarly, there may be a recognition that sometimes persons do not fully possess themselves, such as in states of rage, which would modify responsibility assignments.

2. This area is the case when individuals are exclusively legal persons. As we consider natural persons here, these are liminal cases. For example, in debates about abortion, it is by legal assignment whether embryos below a certain age are recognized as persons. This stands in tension with the possible claim of possession by mothers since the embryo is a part of their body, such as connected to the

42 Anthropologists have coined the notion of "dividual" self that Chao (2022) extends beyond the human / non-human divide.

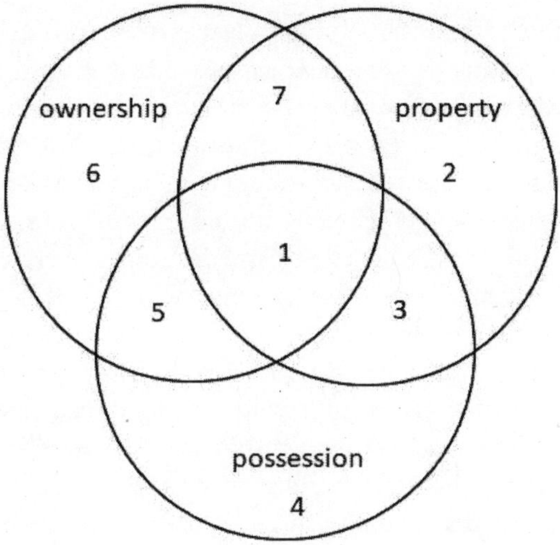

Figure 5.3: Structual modes of havings and the constitution of agents
Source: author's diagram

mother's blood circulation. However, the embryo could also be treated as another member of the holobiont. Then, it is an empirical issue when the criteria of sentience and autonomy apply to the embryo.

3. Continuing with the embryo example, the mother can be seen as a possessor and has full rights of property, so in the case of abortion, the mother solely would have the right to decide. We can also subsume cases of certain mental disorders here, as such individuals certainly possess their bodies and may be recognized, therefore, as having property. However, they still do not fully own it, lacking a unified identity.

4. Mere possession applies to cases when individuals with limited mental capacities would also be denied rights. This includes cases such as possession of the body by other human agents, say, treating a person in a coma with no expectation of return to consciousness as a mere organism and possibly turning off life support systems. Possession also applies to holobiont members as long as we do not assign rights to them. In contrast, ownership is a complex issue as holobiont members interact in constituting the person.

5. The case against slavery is the classic case of combining ownership with possession while denying rights as property of the body. This also applies to body parts: In most countries, even though we own and possess our body parts, we have

no right to trade them in the marketplace. Similarly, we do not have the right to sell ourselves into slavery.

6. Ownership without possession and property is another rare liminal case. One scenario is that a paraplegic person would be denied rights, for example, if also mentally incapacitated or just for any other reason. Another scenario is a state of intoxication where an individual is dispossessed of herself, and this is also recognized as losing property, in this case, for example, losing full legal responsibility for one's actions. Yet, ownership of the body is still being recognized.

7. In contrast, this area defines a state of intoxication which retains full legal responsibility by assignment.

When confronting human property with non-human property, we can conclude that only calling for a straw man justifies denying property to other species, as the constellation of human agency of having is complex and shows the same plurality as that of non-humans. We can identify a similar constellation of modes for humans as for other species and, therefore, adopt a parallelism in the ecological perspective. The critical insight of this discussion is that ownership is not necessarily linked to the idea of a unified natural person but to assemblages involving both internal and external entities. Ownership is an emergent phenomenon that essentially consists of the formation of identity. That means, in the same way as we can deconstruct humans as holobionts and can nevertheless treat ownership as an emergent feature of that holobiont, for example, biologically manifest in the individuality of the immune system, we can also speak of ownership of an ecosystem on a higher systemic level.

Next, property is a matter of assignment and recognition and plays an essential role in creating the status of an actor in the Hegelian sense. We do not assign property to the holobiont members but to the human individual. In this sense, property defines the human person as the steward of the holobiont. Since property involves specifically human phenomena such as language, all non-human havings may or may not include this property assignment. As we will see, ecosystem ownership may be recognized by assigning property to the ecosystem. Finally, co-possession is a universal phenomenon on all levels, involving synergistic co-habitation. In sum, the concept of havings is profoundly relational across ontological levels, resulting in a specific institutional design of property: The universal commons.

5. The universal commons

I will now claim that the constellation of havings that adequately reflects the previous insights is the commons as the fundamental form of relational having. That means I regard the commons as the alternative to "private property" as commonly understood, hence the "universal commons."[43] I approach the commons in economics inspired by Elinor Ostrom's views but radically extending the concept's reach.[44] In this exposition, I concentrate on land havings, which are also salient in Ostrom's work. Still, the concept applies to all other kinds of resources, if only because all of them are spatially located.[45] In general, a commons is a regime of co-possession where the community is the owner and property is assigned to the community but can be divided into possession rights assigned to members of the commons and thereby may even turn certain forms of possession into partial property rights. That is, the commons has layers of possession, and the relationship between different possessors is regulated on the commons level, thus constituting a regime of co-possession. In human commons, this regulation is a political process resulting from negotiations and deliberations among the community members.

For example, in many human societies, forests have been conceived as commons, meaning that the community who lives there has ownership of the forest and no single individuals. Whether property is also assigned to the community is a question of recognition. Many communities would not even assign property to the community, treating the commons as inalienable.[46] However, as in Europe and elsewhere, political bodies may even forcefully assign property to the community and legally recognize that, thereby enabling communities to alienate its ownership.[47] The commons recognize possession of members, such as traditional use rights of members, or may employ a regular procedure of assigning such rights to members. This is co-possession as these assignments consider preserving the joint ownership, such as imposing limitations to logging to keep the forest sus-

---

43 Herrmann-Pillath 2023. An important difference is the treatment of ownership, where Ostrom basically follows the economics literature on property rights. Ownership as inalienable havings eschews this view and is hence compatible with the anthropological critique of the economics notion of commons; Wagner and Talakai 2007.

44 Ostrom 2015.

45 This relates to the literature on "commoning" that explores the performative powers of having; for example, Helfrich and Euler 2021, Micken and Moldenhauer 2021. "Commoning" endogenizes having in the same way as "private property" is reflexive and performative, implying that, in principle, any object can become a commons.

46 As we have seen, in Indigenous views, the commons are the property of spiritual entities, with chiefs only representing them; Brightman, Fausto, and Grotti 2016.

47 De Moor 2018.

tainable. The commons may also assign property rights to members, such as allowing for logging and selling the harvest on the market.

However, this concept of commons focuses on humans only. The critical turn in my argument is that the ecosystem is the owner of the commons, or the ecosystem is the commons. So, the forest is the owner, not the humans, who are only members of the forest, among many other species. The forest is not just the assemblage of trees but the assemblage of all living beings cohabitating in the forest. Accordingly, all members, human and non-human, have possession of parts of the forest, which is relational, as the interaction between its members defines the forest.[48]

A significant consequence of this view is that the forest is necessarily inalienable via property, or the ecosystem cannot become proprietor, with a caveat, as we will see soon. It is physically impossible to move an ecosystem to another place or to substitute all members of an ecosystem with another ecosystem's members who would acquire the ecosystem. This is different in the case of human commons, where, in principle, it is possible that the human community, who is the proprietor of the forest, sells it completely and collectively moves to another place as long as this property is not conceptualized as relational, hence excluding all other species from the property. However, selling the forest is impossible for all the other ecosystem members. This is practically relevant when considering the Amazonia rainforest: Humans may appropriate part of the forest for agriculture, but this means destruction, as one cannot move it elsewhere or recreate it. This fact renders ecocompensation schemes meaningless, too, as these cannot compensate for the losses of all ecosystem members.

This constellation has an equivalent in human law, which is the endowment or the trust, depending on the legal regime, especially in forms today mostly outlawed as the "dead hand." Therefore, we can distinguish between those forms of property which allow for alienation and the trust as the form that translates ownership into a legal construct by which the ecosystem commons becomes a legal person.[49] Trusts count as a form of property, so modifying our previous conclusion that the ecosystem cannot become property. Yet, the trust is a special form as it drives a perpetual wedge between ownership, possession and property.[50] It makes the underlying property object inaccessible to appropriation by any of the three parties: the owners, the possessors, and the proprietors.

48 For a fascinating account of forests as more-than-human communities, see Kohn 2013.

49 Bradshaw 2020 develops this legal view in detail.

50 The trust is a legal form peculiar to common law, reflecting its feudal roots, and has been the topic of debates in jurisprudence for more than a century since it is not easily compatible with civil law, Braun 2017.

The trust is the legal interface between the ecosystem and the human society, economy and politics as distinctly human institutions. This interface function requires representation of the trust by humans as trustees. The legal form of trustee is already applied on animal property, such as when humans designate pets as heirs.[51] This raises the question of how the trustee can adequately pursue the interests of the ecosystem community. There are two ways. Strict legal criteria define trusteeship, and the interests of the ecosystem community can be specified based on the relevant scientific knowledge about the needs of ecosystem members, most generally as the conditions of shared flourishing. This also allows for adequate regulation and supervision of trusts by government bodies and civil society. The model can be detailed in many ways, such as defining professional standards and codes of conduct for trustees. The alternative is installing a democratic procedure, as in the case of human commons. I come back on this below.

Even if the more-than-human commons are inalienable, this does not preclude assigning property rights and possession to members. The "tragedy of the commons" scenario refers to the mode of appropriation only, assuming there are no constraints on individual behavior. In contrast, the Ostrom model builds on the mode of assignment first. This means recognizing possession, such as in the human case, recognizing the traditional claims of members. The same applies to the ecosystem commons in terms of recognizing specific sustainable use patterns of its members. However, I emphasize that this does not mean that property rights are assigned to parts of the underlying object of ownership cast into the legal form of trust, but only to benefits physically linked to it, in the sense of *usus* and *fructus*.

If we consider land, we must conclude that the universal form of commons cannot be human-only as the land is co-possessed unless all other ecosystem members are eradicated. For example, an airfield may be seen as a human-only possession, but even here, the effort is necessary to keep the land "clean" from other plants invading its most minor cracks and holes, accompanied by insects, which will attract predators such as birds, and so forth. If we consider an ecosystem in general, the commons will require that if humans plan to use land for their purposes, they must negotiate with co-possessors. The most general expression of this is applying a principle of reciprocity among all members. This seems to approach the idea of ecocompensation but is much narrower because reciprocity would be constrained to the internal relations in the commons.[52]

The question is how a commons can establish a regulatory process engaging humans and other species in reciprocity. The human commons is based on the

51 Deckha 2021,

52 Herrmann-Pillath 2024. Financial ecocompensation would not be feasible unless humans invest locally in the interest of the incumbent species.

principle of democracy and a deliberative process mediated by language, with the classical *agora* model in the polis. This seems to exclude other species. As argued above for the external relations of the ecosystem commons, this would favor an expert-based internal regulation with humans as stewards who represent the members politically. This differs from assigning property but applies the same model. Beyond possession, property rights would also require linguistic communication. That means one approach is establishing a structure of internal trusteeships representing certain ecosystem members. The advantage of this model is that there can be collective representation. For example, an internal trustee may represent the shrimps if the ecosystem commons is a Wadden Sea coastal area. This would apply to both the internal process and property assignments. As in the case of the commons trustee in external relations, internal trustees may be selected according to specific standards, such as familiarity with the area and the species they represent, scientific expertise, etc.

There is another, more radical way to establish a democratic procedure.[53] The conventional idea of democracy is about a procedure of collective decision-making.[54] Alternative conceptions define democracy in a broader sense, starting from the political body as social cooperation and a learning community.[55] Moreover, deliberation emphasizes speaking. If we equally emphasize listening and the adequate action taken as a response, then human language loses its special status. In contrast, we can include all kinds of expressive behavior as amenable to listening, understanding and responding. For example, suppose humans expropriate a forest community and endanger the survival of certain mammals that need a habitat of a minimal size. In that case, these animals may start approaching human settlements despite their natural tendency to avoid humans. Humans can interpret this action as a sign, equivalent to speech, and listen in the sense of recognizing the reasons for this behavior. They would not see this as appropriating human territory but realize that this action is a response to human appropriation of forest territory. They can now respond. One response is just shooting the intruders to protect human property. In contrast, in the ecosystem commons, the basic principle is cooperation; hence, humans would respond by restraining their activities.

As we see, the general idea is that meaningful action can be functionally equivalent to speech. This is an eco-semiotic view on communication that matches with

53 I am indebted to my colleagues Simo Sarkki and Juha Hiedanpää for inspiration from our joint work on ecocentric democracy. A detailed discussion is Meijer 2019.

54 Christiano and Bajaj 2024.

55 This is Dewey's influential conception, overview in Festenstein 2023.

views on democracy as action.[56] Indeed, in line with previous discussions, we can even say that defining democracy by language is speciesist, analogous to excluding specific languages of oppressed minorities from human democracy, for example, denying their use in parliament. Democracy, as an effort to establish equality, means essentially stating claims in the form of action and not speech in the formally recognized arena. Human minorities claim their voice through actions such as demonstrations. Humans can also recognize claims by interpreting other species' actions as signs with a political meaning.

This view can be combined with the trustee model, but it can also work in a less structured community, provided that humans adequately listen. The primary condition is empathy, which is the sense that humans can understand the inner states of other species.[57] If this appears as tricky, consider the reverse: The shocking capability of humans to dehumanize other humans, for example, as "cockroaches," and then proceed with mass murder. The other way around, humans can also empathize with others. In a Smithian fashion, this would enable them to develop a position of impartiality and justice, a necessary condition for democratic deliberation.[58]

In the context of property, we can significantly build this argument on the capability approach to needs and justice.[59] Humans can empathize with other species because life shares specific basic needs and functions, such as shelter, food, or procreation. We can assess the capabilities of other species in relation to such functionings, and we can, therefore, cognitively empathize with their lives.[60] For example, if we cut all trees in the forest, we can understand what that means for all other species that rely on trees for essential life functions and translate this into human language. This is not anthropomorphism but the reverse: Humans share needs and functions with all life; therefore, we can empathize with all life.

The upshot is that beyond expert knowledge, humans can develop a sense of justice for other species and, therefore, take heed of their needs in a democratic process which still only involves humans when it comes to the final design of policies.[61] As said, this may be institutionalized via trusteeship, but it is not necessarily so. We can imagine a variety of internal functions of organizing an ecosystem commons, which allows us to reach impartiality in political decisions. This includes assigning and recognizing havings of other species. However, a funda-

56 Rancière 2004. For an overview, see Chambers 2011. On ecosemiotics, see Maran 2020.

57 Young, Khalil, and Wharton 2018.

58 Sen 2009.

59 Robeyns and Byskov 2023 overviews the concept, seminally developed by Amartya Sen and Martha Nussbaum.

60 Parker, Soanes, and Roudavski 2022.

61 Celermajer et al. 2023.

mental difference exists between recognizing possession and property, as the latter requires human trusteeship. For example, the ecosystem commons may recognize the nesting places for migratory birds as a form of temporary possession, such as a nest on a building. This means that the human proprietor of the building must respect this right. The right can also obtain the form of property, which might be necessary for negotiating compensation when the proprietor wants to demolish his building and, thereby, the nesting site. This compensation cannot be directly negotiated with the bird, even though there is also the possibility that experts such as ornithologists may figure out compensation. If possession is property, a negotiation can start about the specific financial requirements for doing that.

Summing up, the Universal Commons avoids the dilemmas of thinking about property as individualized assignments to other species. In the framework of having, we can retain individualization regarding possession, which implies that in considering justice, every individual counts as the locus of sentiency and autonomy. The individual slug feels and acts and, hence, is a possessor. However, this does not mean that property must be assigned to individuals only, as we can distinguish natural and legal persons, like in the human domain. So, a species may be assigned property as a legal person, but not the individuals, within the domain of the commons. Finally, ownership is assigned to the ecosystem level. This expresses the fundamental interrelatedness of all life in the ecosystem, which means that individual living beings possess others for their own benefit. This includes even killing others for survival. However, this action is an element in the wider network of actions that sustain the ecosystem to benefit all, including the prey species.

This observation also helps to resolve a moral quandary for humans. We met one manifestation when considering the killing of invasive alien species. In general, human actions, especially appropriative, must be morally judged in relation to their contribution to sustaining the flourishing of the ecosystem and all of its members, including the humans themselves. So, if humans raise vegetables to sustain themselves, and slugs invade, threatening the destruction of the crops, humans have the right to police this action, as it amounts to theft if going beyond some minor damages. The ecosystem commons may vote to legitimize policing slugs, however, considering which kind of action is least harmful to them. Hence, the theory of havings resolves some puzzles in the confrontation between environmentalism and animal rights.

6. Conclusion

The theory of havings goes beyond the philosophically dominant view that having is necessary to enact human freedom. All sentient and autonomous beings need havings to realize their unique way of life. We can acknowledge this straightforwardly, but the challenge is institutionalizing these havings in the human domain. Since humans have not yet included non-human havings in their constitutions and laws, at least in hegemonic societies, a fundamental political transformation is necessary, which must be done by the humans themselves. The process is akin to slaveholders freeing the slaves unilaterally. However, slaveholders could talk to slaves. Hence, the institutional enactment of more-than-human havings poses the challenge of expanding our human language of havings to include other species' ways of life and communication. Humans explore outer space: exploring the many worlds of other species is even more daunting, and we have just started to do so.[62]

The ecosystem commons requires the transformation of human culture in ways that have been dubbed "natureculture"[63] or "co-culture,"[64] thus moving beyond the domain of the economy, broader spoken. Indigenous spirituality can inform this transformation without implying that religious ontologies are adopted that would appear to contradict scientific knowledge.[65] The mediums are the arts, literature, music, and all kinds of aesthetic practices, which are autonomous domains of knowing and experience.[66] In the ecosystem commons, the relationship between humans and other species would be embedded in shared patterns of meanings that materialize in aesthetic practices that do not only cater for the tastes of humans but also those of other species and which nurture shared flourishing.[67]

62 Despret 2021, Yong 2022.
63 Haraway 2016.
64 Sueur and Huffman 2024.
65 Alexander 2013, Wheeler 2016.
66 Dewey 2005.
67 Herrmann-Pillath et al. 2024.

Postscript: Havings in the economy of the future

Modern capitalism puts property at the center of its institutional framework, though, as we have seen, in a specific legal form that combines strong dispositional powers with a high degree of externalization. We can approach the latter as the institutional manifestation of disembedding property in the Polanyian sense, namely, thinning the link between property and society and abstracting markets from the body politic.[1] This form of property is what we may refer to as "private property." Following Polanyi, I regard private property less as a concrete institutional form but as an idea that is part and parcel of capitalism as the utopia of Political Economy, i.e., economics as it emerged in the 19th century. As an institutional form, our argument goes full circle back to Max Weber, who defined *Eigentum* by two criteria: free alienation and free bequest.

The idea of private property emerged first in early Roman times, when the law of the Twelve Tables defined the right to free bequest by the property holder. This individual right disembedded property from family relationships, triggering struggles over the claims of family members to inherit parts of the wealth.[2] Free alienation was constrained by social obligations, and only ritual procedures upheld patterns of embeddedness, though gradually eroding.[3] The disembedding of property assumed full force in the Roman provinces where, paradoxically, state tenancy became the institutional form of private property: The recurrent historical pattern of mapping land emerged when Imperial land surveyors abstracted land as an entity which became the object of legitimate possession by tenants of the Empire.[4] The rent became institutionalized as tax, and the tenant morphed into a proprietor who could act freely on the land market; once the

1 For an extensive discussion of abstraction, see Basso and Herrmann-Pillath 2024.

2 Harke (2023) discusses the legal construct extensively when family members claimed that bequests were made by "insane" individuals.

3 Von der Weth 2024. These developments were mainly unfolding via judicial practice, where praetors recognized transactions as equally valid, with or without the traditional ritual of *mancipatio*.

4 As seen in Chapter 1, this nexus is the topic of Weber's habilitation thesis; Weber 2014a.

rights of tenants also included free bequest on the condition of paying tax, the land was entirely freed from the ritual constraints of the Italian heartlands and hence became the object of private property, Weberian sense. Roman jurists reflected this as a minor form of *dominium*.[5] Hence, key features of *dominium* also shaped the emerging private property, especially the absolute rule of the male household head over all constituents of his property. Considering that these developments concurred with the factual erosion of traditional rituals in the Italian regions, we can conclude that private property diffused as an institutional form across Roman Europe, and the definitive Justinian reforms just formalized and systematized a practice that had existed for centuries. These processes unfolded alongside the rise of Christianity.[6] With the Christianization of Rome, private property became imbued by a distinct metaphysics and form of spirituality. The idea of private property now included metaphysical assumptions dividing mind from body and man (gender intended) from nature, thus extending the Roman notion of *dominium* to the belief that Christians are entitled to subject the world to their rule in the form of property. Christians distinguished and distanced themselves sharply from Jews who upheld tight ritual constraints on property. Therefore, they could easily combine their beliefs with the practices of Roman law.

After the demise of the Roman Empire, Roman private property as an idea coexisted with many other institutional forms in the legal pluralism of medieval and early modern times, in the form of the *ius commune* and the legal scholarship that spread across Europe from Italy. Philosophers began exploring property as a natural right, and eventually, the idea was seen as a key element in overcoming the regimes of feudalism and absolutism. The revolutionary transformations resulted in adopting private property as a universal legal form in Europe and enforcing it against all other forms of having. As a corollary, the legal scholarship on property also included a strong revival of interest in Roman law. Incipient private property had already been the institutional form of pushing colonial dispossession across the globe, and its codifications were enforced globally, either by the colonial rulers or by modernizing elites in independent countries that vied to catch up with the West. In the 20th century, private property became the target of communist revolutions. As a defensive move, the capitalist countries pushed the agenda of re-embedding private property in society via laws and regulations targetting the externalities. After the collapse of most socialist systems in 1989, the idea became powerful again, and even socialist countries such as China adopted legal forms of civil law to promote private property in society.

5 Kantor 2017.

6 Vinzent 2024.

This brief overview of the larger historical trends shows that private property as an idea never was "natural" or the outcome of economic forces that unfolded in a law-like form.[7] Since Roman times, private property ideationally and literally colonized a much more diverse world of havings. As we see in this book, if we approach the social and economic reality with the analytical lens of the theory of havings, we clearly realize that private property is an idea that is enforced by certain powerful groups in society in a Weberian struggle. This enforcement rarely meant that the multimodality of having was shrinking to the institutional form as prescribed by the idea. Radical disembedding only happens in specific institutional settings, such as in modern financial markets, in the form of assetification. This insight concludes that if we eschew the hegemonic language of property, we can build an alternative "realistic utopia" of the multimodality of having and havings.[8]

The theory of havings has significant and manifold consequences for designing economic institutions and policies. It overcomes many obstacles to societal improvements that were rooted in the ideological divisions inherited from the creation of the modern form of private property in the early 19th century. Economics manifests and scientifically systematizes the core concern of this political revolution: Making the economy's institutions endogenous to markets, which presupposes abolishing all forms of inalienability and constraints on including economic objects in the market process. This is what the Marx-inspired literature calls "commodification." Property is the legal form of commodification. As a result, the economic theory of property focuses on this endogenous expansion of markets and how certain economic parameters, such as transaction costs, impact the evolution of property rights. Criteria of equity are neutralized because of the assumption that this process results in efficiency gains that increase welfare for all.

The theory of havings denies this primacy of economic determinants in institutional evolution and instead emphasizes the Weberian role of struggle. Property plays a critical role here, as property is power. This is the fundamental paradox of markets: Markets drive the evolution of property, but property also contains, even spoils, markets by allowing for the simultaneous and endogenous emergence of market power. Market power easily allies with sociopolitical power, thus creating the arena for Weberian struggle. The systematic expression of this paradox is

7 This is also the conclusion of Widerquist and McCall 2021.

8 Basso and Herrmann-Pillath (2024) develop this in detail, following the lines of Ernst Bloch's views on utopia.

that property always and necessarily creates two forces, one enhancing and one diminishing economic efficiency:[9]

- Proprietors are always interested in deploying their property in the most profitable way, which fosters competition over the control of property and hence, the efficiency of outcomes; however,
- proprietors can enhance profitability by externalizing as many costs as possible to other actors, which results in a loss of efficiency.

This is not just the contradiction between private and social efficiency; both actions contribute to social welfare. After all, factories that pollute the river offer cheap goods to the people. This is the point where the theory of havings steps in with full force: We observe two movements; one is appropriation through property. The resulting externalities require institutional measures in another mode: This is the assignment of liability to the proprietor. The Coasean argument that this assignment is governed by transaction costs violates a fundamental principle of responsibility in enacting agency. Whether neighbors or the factory owner have the right to contain or allow for pollution is not a neutral choice, only considering the relative costs of organizing collective actions and negotiations. The proprietor is the causal agent, so the agent must be assigned liability. We cannot expect that proprietors will always be morally motivated to assume responsibility from the individual perspective. Only as members in a community where liabilities are assigned to individuals, legally, by social norms and moral education, will proprietors act responsibly. This is Hegel's ethical life, *Sittlichkeit*. In the view of havings, the modes of appropriation and assignment interplay so that all concerned parties recognize the arrangement. Recognition trumps efficiency.

This simple analysis has far-reaching consequences for designing economic institutions. Since proprietors are often also powerful political interest groups, they can bias institutional change in the direction of enhancing their powers to appropriate gains and externalize costs. This is a, if not the critical feature of property in capitalism: Society bears much of the externalized costs of business, such as the taxpayers the burden of cleaning up the mess of financial crises. Economics mainly discusses phenomena such as pollution, but the reach of the externalities concept is much further.[10] As in the example of financial crises, the general observation is that the current institutions of property allow for externalizing costs of risk-taking in business. This is possible because there is an asymmetry between the institutional treatment of havings.

9 For a more detailed exposition, see Herrmann-Pillath and Hederer 2023, 111 ff.

10 For a detailed and systematic argument, see Basso and Herrmann-Pillath 2024, 488 ff.

Consider the core process of capitalism: innovation. A successful entrepreneur can create a new technology that is highly successful in the market and meets social demand. However, a side effect is that proprietors of assets no longer usable in this technology lose their monetary value: After the invention of the PC, they own the typewriter, but it is worthless.[11] Economists commonly argue that these pecuniary externalities are necessary for driving market efficiency and innovation and, hence, are neutral in terms of welfare. However, this is only valid viewed from the perspective of an external observer: Those who lose feel the pain. For a real-world society, these costs matter.[12]

One of the critical aspects of this ambivalence of innovation can be grasped by the duality of ownership and property in the theory of havings. Consider a worker negatively affected by innovation since her skills are devalued and her job type (profession) vanishes. In the common understanding of property in economics, these skills are not property; hence, the damage does not fall under tort law, which is different from the case of pollution. Indeed, the worker cannot sell the skills and buy new ones because they are embodied: The worker owns the skills, and even more, she might feel like owning the job if, for example, for many years she has been an employee of the firm that now goes bust. The modern welfare state can be seen as endorsing the capitalist asymmetry of property in creating a social safety net for the unemployed. However, we can imagine another regime in which the proprietor directly compensates the laid-off worker for the damage done to her havings. The new industrialists would have paid off the Luddites.

Economists would immediately argue that this would slow down the pace of innovation. That is true, but how do we know the current pace is desirable, watching how the capitalist system drives the planet into climate catastrophe? Indeed, we have seen in Chapter 5 that the theory of havings would vastly enhance the possible scope of compensations for externalities of innovations since havings of other species would be recognized. The theory of havings suggests an institutionalized form of de-growth.[13]

The example demonstrates a general consequence of the theory of havings: The distinction between ownership and property allows for recognizing many types of havings that, from the angle of economics, are deemed irrelevant for designing the economy. Consider the point of ownership of skills and jobs again. In the standard view of corporate governance of listed companies, the shareholders

11 My argument follows Witt 1996.

12 Sen 2009 distinguishes between two ways to judge institutions, transcendental institutionalism and realization-focused comparisons. The standard economic welfare theory adopts the former, whereas Sen argues that only the latter can meet the criteria of justice and equity. I follow the latter here.

13 This concept had been already envisaged by John Stuart Mill in his famous scenario of steady-state economy of the future.

are the proprietors, and the employees are just wage earners. However, in many technologically advanced companies, employees accumulate a substantial stock of knowledge, aka human capital, which is company-specific.[14] Some of this capital is even tacit knowledge; hence, a significant part of it is inalienable and non-tradable via markets. However, its productive contribution is reflected in the company's valuation on the capital market, where shareholders can appropriate the gains without even possessing the employees' human capital. Hence, the structure of havings combined with the current legal property design allows for a substantial redistribution from employees to shareholders. From this point of view, the current compensation schemes for top managers do not serve to enhance motivation and efficiency but to drive a wedge between managers and employees, aligning the interests of the former with the shareholders' interests in factually appropriating gains from the human capital of employees. In an alternative corporate governance structure that recognizes havings of employees, managers would obtain the role of mediators between two different groups having the company in different structural modes, ownership and property.

As we can see, the theory of havings implies a substantial reform of corporate governance structures, strengthening the role of employees in decision-making and further developing models such as the German *Mitbestimmung*.[15] Economists often argue that employees need to become shareholders. Still, similar asymmetries hold here since employees are much less flexible than outside investors in exerting their rights as proprietors, such as selling those stocks while remaining company employees.

The duality of ownership and property can be fruitfully deployed in many other contexts. In general, the economic theory of property always suggests a clear borderline between the sides of the market and the respective property, as in the case of shareholders vis-à-vis employees. A similar constellation applies to the duality of producers and consumers. Consider innovation again. Economics treats the producer as the proprietor of an innovation who has the right to appropriate the gains from selling the new product. The theory is that the producer meets consumers' preferences, so consumers are passive recipients of the innovation. In fact, consumers also actively contribute to the innovation, especially those in the first stage of the diffusion of the innovation: Early adopters are innovators in their own right. We can refer to this constellation as consumers owning the innovation,

14 The following argument has been fully developed in Aoki 2010.

15 Today, some mainstream economists have also adopted this view for similar reasons, for instance, Collier (2019) defends the idea of the "ethical firm."

such as adapting their habits.[16] Consumers often invent uses of the innovation that the producers did not consider. This raises the question of whether and how consumers may partake in the profits that innovators reap from the innovation. However, the market process works differently: Companies aim to create strong brand identities, attach consumers to the brand, and enable high pricing.

We have already discussed ownership concerning intellectual property. Innovators reap gains by claiming this type of property. Again, the question is, to what extent do users contribute to innovation, and how far can they contribute to its further development? One example is the development of copyrights in the media industry. Consumers may love certain fictitious characters to the degree that they incorporate them into their daily lives. Why can't they express ownership of these characters when doing their creative work? This would activate a vast reservoir of social creativity.[17] As argued earlier, the theory of havings would allow for institutional designs in which the possession of characters is open to everyone but with a fee to be paid to the proprietor. After all, many creative businesses exploit the vast cultural reservoirs of peoples of the world, such as Disney German fairy tales, without paying (think of mandatory donations for African people recognizing the use of their cultural heritage).

As we see, the future economy would assume a very different shape if its institutional design followed the theory of havings. The current construct that mainly focuses on property has many harmful consequences for humans and other species. One glaring example is the exploitation of mineral resources in countries where human rights are trampled, and corrupt elites appropriate the riches.[18] This example is particularly worrying because today, these resources are critical for greening the capitalist world economy. The global institutions of property allow for the transformation of theft into legal property when these resources enter international trade, following international law. This is only an extreme version of the fundamental problem of rent extraction from natural resources by what are arbitrary property arrangements. These arrangements lead to the destruction of nature and glaring injustice among humans.

Perhaps the most significant result of the theory of havings is that it eschews anthropocentrism of the conventional view of property. Since this means radically transforming the relationship between humans and nature, there are also many consequences for how humans manage their economic systems, firms, and

16 A large literature in business studies and management sciences is defending this argument, following seminal contributions such as Baldwin and von Hippel 2011. One field where this is extensively theorized is the digital economy and creative industries, for example, Hartley 2021.

17 On this argument, see Boldrin and Levine 2008.

18 Wenar 2017.

households. Recognizing non-human havings means reconstituting Indigenous worldviews and practices globally in an intellectual adventure of "two-eyed seeing."[19] In a vastly expanded world of more-than-human having, humans must find their place for peaceful cohabitation to their own advantage, fostering the good life of future generations.

19 Bartlett, Marshall, and Marshall 2012.

References

Acemoglu, Daron, Simon Johnson, and James A Robinson. 2001. "The Colonial Origins of Comparative Development: An Empirical Investigation." *American Economic Review* 91(5): 1369–1401. doi:10.1257/aer.91.5.1369.

Aikhenvald, Alexandra Y. 2012. "Possession and Ownership: A Cross Linguistic Perspective." In *Possession and Ownership*, eds. Alexandra Y. Aikhenvald and R. M. W. Dixon: 1–64. Oxford University Press, doi:10.1093/acprof:oso/9780199660223.003.0001.

Alchian, Armen A. 2008. "Property Rights." In *The New Palgrave Dictionary of Economics*, ed. Palgrave Macmillan. London: Palgrave Macmillan UK, 1–6. doi:10.1057/978-1-349-95121-5_1814-2.

Alexander, Gregory S., Eduardo Moisés Peñalver, Joseph W. Singer, and Laura S. Underkuffler. 2009. "A Statement of Progressive Property." *Cornell Law Faculty Publications* 11. http://scholarship.law.cornell.edu/facpub/11.

Alexander, Thomas M. 2013. *The human eros: eco-ontology and the aesthetics of existence*. New York: Fordham University Press.

Allen, Douglas W. 2015. "On Hodgson on Property Rights." *Journal of Institutional Economics* 11(4): 711–17. doi:10.1017/S1744137415000132.

Aluffi, Roberta, and Domenico Francavilla. 2017. "Property and the Religious Sphere." In eds. Michelle Graziadei and Lionel Smith, *Comparative Property Law. Global Perspectives*: 355–373, Cheltenham, UK, Northampton, MA: Edward Elgar Publishing

Anderson, Elizabeth. 2019. *Private Government: How Employers Rule Our Lives (and Why We Don't Talk about It)*. Princeton: Princeton University Press.

Andrews, Kristin, and Susana Monsó. 2021. "Animal Cognition". In *The Stanford Encyclopedia of Philosophy*, ed. Edward N. Zalta, Spring 2021. Metaphysics Research Lab, Stanford University, 2021. https://plato.stanford.edu/archives/spr2021/entries/cognition-animal/.

Aoki, Masahiko. 2001. *Toward a Comparative Institutional Analysis*. Cambridge, Mass: MIT Press.

Aoki, Masahiko. 2011. "Institutions as Cognitive Media between Strategic Interactions and Individual Beliefs." *Journal of Economic Behavior and Organization* 79(1): 20–34. doi:10.1016/j.jebo.2011.01.025.

Aoki, Masahiko. 2019. *Corporations in Evolving Diversity: Cognition, Governance, and Institutions*. Oxford: Oxford University Pres.

Apfelbeck, Beate, Robbert P.H. Snep, Thomas E. Hauck, Joanna Ferguson, Mona Holy, Christine Jakoby, J. Scott MacIvor, et al. 2020. "Designing Wildlife-Inclusive Cities That Support

Human-Animal Co-Existence." *Landscape and Urban Planning* 200: 103817. doi:10.1016/j.landurbplan.2020.103817.

Apicella, Coren L., Eduardo M. Azevedo, Nicholas A. Christakis, and James H. Fowler. 2014. "Evolutionary Origins of the Endowment Effect: Evidence from Hunter-Gatherers." *American Economic Review* 104(6): 1793–1805. doi:10.1257/aer.104.6.1793.

Arendt, Hannah. 2018 [1958]. *The Human Condition*. Second edition. Chicago, London: The University of Chicago Press.

Armbrüster, Thomas. 2005. *Management and Organization in Germany*. Aldershot, England, Burlington, VT: Ashgate.

Baldwin, Carliss, and Eric von Hippel. 2011. "Modeling a Paradigm Shift: From Producer Innovation to User and Open Collaborative Innovation." *Organization Science* 22(6): 1399–1417. doi:10.1287/orsc.1100.0618.

Bannas, Stephan, and Carsten Herrmann-Pillath. 2020. *Marktwirtschaft: Zu einer neuen Wirklichkeit: 30 Thesen zur Transformation unserer Wirtschaftsordnung*. Stuttgart: Schäffer-Poeschel Verlag.

Barad, Karen Michelle. 2007. *Meeting the Universe Halfway: Quantum Physics and the Entanglement of Matter and Meaning*. Durham: Duke University Press.

Bartlett, Cheryl, Murdena Marshall, and Albert Marshall. 2012. "Two-Eyed Seeing and Other Lessons Learned within a Co-Learning Journey of Bringing Together Indigenous and Mainstream Knowledges and Ways of Knowing." *Journal of Environmental Studies and Sciences* 2(4): 331–40. doi:10.1007/s13412-012-0086-8.

Barzel, Yoram. 2012. *A Theory of the State: Economic Rights, Legal Rights, and the Scope of the State*. 2. ed. Cambridge: Cambridge Univ. Press.

Basso, Frédéric, and Carsten Herrmann-Pillath. 2024. *Embodiment, Political Economy and Human Flourishing: An Embodied Cognition Approach to Economic Life*. Cham: Palgrave Macmillan.

Bateman, Ian J., and Georgina M. Mace. 2020. "The Natural Capital Framework for Sustainably Efficient and Equitable Decision Making." *Nature Sustainability* 3(10): 776–83. doi:10.1038/s41893-020-0552-3.

Beck, Kasper Ingeman, and Kjeld Erik Brødsgaard. 2022. "Corporate Governance with Chinese Characteristics: Party Organization in State-Owned Enterprises." *The China Quarterly* 250: 486–508. doi:10.1017/S0305741021001351.

Benda-Beckmann, Franz von, Keebet von Benda-Beckmann, and Melanie G. Wiber. 2006. "Changing Properties of Property." In eds. Franz von Benda-Beckmann, Keebet von Benda-Beckmann, and Melanie Wiber: 1–39. New York and Oxford: Berghahn Books doi:10.1515/9780857455284-002.

Benjamin, Solomon, and Bhuvaneswari Raman. 2011. "Illegible Claims, Legal Titles, and the Worlding of Bangalore." *Revue Tiers Monde* 206(2): 37. doi:10.3917/rtm.206.0037.

Berrone, Pascual, Cristina Cruz, and Luis R. Gomez-Mejia. 2012. "Socioemotional Wealth in Family Firms: Theoretical Dimensions, Assessment Approaches, and Agenda for Future Research." *Family Business Review* 25(3): 258–79. doi:10.1177/0894486511435355.

Bhandar, Brenna. 2018. *Colonial Lives of Property: Law, Land, and Racial Regimes of Ownership*. Durham London: Duke University Press.

Bianchi Mancini, Sofia, Helen A. Gibson, Dirk Schuck, and Markus Vinzent, eds. 2024. *Relating to Landed Property*. Frankfurt: Campus.

Blanchette, Jude. 2020. "From "China Inc." to "CCP Inc.": A New Paradigm for Chinese State Capitalism". *China Leadership Monitor*, https://www.prcleader.org/post/from-china-inc-to-ccp-inc-a-new-paradigm-for-chinese-state-capitalism

Bloch, David J. 2006. "Res Sanctae in Gaius and the Founding of the City." *Roman Legal Tradition* 3: 48–62.

Blumenfeld, Jacob. 2024. *The Concept of Property in Kant, Fichte, and Hegel: Freedom, Right, and Recognition*. New York London: Routledge.

Bogdan, Radu J. 2010. *Our Own Minds: Sociocultural Grounds for Self-Consciousness*. Cambridge, Mass: MIT Press.

Boldrin, Michele, and David K. Levine. 2008. *Against Intellectual Monopoly*. New York: Cambridge University Press.

Bourdieu, Pierre. 2019a. *Sociologie générale volume 1*. Paris : Éditions Points.

Bourdieu, Pierre. 2019b. *Sociologie générale volume 2*. Paris : Éditions Points.

Boyd, David R. 2017. *The Rights of Nature: A Legal Revolution That Could Save the World*. Toronto, ON: ECW Press.

Boydell, Spike. 2010. "South Pacific Land: An Alternative Perspective on Tenure Traditions, Business, and Conflict." *Georgetown Journal of International Affairs* 11(1): 17–25.

Bradshaw, Karen. 2020. *Wildlife as Property Owners: A New Conception of Animal Rights*. Chicago: University of Chicago Press.

Bresson, Alain. 2014. "Capitalism and the Ancient Greek Economy." In *The Cambridge History of Capitalism: Volume 1: The Rise of Capitalism: From Ancient Origins to 1848*, eds. Larry Neal and Jeffrey G. Williamson. Cambridge: Cambridge University Press: 43–74. doi:10.1017/CHO9781139095099.003.

Bridle, James. 2022. *Ways of Being: Beyond Human Intelligence*. London: Allen Lane.

Brightman, Marc, Carlos Fausto, and Vanessa Elisa Grotti. 2016a. "Altering Ownership in Amazonia." In eds. Brightman, Marc, Carlos Fausto, and Vanessa Elisa Grotti, *Ownership and Nurture. Studies in Native Amazonian Property Relations*: 19–71, New York, Oxford: Berghahn Books.

Brightman, Marc, Carlos Fausto, and Vanessa Elisa Grotti, eds. 2016b. *Ownership and Nurture: Studies in Native Amazonian Property Relations*. New York, Oxford: Berghahn Books.

Bruton, Garry D., Mike W. Peng, David Ahlstrom, Ciprian Stan, and Kehan Xu. 2015. "State-owned Enterprises around the World as Hybrid Organizations". *Academy of Management Perspectives* 29(1): 92–114.

Cai, Changkun, Ying Liu, and Weiqi Jiang. 2023. "Bringing the Party Back into the Community: Restructuring Grassroots Governance in Shenzhen." *The China Quarterly* 254: 412–28. doi:10.1017/S0305741023000176.

Cai, Meina, Ilia Murtazashvili, and Jennifer Murtazashvili. 2020. "The Politics of Land Property Rights." *Journal of Institutional Economics* 16(2): 151–67. doi:10.1017/S1744137419000158.

Candlish, Stewart, and George Wrisley. 2019. "Private Language." In *The Stanford Encyclopedia of Philosophy*, ed. Edward N. Zalta. Metaphysics Research Lab, Stanford University. https://plato.stanford.edu/archives/fall2019/entries/private-language/.

Capraro, Valerio, Joseph Y. Halpern, and Matjaž Perc. 2024. "From Outcome-Based to Language-Based Preferences." *Journal of Economic Literature* 62(1): 115–54. doi:10.1257/jel.20221613.

Celermajer, Danielle, David Schlosberg, Dinesh Wadiwel, and Christine Winter. 2023. "A Political Theory for a Multispecies, Climate-Challenged World: 2050." *Political Theory* 51(1): 39–53. doi:10.1177/00905917221128833.

Cesarino, Pedro de Niemeyer. 2016. "Doubles and Owners: Relations of Knowledge, Property and Authorship Among the Marubo." In eds. Brightman, Marc, Carlos Fausto, and Vanessa Elisa Grotti, *Ownership and Nurture. Studies in Native Amazonian Property Relations:* 295–3.28 New York, Oxford: Berghahn Books.

Chambers, Samuel A. 2011. "Jacques Rancière and the Problem of Pure Politics." *European Journal of Political Theory* 10(3): 303–26. doi:10.1177/1474885111406386.

Chan, Anita, Richard Madsen, Jonathan Unger, and Anita Chan. 2009. *Chen Village: Revolution to Globalization*. 3rd ed. Berkeley: University of California Press.

Chao, Sophie. 2022. *In the Shadow of the Palms: More-than-Human Becomings in West Papua*. Durham: Duke University Press.

Chapron, Guillaume, Yaffa Epstein, and José Vicente López-Bao. 2019. "A Rights Revolution for Nature." *Science* 363(6434): 1392–93. doi:10.1126/science.aav5601.

Cheng, Jing, Carsten Herrmann Pillath, Ling Li, and Man Guo. 2024. "Shareholding Cooperatives in Shenzhen and the Revival of 'Filial Piety' as a Core Value of Chinese Ethical Life." In eds. Carsten Herrmann-Pillath and Qian Zhao, *East Asian Ethical Life and Socio-Economic Transformation in the Twenty-First Century The Ethical Sources of the Entrepreneurial Renewal of Companies and Communities*, Abingdon and London: Routledge.

Cheng, Jing, Carsten Herrmann-Pillath, and Ling Li. 2022. "The Three Modes of Appropriation Lessons of Chinese Practice for Theorizing Property." *Sonderforschungsbereich/Transregio 294»Strukturwandel des Eigentums«*. Working Paper Nr. 1. https://sfb294-eigentum.de/media/filer_public/30/2b/302b1677-d0 ff-4390-aa31-4bcae0d5971 f/wp_01_final_issn.pdf.

Chimhowu, Admos. 2019. "The 'New' African Customary Land Tenure. Characteristic, Features and Policy Implications of a New Paradigm." *Land Use Policy* 81: 897–903. doi:10.1016/j.landusepol.2018.04.014.

Chimhowu, Admos, and Phil Woodhouse. 2006. "Customary vs Private Property Rights? Dynamics and Trajectories of Vernacular Land Markets in Sub-Saharan Africa." *Journal of Agrarian Change* 6(3): 346–71. doi:10.1111/j.1471-0366.2006.00125.x.

Chong, Isis, and Robert W. Proctor. 2020. "On the Evolution of a Radical Concept: Affordances According to Gibson and Their Subsequent Use and Development." *Perspectives on Psychological Science* 15(1): 117–32. doi:10.1177/1745691619868207.

Christiano, Tom, and Sameer Bajaj. 2024. "Democracy." In *The Stanford Encyclopedia of Philosophy*, eds. Edward N. Zalta and Uri Nodelman. Metaphysics Research Lab, Stanford University. https://plato.stanford.edu/archives/spr2024/entries/democracy/.

Clark, Andy. 2011. *Supersizing the Mind: Embodiment, Action, and Cognitive Extension*. Oxford: Oxford University Press.

Clark, Andy. 2023. *The Experience Machine: How Our Minds Predict and Shape Reality*. UK: Allen Lane.

Coase, R. H. 1960. "The Problem of Social Cost." *The Journal of Law & Economics* 3: 1–44.

Cohen, Myron L. 1992. "Family Management and Family Division in Contemporary Rural China." *The China Quarterly* 130: 357–77. doi:10.1017/S0305741000040777.

Coleman, James S. 1990. *Foundations of Social Theory*. Cambridge, Mass: Belknap Press.

Collier, Paul. 2019. *The Future of Capitalism: Facing the New Anxieties*. New York: HarperCollins.

Costa, Luis. 2016. "Fabricating Necessity. Feeding and Commensality in Western Amazonia." In eds. Brightman, Marc, Carlos Fausto, and Vanessa Elisa Grotti, *Ownership and Nurture. Studies in Native Amazonian Property Relations:* 141–83. New York and Oxford: Berghahn Books.

Dagan, Ḥanokh. 2021. *A Liberal Theory of Property*. Cambridge, New York, NY: Cambridge University Press.

Damasio, Antonio R. 2010. *Self Comes to Mind: Constructing the Conscious Brain*. New York: Pantheon Books.

Dawkins, Sarah, Amy Wei Tian, Alexander Newman, and Angela Martin. 2017. "Psychological Ownership: A Review and Research Agenda." *Journal of Organizational Behavior* 38(2): 163–83. doi:10.1002/job.2057.

Deckha, Maneesha. 2021. *Animals as Legal Beings: Contesting Anthropocentric Legal Orders*. Toronto : University of Toronto Press.

Demoulin-Auzary, Florence. 2005. "Dominium et Proprietas Dans Le Décret de Gratien." *Revue historique de droit français et étranger (1922-)* 83(4) : 647–55.

Demsetz, Harold. 1967. "Toward a Theory of Property Rights." *The American Economic Review* 57(2): 347–59.

Despret, Vinciane. 2019. *Habiter En Oiseau*. Arles : Actes sud.

Despret, Vinciane. 2021. *Autobiographie d'un poulpe: et autres récits d'anticipation*. Arles : Actes Sud, 2021.

Dewey, John. 2005 [1934]. *Art as Experience.* New York: Berkeley Publ. Group.

Dixon, R. M. W. 2012. "Possession and Also Ownership—Vignettes." In *Possession and Ownership*, eds. Alexandra Y. Aikhenvald and R. M. W. Dixon. Oxford University Press: 291–308, doi:10.1093/acprof:oso/9780199660223.003.0014.

Dyk, Silke van, Tilman Reitz, and Hartmut Rosa. 2023. *Nach dem Privateigentum? Güter, Infrastrukturen und Weltverhältnisse im Kapitalismus des 21. Jahrhunderts*. Frankfurt: Campus.

Earle, Timothy. 2017. "Property in Prehistory." In *Comparative Property Law*, Edward Elgar Publishing, 3–25. doi:10.4337/9781785369162.00008.

Economou, Emmanouil M. L., and Nicholas C. Kyriazis. 2017. "The Emergence and the Evolution of Property Rights in Ancient Greece." *Journal of Institutional Economics* 13(1): 53–77. doi:10.1017/S1744137416000205.

Ekelund, Robert B., and Douglas M. Walker. 1996. "J. S. Mill on the Income Tax Exemption and Inheritance Taxes: The Evidence Reconsidered." *History of Political Economy* 28(4): 559–81. doi:10.1215/00182702-28-4-559.

Ellickson, Robert C. 1994. *Order without Law: How Neighbors Settle Disputes*. Cambridge, Mass.: Harvard University Press.

Emerich, Yaell. 2017. "Possession." In eds. Michelle Graziadei and Lionel Smith, *Comparative Property Law: Global Perspectives*: 171–91. Cheltenham, Northhampton: Edward Elgar,

Eucken, Walter. 2004 [1959]. *Grundsätze der Wirtschaftspolitik*. 7. Aufl. Tübingen: Mohr Siebeck.

Faure, David. 2007. *Emperor and Ancestor: State and Lineage in South China*. Stanford, Calif: Stanford University Press.

Federici, Silvia. 2021 [2004]. *Caliban and the Witch: Women, the Body and Primitive Accumulation*. London: Penguin Book.

Federici, Silvia, and Peter Linebaugh. 2019. *Re-Enchanting the World: Feminism and the Politics of the Commons*. Oakland, California: PM Press.

Feng, Yi, Fulong Wu, and Fangzhu Zhang. 2022. "Changing Roles of the State in the Financialization of Urban Development through *Chengtou* in China." *Regional Studies* 56(8): 1259–70. doi:10.1080/00343404.2021.1900558.

Festenstein, Matthew. 2023. "Dewey's Political Philosophy." In *The Stanford Encyclopedia of Philosophy*, eds. Edward N. Zalta and Uri Nodelman. Metaphysics Research Lab, Stanford University. https://plato.stanford.edu/archives/spr2023/entries/dewey-political/ (March 13, 2024).

Fligstein, Neil, and Doug McAdam. 2012. *A Theory of Fields*. New York: Oxford University Press.

Ford, Laura R. 2010. "Max Weber on Property: An Effort in Interpretive Understanding." SSRN Electronic Journal. doi:10.2139/ssrn.1560042.

Frühbrodt, Prof Lutz. 2021. "Initiative Neue Authentische Marktwirtschaft: Zurück in die Zukunft?" *Die Zweite Aufklärung*. https://www.zweite-aufklaerung.de/marktwirtschaft-bannas-herrmann-pillath-rezension/ (April 15, 2024).

Frye, Timothy. 2006. "Original Sin, Good Works, and Property Rights in Russia." *World Politics* 58(4): 479–504. doi:10.1353/wp. 2007.0007.

Gastineau, Pascal, Pascal Mossay, and Emmanuelle Taugourdeau. 2021. "Ecological Compensation: How Much and Where?" *Ecological Economics* 190: 107191. doi:10.1016/j.ecolecon.2021.107191.

Gates, Hill. 1996. *China's Motor: A Thousand Years of Petty Capitalism*. Ithaca: Cornell University Press.

George, Henry. 1879. *Progress and Poverty.* |Online Library of Liberty. https://oll.libertyfund.org/titles/george-progress-and-poverty (April 29, 2024).

Gesell, Silvio. 2022 [1919]. *Die natürliche Wirtschaftsordnung durch Freigeld und Freiland (classics reprint)*. S.l.: Forgotten books.

Gibson, Johanna. 2021. *Owned, an Ethological Jurisprudence of Property: From the Cave to the Commons*. London and New York: Routledge.

Giglio, Francesco. 2018. "The Concept of Ownership in Roman Law." 135(1): 76–107. doi:10.26498/zrgra-2018-1350106.

Gintis, Herbert. 2007. "The Evolution of Private Property." *Journal of Economic Behavior & Organization* 64(1): 1–16. doi:10.1016/j.jebo.2006.02.002.

Godfrey-Smith, Peter. 2017. *Other Minds: The Octopus and the Evolution of Intelligent Life*. London: William Collins.

Godfrey-Smith, Peter. 2020. *Metazoa: Animal Minds and the Birth of Consciousness*. London: William Collins.

Goetzmann, William N. 2017. *Money Changes Everything: How Finance Made Civilization Possible*. Princeton, New Jersey Oxford: Princeton University Press.

Goody, Jack. 1983. *The Development of the Family and Marriage in Europe*. Cambridge: Cambridge University Press.

Gordon, Cesar. 2016. "Ownership and Well-Being among the Mebengokre-Xikrin. Differentiation and Ritual Crisis." In eds. Brightman, Marc, Carlos Fausto, and Vanessa Elisa Grotti, *Ownership and Nurture. Studies in Native Amazonian Property Relations*: 330—363, New York, Oxford: Berghahn Books.

Gottesman, Alex. 2010. "The Beggar and the Clod: The Mythic Notion of Property in Ancient Greece." *Transactions of the American Philological Association*140(2): 287–322.

Graeber, David. 2014. *Debt: the first 5,000 years.* Brooklyn: Melville House.

Granick, David. 1990. *Chinese State Enterprises: A Regional Property Rights Analysis*. Chicago: University of Chicago Press.

Graziadei, Michele. 2017. "The Structure of Property Ownership and the Common Law/Civil Law Divide." In eds. Michelle Graziadei and Lionel Smith, *Comparative Property Law*: 71–99. Cheltenham and Northhampton, Edward Elgar Publishing, doi:10.4337/9781785369162.00012.

Greer, Allan. 2017. *Property and Dispossession: Natives, Empires and Land in Early Modern North America*. Cambridge; New York, NY: Cambridge University Press.

Gretton, George L. 2007. "Ownership and its Objects." *Rabels Zeitschrift für ausländisches und internationales Privatrecht* 71(4): 802. doi:10.1628/003372507782419462.

Guo, Man, and Carsten Herrmann-Pillath. 2019a. "Exploring Extended Kinship in Twenty-First-Century China: A Conceptual Case Study." *Journal of Current Chinese Affairs* 48(1): 50–75. doi:10.1177/1868102619845244.

Guo, Man, and Carsten Herrmann-Pillath. 2019b. "Lineage, Food and Ritual in a Chinese Metropolis." *Anthropos* 114(1): 195–208. doi:10.5771/0257-9774-2019-1-195.

Hadley, John. 2015. *Animal Property Rights: A Theory of Habitat Rights for Wild Animals*. Lanham: Lexington Books.

Hann, Chris. 2007. "A New Double Movement? Anthropological Perspectives on Property in the Age of Neoliberalism." *Socio-Economic Review* 5(2): 287–318. doi:10.1093/ser/mwl027.

Haraway, Donna J. 2016. *Staying with the Trouble: Making Kin in the Chthulucene. Experimental futures: Technological Lives, Scientific Arts, Anthropological Voices*. Durham: Duke University Press

Harke, Jan Dirk. 2016. *Römisches Recht: von der klassischen Zeit bis zu den modernen Kodifikationen*. 2., überarbeitete Auflage. München: C.H. Beck.

Harke, Jan Dirk. 2020. "Eigentum und Erbrecht". *Der Staat* 198, Nr. 3: 397–420. https://doi.org/10.3790/staa.59.3.397.

Harke, Jan Dirk. 2023. *Pflicht und Freiheit des Erblassers: Pflichtteil und Wahnsinnsfiktion im klassischen römischen Erbrecht*. Frankfurt: Campus, 2023.

Hartley, John. 2021. *Advanced Introduction to Creative Industries*. Northampton: Edward Elgar Publishing.

Hase, P. H. 2013. *Custom, Land and Livelihood in Rural South China: The Traditional Land Law of Hong Kong's New Territories, 1750–1950*. Hong Kong: Hong Kong University Press.

Hausman, Daniel M. 2021. "Philosophy of Economics." In *The Stanford Encyclopedia of Philosophy*, ed. Edward N. Zalta. Metaphysics Research Lab, Stanford University. https://plato.stanford.edu/archives/win2021/entries/economics/ (May 10, 2024).

Hegel, Georg Wilhelm Friedrich. 2009 [1821]. *Grundlinien der Philosophie des Rechts oder Naturrecht und Staatswissenschaft im Grundrisse*. Stuttgart: Reclam.

Helfrich, Silke, and Johannes Euler. 2021. "Die Neufassung der Commons: Commoning als gemeinwohlorientiertes Gemeinwirtschaften". *Zeitschrift für Gemeinwirtschaft und Gemeinwohl* 1, 1: 41–58. https://doi.org/10.5771/2701-4193-2021-1-41.

Heller, Michael A. 1998. "The Tragedy of the Anticommons: Property in the Transition from Marx to Markets." *Harvard Law Review* 111, no. 3: 621–88.

Henning, Christoph. 2023. "Values of Exchange, Value of Sharing." In eds. Bettina Hollstein, Hartmut Rosa and Jörg Rüpke, *"Weltbeziehung": The Study of Our Relation to the World*: 235–258. Frankfurt New York: Campus.

Henry, Rosita. 2012. "Being and Belonging: Exchange, Value, and Land Ownership in the Western Highlands of Papua New Guinea." In *Possession and Ownership*, eds. Alexandra Y. Aikhenvald and R. M. W. Dixon. Oxford University Press, 0. doi:10.1093/acprof:oso/9780199660223.003.0013.

Herrmann-Pillath, Carsten. 1991. *Institutioneller Wandel, Macht und Inflation in China: Ordnungstheoretische Analysen zur Politischen Ökonomie eines Transformationsprozesses*. Baden-Baden: Nomos.

Herrmann-Pillath, Carsten. 2013. *Foundations of Economic Evolution: A Treatise on the Natural Philosophy of Economics*. Cheltenham, UK: Edward Elgar.

Herrmann-Pillath, Carsten. 2016. "Performative Mechanisms". In *Enacting Dismal Science*, eds. Ivan Boldyrev and Ekaterina Svetlova, 53–86. New York: Palgrave Macmillan. https://doi.org/10.1057/978-1-137-48876-3_3.

Herrmann-Pillath, Carsten. 2017a. *China's Economic Culture: The Ritual Order of State and Markets*. Abingdon, Oxon, New York, NY: Routledge.

Herrmann-Pillath, Carsten. 2017b. "Institutional Naturalism: Reflections on Masahiko Aoki's Contribution to Institutional Economics." *Evolutionary and Institutional Economics Review* 14(2): 501–22. doi:10.1007/s40844-016-0037-2.

Herrmann-Pillath, Carsten. 2019. "Power, Ideas and Culture in the 'Longue Durée' of Institutional Evolution: Theory and Application on the Revolutions of Property Rights in Russia." *Journal of Evolutionary Economics* 29(5): 1483–1506. doi:10.1007/s00191-019-00624-z.

Herrmann-Pillath, Carsten. 2023. "The Universal Commons: An Economic Theory of Ecosystem Ownership." *Ecological Economics* 208: 107822. doi:10.1016/j.ecolecon.2023.107822.

Herrmann-Pillath, Carsten. 2024. "Rituals as Nature-Based Governance of Reciprocity between People and Nature." *Open Research Europe* 4: 66. doi:10.12688/openreseurope.17206.1.

Herrmann-Pillath, Carsten, and I. A. Boldyrev. 2014. *Hegel, Institutions, and Economics: Performing the Social*. London, New York: Routledge.

Herrmann-Pillath, Carsten, Han Xu, Pan Liqun, Ren Yuxuan, Peng Ying, Cheng Jing, Li Ling, and Guo Man. 2024. "Green Infrastructure, Ritual Spaces, and Socialist Property Regimes in Shenzhen", forthcoming *Berliner Journal für Soziologie*.

Herrmann-Pillath, Carsten, Man Guo, and Xingyuan Feng. 2021. *Ritual and Economy in Metropolitan China: A Global Social Science Approach*. London, New York: Routledge, Taylor & Francis Group.

Herrmann-Pillath, Carsten, and Christian Hederer. 2023. *A New Principles of Economics: The Science of Markets*. Abingdon and New York, NY: Routledge.

Herrmann-Pillath, Carsten, Simo Sarkki, Timo Maran, Katriina Soini, und Juha Hiedanpää. 2023. "Nature-based Solutions as More-than-human Art: Co-evolutionary and Co-creative Design Approaches". *Nature-Based Solutions* 4: 100081. https://doi.org/10.1016/j.nbsj.2023.100081.

Herrmann-Pillath, Carsten, and Qian Zhao. 2023. "The Cultural Meaning of 'Market' in China and the Western Tradition: Worlds Apart?"In eds. Bettina Hollstein, Hartmut Rosa and Jörg Rüpke, *Weltbeziehungen. The Study of our Relationship to the World*: 157–188. Frankfurt am Main: Campus. https://doi.org/10.12907/978-3-593-45587-7_008.

Ho, Peter. 2001. "Who Owns China's Land? Policies, Property Rights and Deliberate Institutional Ambiguity." *The China Quarterly* 166. doi:10.1017/S0009443901000195.

Ho, Peter. 2013. "In Defense of Endogenous, Spontaneously Ordered Development: Institutional Functionalism and Chinese Property Rights." *Journal of Peasant Studies* 40(6): 1087–1118. doi:10.1080/03066150.2013.866553.

Hodgson, Geoffrey M. 2015. "Much of the 'Economics of Property Rights' Devalues Property and Legal Rights." *Journal of Institutional Economics* 11(4): 683–709. doi:10.1017/S1744137414000630.

Hohfeld, Wesley Newcomb. 2022 [1919]. *Fundamental Legal Conceptions as Applied in Judicial Reasoning and Other Legal Essays (Classic Reprint)*. S.l.: Forgotten books.

Holm, Petter, and Kåre Nolde Nielsen. 2007. "Framing Fish, Making Markets: The Construction of Individual Transferable Quotas (ITQs)." *The Sociological Review* 55(2_suppl): 173–95. doi:10.1111/j.1467-954X.2007.00735.x.

Honoré, A. M. 1961. "Ownership." In *Oxford Essays in Jurisprudence*, Oxford: Oxford University Press, 107–47.

Hsing, You-tien. 2006. "Land and Territorial Politics in Urban China." *The China Quarterly* 187: 575–91. doi:10.1017/S0305741006000385.

Huang, Philip C. C. 2006. "Civil Adjudication in China, Past and Present." *Modern China* 32(2): 135–80. doi:10.1177/0097700405285397.

Hübner, Jonas. 2020. *Gemein und ungleich: Ländliches Gemeingut und ständische Gesellschaft in einem frühneuzeitlichen Markenverband: Die Essener Mark bei Osnabrück*. Göttingen: Wallstein Verlag.

Ireland, P. 2010. "Limited Liability, Shareholder Rights and the Problem of Corporate Irresponsibility." *Cambridge Journal of Economics* 34(5): 837–56. doi:10.1093/cje/ben040.

Islam, Muhammad Wohidul. 1999. "Al-Mal: The Concept of Property in Islamic Legal Thought." *Arab Law Quarterly* 14(4): 361–68.

Ivanchikova, Julia S. 2018. "The Concepts of «Property», «Strength», «Power» in the Semantic Structure of the Semantic-Etymological Field 'Property' (on the Material of the Russian Language)." *Journal of the Belarusian State University. Philology.* 2018(3): 110–19.

Jablonka, Eva, Marion J. Lamb, and Anna Zeligowski. 2014. *Evolution in Four Dimensions: Genetic, Epigenetic, Behavioral, and Symbolic Variation in the History of Life*. Revised edition. Cambridge, Massachusetts, London, England: A Bradford Book, The MIT Press.

Jasanoff, Alan. 2018. *The Biological Mind: How Brain, Body, and Environment Collaborate to Make Us Who We Are*. New York: Basic Books.

Jenkins, David G., Helmut Haberl, Karl-Heinz Erb, and Andrew L. Nevai. 2020. "Global Human 'Predation' on Plant Growth and Biomass" *Global Ecology and Biogeography* 29(6): 1052–64. doi:10.1111/geb.13087.

Jiang, Shigong. 2010. "Written and Unwritten Constitutions: A New Approach to the Study of Constitutional Government in China." *Modern China* 36(1): 12–46. doi:10.1177/0097700409349703.

Jin, Keyu. 2023. *The New China Playbook: Beyond Socialism and Capitalism*. New York: Viking.

Jin, Xiankun, Liping Xu, Yu Xin, and Ajay Adhikari. 2022. "Political Governance in China's State-Owned Enterprises." *China Journal of Accounting Research* 15(2): 100236. doi:10.1016/j.cjar.2022.100236.

Jones-Rogers, Stephanie E. 2019. *They Were Her Property: White Women as Slave Owners in the American South*. New Haven, London: Yale University Press.

Jursa, Michael. 2014. "Babylonia in the First Millennium bce– Economic Growth in Times of Empire." In eds. Larry Neal and Jeffrey G. Williamson *The Cambridge History of Capitalism: Volume 1: The Rise of Capitalism: From Ancient Origins to 1848*: 24–42. Cambridge: Cambridge University Press,. doi:10.1017/CHO9781139095099.002.

Kahneman, Daniel. 2012. *Thinking, Fast and Slow*. London: Penguin Books.

Kan, Karita. 2019. "A Weapon of the Weak? Shareholding, Property Rights and Villager Empowerment in China." *The China Quarterly* 237: 131–52. doi:10.1017/S0305741018001352.

Kantor, Georgy. 2017. "Property in Land in Roman Provinces." In eds. Georgy Kantor, Tom Lambert, and Hannah Skoda *Legalism: Property and Ownership*: 55–74, Oxford University Press, doi:10.1093/oso/9780198813415.003.0003.

Kaser, Max. 1985. "I. Über relatives Eigentum im Altrömischen Recht." *Zeitschrift der Savigny-Stiftung für Rechtsgeschichte: Romanistische Abteilung* 102(1): 1–39.

Kauffman, Stuart A. 2000. *Investigations*. New York: Oxford University Press.

Kauffmann, Matthias. 2005. "Das Recht auf Eigentum im Mittelalter." In eds. Andreas Eckl and Bernd Ludwig, *Was ist Eigentum? Philosophische Theorien des Eigentums von Platon bis Habermas*: 73–78, München: C.H. Beck.

Keenan, Sarah. 2015. *Subversive Property: Law and the Production of Spaces of Belonging*. Milton Park, Abingdon, Oxonand New York, NY: Routledge.

Kendal, Jeremy, Jamshid J. Tehrani, and John Odling-Smee. 2011. "Human Niche Construction in Interdisciplinary Focus." *Philosophical Transactions of the Royal Society B: Biological Sciences* 366(1566): 785–92. doi:10.1098/rstb.2010.0306.

Kennedy, David. 2011. "Some Caution about Property Rights as a Recipe for Economic Development." *Accounting, Economics, and Law* 1(1). doi:10.2202/2152-2820.1006.

Kennedy, David, and Joseph E. Stiglitz, eds. 2013. *Law and Economics with Chinese Characteristics: Institutions for Promoting Development in the Twenty-First Century*. Oxford: Oxford University Press.

Kimmerer, Robin Wall. 2020. *Braiding Sweetgrass: Indigenous Wisdom, Scientific Knowledge and the Teachings of Plants*. London: Penguin Books.

Kingreen, Thorsten. 2016. "Die Eigentumsgarantie (Art. 14 GG)." *JURA – Juristische Ausbildung* 38(4). doi:10.1515/jura-2016-0079.

Knauß, Stefan. 2018. "Conceptualizing Human Stewardship in the Anthropocene: The Rights of Nature in Ecuador, New Zealand and India." *Journal of Agricultural and Environmental Ethics* 31(6): 703–22. doi:10.1007/s10806-018-9731-x.

Kohn, Eduardo. 2013. *How Forests Think: Toward an Anthropology beyond the Human*. Berkeley: University of California Press.

Kolchinsky, Artemy, and David H. Wolpert. 2018. "Semantic Information, Autonomous Agency and Non-Equilibrium Statistical Physics." *Interface Focus* 8(6): 20180041. doi:10.1098/rsfs. 2018.0041.

Krausmann, F., K.-H. Erb, S. Gingrich, H. Haberl, A. Bondeau, V. Gaube, C. Lauk, C. Plutzar, and T. D. Searchinger. 2013. "Global Human Appropriation of Net Primary Production Doubled in the 20th Century." *Proceedings of the National Academy of Sciences* 110(25): 10324–29. doi:10.1073/pnas. 1211349110.

Kroker, E.J.M. 1958. *The Concept of Property in Chinese Customary Law*. Asiatic Society of Japan. https://books.google.de/books?id=iZg9ywAACAAJ.

Krüsselberg, Hans-Günter. 1984. "Vermögen, Kapital, Eigentum – Schlüsselbegriffe der Ordnungstheorie?" In ed. Hans Günter Krüsselberg, *Vermögen im Systemvergleich*, 37–60. Berlin, Boston: De Gruyter Oldenbourg. https://doi.org/10.1515/9783110510584-005.

Kuran, Timur. 1997. *Private Truths, Public Lies: The Social Consequences of Preference Falsification*. Cambridge, Mass.: Harvard University Press.

Kurz, Heinz D. 2020. "Über die scheinbare Paradoxie von Weltablehnung und Erwerbsvirtuosität: Zum 100. Todestag von Max Weber." *Perspektiven der Wirtschaftspolitik* 21(4): 326–52. doi:10.1515/pwp-2020-0054.

Lagerwey, John. 2010. *China: A Religious State*. Hong Kong: Hong Kong University Press.

Lai, Yani, Edwin Hon Wan Chan, and Lennon Choy. 2017. "Village-Led Land Development under State-Led Institutional Arrangements in Urbanising China: The Case of Shenzhen." *Urban Studies* 54(7): 1736–59. doi:10.1177/0042098016629325.

Lai, Yani, Yang Chen, Yidan Gui, Shifu Wang, Lingman Chen, and Xuan Liu. 2023. "Cooperating and Competing for Land-Based Interests in the Growth Coalition of Market-Oriented Urban Redevelopment: The Case of Longsheng Village, Shenzhen." *Journal of Urban Affairs*: 1–26. doi:10.1080/07352166.2023.2245075.

Lai, Yani, Jiayuan Wang, and Waiming Lok. 2017. "Redefining Property Rights over Collective Land in the Urban Redevelopment of Shenzhen, China." *Land Use Policy* 69: 485–93. doi:10.1016/j.landusepol.2017.09.046.

Lai, Yani, Xian Zheng, Lennon H.T. Choy, and Jiayuan Wang. 2017. "Property Rights and Housing Prices: An Empirical Study of Small Property Rights Housing in Shenzhen, China." *Land Use Policy* 68: 429–37. doi:10.1016/j.landusepol.2017.08.010.

Larson, Anne M., Iliana Monterosso, Mani Ram Banjade, and Esther Mwangi. 2017. "Community Rights to Forests in the Tropics." In eds. Michelle Graziadei and Lionel Smith *Comparative Property Law. A Global Perspective*: 435–57. Cheltenham, Northhampton: Edward Elgar.

Li, Lixing. 2020. "Changing Ownership Structure of the Economy." In eds. David Dollar, Yiping Huang and Yang Yao, *China 2049, Economic Challenges of a Rising Global Power*: 183–206, New York: Brookings Institution Press. http://www.jstor.org/stable/10.7864/j.ctvktrz58.11

Lieber, Michael D., and Michael A. Rynkiewich. 2007. "Conclusion: Oceanic Conceptions of the Relationship between People and Property." *Human Organization* 66(1): 90–97.

Lomasky, Loren E. 1989. *Persons, Rights, and the Moral Community*. New York: Oxford University Press.

Long, Qinglan. 2009. "Reinterpreting Chinese Property Law." *Southern California Interdisciplinary Law Journal* 19.

Lueck, Dean. 2008. "Property Law, Economics And." In *The New Palgrave Dictionary of Economics*, ed. Palgrave Macmillan. London: Palgrave Macmillan UK, 1–9. doi:10.1057/978-1-349-95121-5_2225-1.

Lund, Christian, and Catherine Boone. 2013. "Introduction: Land Politics in Africa – Constituting Authority over Territory, Property and Persons." *Africa* 83(1): 1–13. doi:10.1017/S000197201200068X.

Macpherson, C. B. 2011[1962]. *The Political Theory of Possessive Individualism: Hobbes to Locke*. Oxford: Oxford University Press.

Madsen, Richard. 1984. *Morality and Power in a Chinese Village*. Berkeley: University of California Press.

Malafouris, Lambros. 2013. *How Things Shape the Mind: A Theory of Material Engagement*. Cambridge, Massachusetts: MIT Press.

Mann, Michael. 2012. *The Sources of Social Power*. New York: Cambridge University Press.

Maran, Timo. 2020. *Ecosemiotics: The Study of Signs in Changing Ecologies*. Cambridge, United Kingdom: Cambridge University Press. doi:10.1017/9781108942850.

Matos Viegas, Susana de. 2016. "Temporalities of Ownership. Land Possession and Its Transformations among the Tupinambá (Bahia, Brazil)." In eds. Brightman, Marc, Carlos Fausto, and Vanessa Elisa Grotti, *Ownership and Nurture. Studies in Native Amazonian Property Relations*: 365–402. New York (N.Y.), Oxford: Berghahn Books.

Mayhew, Robert. 1993. "Aristotle on Property." *The Review of Metaphysics* 46(4): 803–31.

Mazumdar, Sucheta. 2001. "Rights in People, Rights in Land: Concepts of Customary Property in Late Imperial China." *Extrême orient Extrême occident* 23(23): 89–107. doi:10.3406/oroc.2001.1137.

McNeil, Kent. 2017. "Indigenous Territorial Rights in the Common Law." In eds. Michelle Graziadei and Lionel Smith *Comparative Property Law*, Edward Elgar Publishing, 412–34. doi:10.4337/9781785369162.00028.

Meijer, Eva. 2019. *When Animals Speak: Toward an Interspecies Democracy.* New York: New York University Press.

Menary, Richard. 2007. "Writing as Thinking." *Cognitive Dynamics in Language* 29(5): 621–32. doi:10.1016/j.langsci.2007.01.005.

Mendelski, Martin, and Alexander Libman. 2014. "Demand for Litigation in the Absence of Traditions of Rule of Law: An Example of Ottoman and Habsburg Legacies in Romania." *Constitutional Political Economy* 25(2): 177–206. doi:10.1007/s10602-014-9158-y.

Menger, Carl. 1871/2022. *Grundsätze der Volkswirtschaftslehre*. Oeconimus.

Micken, Simon, and Joschka Moldenhauer. 2021. "Zu einem tieferen Verständnis von Gemeingütern durch Commons und Commoning". *Zeitschrift für Gemeinwirtschaft und Gemeinwohl* 44, 2 (2021): 218–35. https://doi.org/10.5771/2701-4193-2021-2-218.

Miller Jr, Fred D. 1986. "Aristotle on Property Rights." *The Society for Ancient Greek Philosophy Newsletter.* 317. https://orb.binghamton.edu/sagp/317.

Möllers, Anna. 2024. "The Construction of Land as Property: Ideas about the Relationship between Land and Humans in Nineteenth-Century Political Economy and Indigenous Counter- Narratives." In eds. Sofia Bianchi Mancini, Helen A. Gibson, Dirk Schuck, Markus Vinzent *Relating to Landed Property*: 157–86. Frankfurt New York: Campus Verlag,

de Moor, Tine. 2018. *Dilemma of the Commoners: Understanding the Use of Common-Pool Resources in Long-Term Perspective.* Cambridge: Cambridge University Press.

Mungello, D. E. 1999. *The Great Encounter of China and the West, 1500–1800*. Lanham, Md: Rowman & Littlefield Publishers.

Myers, Ramon L. 1982. "Customary Law, Markets, and Resource Transactions in Late Imperial China." In *Explorations in the New Economic History*, New York (N.Y.): Academic Press, 273–98.

Naughton, Barry. 2018. *The Chinese Economy: Adaptation and Growth*. Second edition. Cambridge, Massachusetts: MIT Press.

Neuhouser, Frederick. 2008. "Hegel's Social Philosophy." In *The Cambridge Companion to Hegel and Nineteenth-Century Philosophy*, Cambridge Companions to Philosophy, ed. Frederick C. Beiser. Cambridge: Cambridge University Press, 204–29. doi:10.1017/CCOL9780521831673.009.

Nissim, Roger. 2016. *Land Administration and Practice in Hong Kong*. Fourth Edition. Hong Kong: Hong Kong University Press.

North, Douglass C. 1981. *Structure and Change in Economic History*. New York London: W. W. Norton.

North, Douglass C. 1990. *Institutions, Institutional Change, and Economic Performance*. Cambridge and New York: Cambridge University Press.

North, Douglass C., John Joseph Wallis, and Barry R. Weingast. 2009. *Violence and Social Orders: A Conceptual Framework for Interpreting Recorded Human History*. Cambridge; New York: Cambridge University Press.

Nozick, Robert. 1974/2013. *Anarchy, State, and Utopia*. New York, NY: Basic Books.

Ocko, Jonathan. 2004. "The Missing Metaphor: Applying Western Legal Scholarship to the Study of Contract and Property in Early Modern China." In eds. Madeleine Zelin , Jonathan K. Ocko and Robert Gardella *Contract and Property in Early Modern China*: 178–207. Stanford, Stanford University Press,

Odling-Smee, F. John, Kevin N. Laland, and Marcus W. Feldman. 2003. *Niche Construction: The Neglected Process in Evolution*. Princeton: Princeton University Press.

O'Donnell, Mary Ann, Winnie Won Yin Wong, and Jonathan P. G. Bach, eds. 2017. *Learning from Shenzhen: China's Post-Mao Experiment from Special Zone to Model City*. Chicago: The University of Chicago Press.

Osborne, Anne. 2004. "Property, Taxes, and State Protection of Rights." In eds. Madeleine Zelin, Jonathan K. Ocko and Robert Gardella *Contract and Property in Early Modern China*, Stanford, Calif: Stanford University Press, 94–119.

Ostrom, Elinor.1990/ 2015. *Governing the Commons: The Evolution of Institutions for Collective Action*. Cambridge, United Kingdom: Cambridge University Press.

Oswalt, Walter. 2024. *Starker Liberalismus: Geschichte und Aktualität einer politischen Idee zur Begrenzung von Wirtschaftsmacht*. Bielefeld: Transcript, 2024.

Oyama, Susan. 2000. *The Ontogeny of Information: Developmental Systems and Evolution*. Durham, N.C.: Duke University Press.

Padoa Schioppa, Antonio. 2017. *A History of Law in Europe: From the Early Middle Ages to the Twentieth Century*. Cambridge UK and New York: Cambridge University Press.

Pan, Fenghua, Fangzhu Zhang, and Fulong Wu. 2021. "State-Led Financialization in China: The Case of the Government-Guided Investment Fund." *The China Quarterly* 247: 749–72. doi:10.1017/S0305741020000880.

Parker, Dan, Kylie Soanes, and Stanislav Roudavski. 2022. "Interspecies Cultures and Future Design." *Transpositiones* 1(1): 183–236. doi:10.14220/trns. 2022.1.1.183.

Patil, Varun. 2024. "From Bureaucratic Practice to Competing Policy: Examining the Durable and Redistributive Nature of Land Regularization Politics in Bangalore." *City* 28(1–2): 84–100. doi:10.1080/13604813.2024.2324212.

Patil, Varun, and Martin Fuchs. 2024. "Ownership Rights in Practice: Property Dynamics in an Urban Poor Settlement in Mumbai – The Exemplary Case of Dharavi". *Berliner Journal für Soziologie*, 34 (4).

Peters, Florian. 2023. *Von Solidarnosc zur Schocktherapie: Wie der Kapitalismus nach Polen kam*. Berlin: Ch. Links Verlag.

Piketty, Thomas. 2013. *Le capital au XXIe siècle*. Paris: Éditions du Seuil.

Pippin, Robert B. 2008. *Hegel's Practical Philosophy: Rational Agency as Ethical Life*. Cambridge, UK and New York: Cambridge University Press.

Pistor, Katharina. 2019. *The Code of Capital: How the Law Creates Wealth and Inequality*. Princeton: Princeton University Press.

Po, Lanchih. 2012. "Asymmetrical Integration: Public Finance Deprivation in China's Urbanized Villages." *Environment and Planning A* 44(12): 2834–51. doi:10.1068/a44253.

Polanyi, Karl. 2001 [1944]. *The Great Transformation: The Political and Economic Origins of Our Time*. 2nd Beacon Paperback ed. Boston, MA: Beacon Press.

Pomeranz, Kenneth. 2008. "Land Markets in Late Imperial and Republican China." *Continuity and Change* 23(1): 101–50. doi:10.1017/S0268416007006625.

Posner, Eric A., and E. Glen Weyl. 2018. *Radical Markets: Uprooting Capitalism and Democracy for a Just Society*. Princeton: Princeton University Press.

Potter, Sulamith Heins, and Jack M. Potter. 1990. *China's Peasants: The Anthropology of a Revolution*. Cambridge [England]; New York: Cambridge University Press.

Povinelli, Elizabeth A. 2016. *Geontologies: A Requiem to Late Liberalism*. Durham: Duke University Press.

Praduroux, Sabrina. 2017. "Objects of Property Rights: Old and New." In eds. Michelle Graziadei and Lionel Smith *Comparative Property Law*, Edward Elgar Publishing, 51–70. doi:10.4337/9781785369162.00011.

Pravilova, E. A. 2014. *A Public Empire: Property and the Quest for the Common Good in Imperial Russia*. Princeton, Oxford: Princeton University Press.

Preda, Alex. 2005. "The Investor as a Cultural Figure of Global Capitalism." In eds. Karin Knorr Cetina and Alex Preda, *The Sociology of Financial Markets*: 141–61. Oxfordand New York: Oxford University Press,.

Priddat, Birger P. 1990. *Hegel als Ökonom*. Berlin: Duncker & Humblot.

Prum, Richard O. 2017. *The Evolution of Beauty: How Darwin's Forgotten Theory of Mate Choice Shapes the Animal World– and Us*. New York: Doubleday.

Qiao, Shitong. 2018. *Chinese Small Property: The Co-Evolution of Law and Social Norms*. Cambridge: Cambridge University Press. https://doi.org/10.1017/9781316810095.

Qiao, Shitong, and Frank K. Upham. 2017. "China's Changing Property Law Landscape." In eds. Michelle Graziadei and Lionel Smith *Comparative Property Law. Global Perspectives*: 311–31 Cheltenham, UK; Northampton, MA: Edward Elgar Publishing,

Ragavan, Shruti, and Shubangi Srivastava. 2020. "Commoning Infrastructures." https://www.societyandspace.org/articles/commoning-infrastructures (last access September 28, 2023).

Ranasinghe, Prashan. 2019. "Crime, Broken Windows Theory Of." In *The Blackwell Encyclopedia of Sociology*, ed. George Ritzer. Wiley, 1–2. doi:10.1002/9781405165518.wbeosc147.pub2.

Rancière, Jacques. 2004. *Aux bords du politique*. Paris: Gallimard.

Rao, Nitya. 2008. "Good Women Do Not Inherit Land": Politics of Land and Gender in India. New Delhi: Social Science Press.

Reiff, Marvin. 2024. *Verantwortungseigentum: Idee, Umsetzung und Kritik eines alternativen Eigentums an Unternehmen*. Tübingen: Mohr Siebeck. doi:10.1628/9783161633492.

Ritter, Joachim. 2004. "Person and Property in Hegel's Philosophy of Right (§§ 34–81)." In eds. Nicholas Walker, Otfried Höffe, and Robert B. Pippin *Hegel on Ethics and Politics, The German Philosophical Tradition*. Cambridge: Cambridge University Press, 101–23. doi:10.1017/CBO9780511498176.006.

Robeyns, Ingrid, and Morten Fibieger Byskov. 2023. "The Capability Approach." In *The Stanford Encyclopedia of Philosophy*, eds. Edward N. Zalta and Uri Nodelman. Metaphysics Research Lab, Stanford University. https://plato.stanford.edu/archives/sum2023/entries/capability-approach/ (May 29, 2024).

Rose, Carol M. 2019. *Property and Persuasion: Essays on the History, Theory, and Rhetoric of Ownership*. https://www.taylorfrancis.com/books/e/9780429303227 (July 7, 2022).

Ross, Don. 2014. *Philosophy of Economics*. Basingstoke New York: Palgrave Macmillan.

Ross, Don, David Spurrett, Harold Kincaid, and G. Lynn Stephens, eds. 2007. *Distributed Cognition and the Will: Individual Volition and Social Context*. Cambridge, Mass: MIT Press.

Rousset, Denis. 2013. “Sacred Property and Public Property in the Greek City.” *The Journal of Hellenic Studies* 133: 113–33. doi:10.1017/S0075426913000074.

Rüpke, Jörg. 2019. “Roman Gods and Private Property: The Invention of State Religion in Cicero’s Speech on his House.” *Religion in the Roman Empire* 5(2): 292. doi:10.1628/rre-2019-0016.

Ryan, Alan. 1987. “Property.” In *The New Palgrave Dictionary of Economics*, ed. Palgrave Macmillan. London: Palgrave Macmillan UK, 1–4. doi:10.1057/978-1-349-95121-5_1429-1.

Sahlins, Marshall. 2023. *The New Science of the Enchanted Universe: An Anthropology of Most of Humanity*. Princeton Oxford: Princeton University Press.

Santos-Granero, Fernando. 2016. “Masters, Slaves and Real People: Native Understandings of Ownership and Humanness in Tropical American Capturing Societies.” In eds. Brightman, Marc, Carlos Fausto, and Vanessa Elisa Grotti *Ownership and Nurture: Studies in Native Amazonian Property Relations*: 72–112. New York; Oxford: Berghahn Books,.

Sartre, Jean-Paul. 2017 []. *L’être et le néant: essai d’ontologie phénoménologique*. Edition corrigée. Paris: Gallimard.

Sawadogo, Jean-Pierre, and Volker Stamm. 2000. “Local Perceptions of Indigenous Land Tenure Systems: Views of Peasants, Women and Dignitaries in a Rural Province of Burkina Faso.” *The Journal of Modern African Studies* 38(2): 279–94.

Sayın, Yiğit, Amnon Lehavi, Bertil Emrah Oder, Murat Önok, Domenico Francavilla, Victor Torre De Silva, and R. Sudarshan. 2017. “Land Law and Limits on the Right to Property: Historical, Comparative and International Analysis.” *European Property Law Journal* 6(1). doi:10.1515/eplj-2017-0002.

Schlager, Edella, and Elinor Ostrom. 1992. “Property-Rights Regimes and Natural Resources: A Conceptual Analysis.” *Land Economics* 68(3): 249–62. doi:10.2307/3146375.

Schlicht, Ekkehart. 2018. *On Custom in the Economy*. Oxford; New York, NY: Clarendon Press.

Schlömer-Laufen, Nadine, Annika Reiff, and Rosemarie Kay. 2024. “Braucht es eine Gesellschaft mit gebundenem Vermögen?” *Perspektiven der Wirtschaftspolitik* 24(4): 408–13. doi:10.1515/pwp-2023-0037.

Schnädelbach, Herbert. 2000. *Hegels Praktische Philosophie: Ein Kommentar der Texte in der Reihenfolge ihrer Entstehung*. Frankfurt am Main: Suhrkamp.

Schubert, Gunter, and Anna L. Ahlers. 2012. “County and Township Cadres as a Strategic Group: ‘Building a New Socialist Countryside’ in Three Provinces.” *The China Journal* (67): 67–86. doi:10.1086/665740.

Searle, John R. 1995. *The Construction of Social Reality*. New York: Free Press.

Searle, John R. 2011. *Making the Social World: The Structure of Human Civilization*. Oxford: Oxford University Press.

Sen, Amartya. 2009. *The Idea of Justice*. Cambridge, Mass: Belknap Press of Harvard University Press.

Serkin, Christopher. 2016. *The Law of Property*. Second edition. St. Paul, MN: Foundation Press.

Singer, Peter, and Yuval Noaḥ Harari. 2023. *Animal Liberation Now: The Definitive Classic Renewed*. New York: Harper Perennial.

Siu, Helen F. 1989. *Agents and Victims in South China: Accomplices in Rural Revolution*. New Haven: Yale University Press.

Soto, Hernando de. 2001. *The Mystery of Capital: Why Capitalism Triumphs in the West and Fails Everywhere Else*. London: Black Swan.

Benjamin, Solomon, and Bhuvaneswari Raman. 2011. "Illegible Claims, Legal Titles, and the Worlding of Bangalore". *Revue Tiers Monde* 206, 2: 37–54 https://doi.org/10.3917/rtm.206.0037.

Spengler, Robert N. 2021. "Niche Construction Theory in Archaeology: A Critical Review." *Journal of Archaeological Method and Theory* 28(3): 925–55. doi:10.1007/s10816-021-09528-4.

Stienen, Daniel Benedikt. 2022. *Verkauftes Vaterland: Die moralische Ökonomie des Bodenmarktes im östlichen Preussen 1886–1914*. Göttingen: Vandenhoeck & Ruprecht.

Stiglitz, Joseph E. 2013. "The Economics Behind Law in a Market Economy: Alternatives to the Neoliberal Orthodoxy" In eds. David Kennedy and Joseph E. Stiglitz *Law and Economics with Chinese Characteristics: Institutions for Promoting Development in the Twenty-First Century*, Oxford: Oxford University Press, doi:10.1093/acprof:oso/9780199698547.003.0005.

Sueur, Cédric, and Michael A Huffman. 2024. "Co-Cultures: Exploring Interspecies Culture Among Humans and Other Animals". HAL Open Science https://hal.science/hal-04368545/document.

Sundström, Lars. 1974. *The Exchange Economy of Pre-Colonial Tropical Africa*. London: C. Hurst & Company.

Swab, R. Gabrielle, Chelsea Sherlock, Erik Markin, and Clay Dibrell. 2020. "'SEW' What Do We Know and Where Do We Go? A Review of Socioemotional Wealth and a Way Forward." *Family Business Review* 33(4): 424–45. doi:10.1177/0894486520961938.

Takizawa, Hirokazu. 2017. "Masahiko Aoki's Conception of Institutions." *Evolutionary and Institutional Economics Review* 14(2): 523–40. doi:10.1007/s40844-017-0087-0.

Tao Ran. 2023. *Ren di zhi jian: Zhongguo zengzhang moshi xa de chengxiang tudi gaige.*. Shenyang: Liaoning renmin chubanshe.

Taqiyuddin, Hafidz, Mus'idul Millah, and Hikmatul Luthfi. 2023. "Instruments of Property Ownership in Islam: The Study of Inheritance Law." *Journal of Islamic Thought and Civilization* 13(1). doi:10.32350/jitc.131.11.

Taylor, Charles. 1975. *Hegel*. Cambridge: Cambridge University Press. doi:10.1017/CBO9781139171465.

Tellmann, Ute. 2022. "The Politics of Assetization: From Devices of Calculation to Devices of Obligation." *Distinktion: Journal of Social Theory* 23(1): 33–54. doi:10.1080/1600910X.2021.1991419.

Thaler, Richard H. 2016. *Misbehaving: The Making of Behavioural Economics*. New York, London: W. W. Norton & Company.

The Cyrus R. Vance Center. 2020. "Rights of Rivers." *International Rivers*. https://www.internationalrivers.org/resources/reports-and-publications/rights-of-river-report/ (May 6, 2024).

Thomas, Yan. 2011. *Les opérations du droit*. Paris: Gallimard Seuil.

Tomasello, Michael. 2019. *Becoming Human: A Theory of Ontogeny*. Cambridge, Massachusetts: The Belknap Press of Harvard University Press.

Tong, De, Yaying Wu, Ian MacLachlan, and Jieming Zhu. 2021. "The Role of Social Capital in the Collective-Led Development of Urbanising Villages in China: The Case of Shenzhen." *Urban Studies* 58(16): 3335–53. doi:10.1177/0042098021993353.

Trémon, Anne-Christine. 2015. "Local Capitalism and Neoliberalization in a Shenzhen Former Lineage Village." *Focaal* 2015(71). doi:10.3167/fcl.2015.710107.

Tripp, Charles. 2006. *Islam and the Moral Economy: The Challenge of Capitalism*. Cambridge; New York: Cambridge University Press.

Trosper, Ronald L. 2022. *Indigenous Economics: Sustaining Peoples and Their Lands*. Tucson: University of Arizona Press.

Tsai, Lily L. 2007. *Accountability without Democracy: Solidary Groups and Public Goods Provision in Rural China*. New York, NY: Cambridge University Press.

Turner, Bertram. 2017. "The Anthropology of Property." In eds. Michelle Graziadei and Lionel Smith *Comparative Property Law. Global Perspectives*: 26–49. Cheltenham, UK, Northampton, MA: Edward Elgar Publishing,

Uexküll, J. Baron, and G. Kriszat. 1934. *Streifzüge durch die Umwelten von Tieren und Menschen Ein Bilderbuch unsichtbarer Welten*. Berlin, Heidelberg: Springer Berlin Heidelberg. doi:10.1007/978-3-642-98976-6.

Universitas Islam Negeri Sunan Gunung Djati Bandung, Indonesia, and Dudang Gojali. 2023. "Philosophy of Ownership Law in Islam (Analysis of Fiqh Principles)." *International Journal of Social Science and Human Research* 6(08). doi:10.47191/ijsshr/v6-i8-51.

Valguarnera, Filippo. 2017. "Access to Nature." In eds. Michelle Graziadei and Lionel Smith *Comparative Property Law. Global Perspectives*: 258–80, Cheltenham, UK, Northampton, MA: Edward Elgar Publishing,.

Vanuxem, Sarah. 2022. *La Propriété de la terre*. Nouvelle éd. Marseille: Wildproject.

Vinzent, Markus. 2024. "Inheritance of Land—the Origin of Property." In eds. Sofia Bianchi Mancini, Helen A. Gibson, Dirk Schuck, Markus Vinzent. *Relating to Landed Property*, 41–64. Frankfurt New York: Campus Verlag,

Wagner, John, and Malia Talakai. 2007. "Customs, Commons, Property, and Ecology: Case Studies From Oceania." *Human Organization* 66(1): 1–10.

Waldron, Jeremy. 2023. "Property and Ownership." In *The Stanford Encyclopedia of Philosophy*, eds. Edward N. Zalta and Uri Nodelman. Metaphysics Research Lab, Stanford University. https://plato.stanford.edu/archives/fall2023/entries/property/ (August 7, 2023).

Wang, Da Wei David. 2016. *Urban Villages in the New China: Case of Shenzhen*. New York, NY: Palgrave Macmillan.

Wang, Jiangyu. 2014. "The Political Logic of Corporate Governance in China's State-Owned Enterprises." *Cornell International Law Journal* 47: 631–69.

Wang, Li, Tiangui Lv, Xinmin Zhang, Han Hu, and Xiao Cai. 2022. "Global Research Trends and Gaps in Ecological Compensation Studies from 1990 to 2020: A Scientometric Review." *Journal for Nature Conservation* 65: 126097. doi:10.1016/j.jnc.2021.126097.

Wang, Yang, and Beini Li. 2019. "Property System in Traditional China and Its Enlightenment." *Tsinghua China Law Review* 12(1): 88–113.

Waszek, Norbert. 1988. *The Scottish Enlightenment and Hegel's Account of "Civil Society."* Dordrecht: Kluwer.

Watson, James L. 1987. "From the Common Pot: Feasting with Equals in Chinese Society." *Anthropos* 82(4/6): 389–401.

Watson, James L. 2004. "Presidential Address: Virtual Kinship, Real Estat, and Diaspora Formation—The Man Lineage Revisited." *The Journal of Asian Studies* 63(4): 893–910. doi:10.1017/S0021911804002359.

Watson, Rubie S. 2007. *Inequality among Brothers: Class and Kinship in South China*. Cambridge: Cambrige Univ. Press.

Weber, Max. 2012 [1889]. *Zur Geschichte der Handelsgesellschaften im Mittelalter*. Berlin: Heptagon.

Weber, Max. 2014a [1891]. *Die Römische Agrargeschichte in Ihrer Bedeutung für das Staats- und Privatrecht*. S.l.: e-artnow Verlag.

Weber, Max. 2014b. *Wirtschaft und Gesellschaft. soz: Soziologie: unvollendet* 1919–1920. Tübingen: Mohr.

Weber, Max, Guenther Roth, and Claus Wittich. 1978. *Economy and Society: An Outline of Interpretive Sociology*. Berkeley: University of California Press.

Weber, Max, and Keith Tribe. 2019. *Economy and Society: A New Translation*. Cambridge, Massachusetts: Harvard University Press.

Weber, Max, and Johannes Winckelmann. 2009 [1956]. *Wirtschaft und Gesellschaft: Grundriss der verstehenden Soziologie*. 5., rev. Aufl., Studienausg., [Nachdr.]. Tübingen: Mohr Siebeck.

Wenar, Leif. 2017. *Blood Oil: Tyrants, Violence, and the Rules That Run the World*. Oxford: Oxford university press.

Wesche, Tilo. 2023. *Die Rechte der Natur: vom nachhaltigen Eigentum*. Berlin: Suhrkamp.

Weth, Lydia von der. 2024. "Mancipatio: The Starting Point of a Uniform Property System?" In eds. Sofia Bianchi Mancini, Helen A. Gibson, Dirk Schuck, Markus Vinzent *Relating to Landed Property:* 105–26. Frankfurt New York: Campus Verlag,

Wheeler, Wendy. 2016. *Expecting the Earth: Life, Culture, Biosemiotics*. London: Lawrence & Wishart.

White, Richard. 2001. *The Organic Machine: The Remaking of the Columbia River*. New York: Hill and Wang.

Widerquist, Karl, and Grant S. McCall. *The Prehistory of Private Property: Implications for Modern Political Theory*. Edinburgh: Edinburgh University Press, 2021.

Wiener, Jonathan M. 1982. "Max Weber's Marxism: Theory and Method in 'The Agrarian Sociology of Ancient Civilizations'" ed. Max Weber. *Theory and Society* 11(3): 389–401.

Wilson, Bart J. 2022. "The Primacy of Property; or, the Subordination of Property Rights." *Journal of Institutional Economics*: 1–17. doi:10.1017/S1744137422000212.

Wilson, David Sloan. 1998. "Hunting, Sharing, and Multilevel Selection". *Current Anthropology* 39, No. 1 (1998): 73–97. https://doi.org/10.1086/204699.

Wily, Liz Alden. 2017. "Customary Tenure: Remaking Property for the 21st Century." In eds. Michelle Graziadei and Lionel Smith *Comparative Property Law.Global Perspectives*: 458–78.Cheltenham, UK; Northampton, MA: Edward Elgar Publishing,

Witt, Ulrich. 1996. "Innovations, Externalities and the Problem of Economic Progress." *Public Choice* 89(1): 113–30. doi:10.1007/BF00114282.

Wittgenstein, Ludwig. 2009 [1953]. *Philosophical investigations*. Chichester, West Sussex, U.K., Malden, MA: Wiley-Blackwell.

Wolff, Lutz-Christian. 2020. "The Relationship between Contract Law and Property Law." *Common Law World Review* 49(1): 31–55. doi:10.1177/1473779520903729.

Woloson, Wendy A. 2012. *In Hock: Pawning in America from Independence through the Great Depression*. Paperback ed. Chicago: University of Chicago Press.

Wong, Siu Wai. 2015. "Land Requisitions and State–Village Power Restructuring in Southern China." *The China Quarterly* 224: 888–908. doi:10.1017/S0305741015001241.

Wood, Michael. 2012. "Spirits of the Forest, the Wind, and New Wealth: Defining Some of the Possibilities, and Limits, of Kamula Possession." In eds. Alexandra Y. Aikhenvald and R. M. W. Dixon *Possession and Ownership*: 261–273. Oxford University Press, doi:10.1093/acprof:oso/9780199660223.003.0012.

World Economic Forum. 2022. *BiodiverCities by 2030: Transforming Cities' Relationships with Nature*. Geneva: Woröd Economic Forum. https://www.weforum.org/publications/biodivercities-by-2030-transforming-cities-relationship-with-nature/.

Yong, Ed. 2017. *I Contain Multitudes: The Microbes within Us and a Grander View of Life*. London: Vintage.

Yong, Ed. 2022. *An Immense World: How Animal Senses Reveal the Hidden Realms around Us*. London: The Bodley Head Ltd.

Young, Ashley, Kathayoon A. Khalil, and Jim Wharton. 2018. "Empathy for Animals: A Review of the Existing Literature." *Curator: The Museum Journal* 61(2): 327–43. doi:10.1111/cura.12257.

Zanasi, Margherita. 2020. *Economic Thought in Modern China*. New York: Cambridge University Press.

Zawidzki, Tadeusz. 2013. *Mindshaping: A New Framework for Understanding Human Social Cognition*. Cambridge, Mass: MIT Press.

Zelin, Madeleine. 2004. "A Critique of Rights of Property in Prewar China." In Madeleine Zelin , Jonathan K. Ocko and Robert Gardella *Contract and Property in Early Modern China*, Stanford, Calif: Stanford University Press, 17–36.

Figures

Tables

Index